Preservation and
the New Data Landscape

Preservation and
the New Data Landscape

Edited by Erica Avrami

TABLE OF CONTENTS

Introduction

Institutionalizing Data

Co-Producing Knowledge

Building Evidence-Based Narratives

Informing Policy Agendas

Appendices

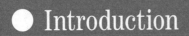 Introduction

1
See appendices for
a literature review
examining these
research avenues.

Heritage Data and the Next Generation
of Preservation Policy

Erica Avrami

Two generations ago, historic preservation secured its foothold in US public policy. The New York City Landmarks Law of 1965—a paragon of municipal preservation legislation—and the federal National Historic Preservation Act of 1966 codified a now widely accepted practice of government action to safeguard places of significance. The emergence of preservation policy infrastructure forged cultural conventions and encouraged public dialogue around heritage and its protection. It fostered and supported strong legal foundations and institutional arrangements—especially at the municipal level, where the power to regulate real property is greatest.

In those same two generations, the context in which preservation policy operates has shifted dramatically. World population has more than doubled, and it has become more urban. Today, most major metropolitan areas in the United States contend with growing and increasingly diverse populations. Urban built environments must accommodate this growth and at the same time meet multiple and often conflicting needs, including protecting open space and cultural resources, reducing energy and land consumption, adapting to climate change, promoting economic vitality, and ensuring social inclusion and community resilience.

These challenges place new demands on heritage preservation: it must demonstrate its value to society and the environment as it competes for political support and scarce financial resources within a complex urban agenda. In response, practitioners and academics are working to demonstrate the economic impacts of heritage protection, from increases in property values to job creation to tourism revenue. New research is also examining the environmental impacts of older buildings and neighborhoods and the affirmative role of existing (historic) structures in the ecological well-being of the planet. Empirical investigations into the role of arts and culture in communities shed additional light on the social value of heritage and the ways in which attachments to places are formed.[1]

Such research represents an important, though still very limited, reorientation of the preservation field toward evidence-based policy evaluation, particularly at the municipal level. Because preservation is often at odds with better financed and politically empowered real estate development interests, studies on the subject are often reactive and geared toward rationalizing investment in heritage by defending the status quo. Despite half a century of local policy experience behind us, there is still much to learn about the positive and negative influence of preservation on the social and physical fabric of cities. A better understanding of that influence can help policy meet contemporary needs more effectively and serve communities more justly.

Some may argue that such policy evaluation and the changes it may prompt constitute "mission creep" for preservation, which should instead focus on designating and regulating historic buildings and sites. Indeed, protection of the formal qualities of significant structures and districts forms the bulk of government-led preservation in cities across the United States. However, the policy rationales of most municipal ordinances, which provide the justification for investing tax-funded resources, reflect much broader mandates. Public education and welfare are certainly included within them, as are economic rationales such as generating tourism, stimulating growth, and increasing property values.[2] These legal justifications fundamentally position preservation as a tool for enhancing quality of life and promoting community-building through the historic built environment.[3] Revisiting that toolbox to improve its efficacy should be part of preservation's remit.

The Urban Heritage, Sustainability, and Social Inclusion initiative—from which this volume developed—is a collaboration between the Columbia University Graduate School of Architecture, Planning, and Preservation, the Earth Institute–Center for Sustainable Urban Development, and the American Assembly, with support from the New York Community Trust. It seeks to build stronger linkages among researchers, policy makers, and practitioners in the heritage field by examining issues at the vanguard of urban preservation decision-making. Many government agencies dealing with preservation lack the mandate and the resources to independently explore emerging questions about policy, and the same is often true for not-for-profit and community groups. Though scholarly research on the topic is expanding, it remains fragmented. This initiative aims to counter that fragmentation and foster communication and collective action toward socially and environmentally responsive change. This new publication series, Issues in Preservation Policy, launches and makes public this exploratory discourse. The first question probed, and the subject of this initial volume, is the changing landscape of preservation-related data as an opportunity for, and foundation of, policy innovation. Two further volumes will discuss historic preservation's relationship to social inclusion and new possibilities for assessing the outcomes of preservation policy.

Technological changes over the past decades have dramatically altered how we analyze and understand the built environment and communities. The existing preservation policy infrastructure was put in place before the advent of digital recording methods, the World Wide Web, and even personal computers. At its inception, it relied largely on visual and historical documentation to inform designation and the design review of formal changes to listed properties. Today, the increased accessibility of geospatial technology, open data laws, urban dashboards, the public engagement and multimedia options afforded by online platforms, and the burgeoning arena of civic tech engender a raft of quantitative and qualitative data, tools, and methods for understanding the relationships between people and their communities, and for informing policy decisions toward just and ecologically sustainable development.

This new data landscape presents a critical opportunity for preservation policy, as it is increasingly possible to analyze long-term effects

2
Erica Avrami, Cherie-Nicole Leo, and Alberto Sanchez-Sanchez, "Confronting Exclusion: Redefining the Intended Outcomes of Historic Preservation," Change Over Time 8, no. 1 (forthcoming).

3
Carol M. Rose, "Preservation and Community: New Directions in the Law of Historic Preservation," Stanford Law Review 33, no. 3 (February 1981): 473–534.

4
J. Mark Schuster, "Information as a Tool of Preservation Action," in *Preserving the Built Heritage: Tools for Implementation*, ed. J. Mark Schuster, John de Monchaux, and Charles A. Riley II (Hanover, NH: University Press of New England, 1997), 100–123; J. Mark Schuster, "Making a List and Checking It Twice: Information as a Tool for Historic Preservation," Cultural Policy Center at the University of Chicago, November 25, 2002, https://culturalpolicy. uchicago.edu/sites/ culturalpolicy.uchicago. edu/files/Schuster14. pdf.

5
Stefan Fisch, "National Approaches to the Administration of Historical Heritage," in *National Approaches to the Governance of Historical Heritage Over Time: A Comparative Report*, ed. Stefan Fisch (Amsterdam: IOS Press, 2008), 1–13; "First International Congress of Architects and Technicians of Historic Monuments, 1931," Athens Charter for the Restoration of Historic Monuments, http:// www.icomos.org/en/ charters-and-texts/179- articles-en-francais/ ressources/charters- and-standards/167-the- athens-charter-for-the- restoration-of-historic- monuments.

6
Advisory Council on Historic Preservation, *The Preserve America Summit Executive Summary: Charting a Future Course for the National Historic Preservation Program* (Washington, DC: ACHP, 2007).

7
Meenakshi Srinivasan, Lisa Kersavage, and Daniel Watts, "NYC Landmarks Preservation Commission's Historic Building Data Project" (PowerPoint presentation, Urban Heritage and Data in the 21st Century Symposium, New York, NY, February 8, 2018).

and to consider criteria for success that are not currently included in decision-making frameworks. Evidence-based policy evaluation hinges on the capacity to forge, navigate, and build upon the potential of data in ways that are germane to preservation and its desired outcomes. The contributors to this volume explore this terrain in an effort to chart new paths of research and practice. Through the Urban Heritage and Data in the 21st Century symposium and the articles and interviews included in this book, a number of themes emerged that can inform the next generation of preservation policy.

● THE POWER OF DATA COLLECTION AND MANAGEMENT

Information is a fundamental preservation policy tool. From the identification of what is *heritage* to documentation, promotion, and technical assistance, information enables collective action for public purpose and validates government decision-making and investment. It serves as a foundation for the application of other public policy tools, such as preservation regulation and incentives. [4]

At the core of government action are the lists or inventories that identify those places and resources worthy of public recognition and warranting some form of protection. As Lisa Ackerman notes, this impetus to classify heritage has a long history, and institutions as well as governments have pushed heritage data into the public arena. Some European governments began generating systematic lists of their historic monuments more than two centuries ago, and in 1931 the Athens Charter for the Restoration of Historic Monuments called for nation-states to create and publish heritage inventories. [5] The importance of collecting and managing such heritage data persists as a policy priority: the top recommendation emerging from the Preserve America Summit, on the occasion of the fortieth anniversary of the National Historic Preservation Act, was to expand and increase the accessibility of heritage inventories. [6]

Such inventories take a range of forms, but increasingly, they capitalize on the geospatial technologies and software now readily available. Not only documenting but also mapping culturally or historically significant elements of the built environment is a powerful way to share information on the level of urban land use and planning, including for environmental review, zoning, transportation design, growth management, and disaster preparedness. Mapping likewise is an important medium for analyzing heritage in relation to demographics and other spatialized data.

Many municipalities are taking part in this new era of transparency as web-based platforms provide access to decades of existing—or legacy— data. The New York City Landmarks Preservation Commission launched an interactive map, Discover New York City Landmarks, which provides detailed information about the city's 1,400 individual landmarks, as well as 34,000 buildings within its 141 historic districts, culled from fifty years' worth of designation reports and other research. This standardization of data allows for filtered searching, facilitates comparative analyses, and also provides a feedback portal for public input. [7]

The City of Los Angeles has taken the municipal heritage inventory even further. As Janet Hansen and Sara Delgadillo Cruz explain, the Historic Resources Office of the Department of City Planning has embarked on an ambitious program to document all of the city's historic resources, designated and not designated alike. By first identifying important themes in Los Angeles history, or "historic contexts," the city has been able to create an innovative public participation and mapping platform called SurveyLA to relate those themes to extant properties. The existing data on designated resources, as well as on those buildings identified through the survey, is all fully accessible and mappable in HistoricPlacesLA, the city's online historic resources inventory and management system.

SurveyLA was an unprecedented effort in municipal heritage data collection, requiring significant human and financial resources, whereas the Discover New York City Landmarks project was an in-house operation on a limited budget. This difference is emblematic of the varying capacities of local governments and the range of data tools available. More sophisticated systems enable more complex spatial characterization and use analysis, allowing, for example, the inclusion of nonparcel resources (the street intersection where an important event occurred, viewsheds, and the like), the threading of sites into narratives, and the incorporation of older—not just designated—architecture and places. This enhanced functionality comes at a cost that may be beyond the reach of many municipalities. As Matthew Hampel emphasizes, from surveying and resurveying to updating data and software, collection and management of heritage information is an ongoing responsibility, not a onetime event (especially given the ever increasing roster of heritage sites). To sustain these systems, simplicity can sometimes be an advantage. Data collection and management, with clear goals in mind, should be internalized as part of the everyday operations of heritage agencies and institutions. Ultimately, these organizations need to focus on operationalizing data for social change.

● DATA AS CIVIC ENGAGEMENT

Technological shifts in historic preservation over the last several decades have paralleled theoretical shifts in the field. Whereas heritage was traditionally viewed as having inherent value discernible only to experts, there is now an increased awareness of how society "creates" heritage by ascribing present-day values to places of the past. By valorizing particular styles, materials, people, events, narratives, and more, each generation influences the ways in which preservation policy is developed and implemented. Greater understanding of heritage as both a social process and a social construct has helped to foster broader public participation in decision-making about what to preserve and how.

In the same way that significance is not objectively ascertained, data does not simply exist "out there" to be objectively collected and analyzed. The breadth of the new data landscape compels us to be vigilantly conscious of bias as we create and use information. It likewise obliges us to be mindful of who participates in surveys and data collection, analysis, and management and of the risks of exclusion. Empowering communities to access and use existing data as well as to co-create new data is thus a topic described by multiple contributors to this volume. Vicki Weiner, for example, describes the Pratt Center's Neighborhood Data Portal as a tool to democratize information by making existing datasets about New York City's built environment more easily accessible and usable. The goal is to empower diverse publics to improve their data literacy and, in doing so, to become more active participants in decision-making about their communities and built environments.

Several contributors underscore the notion of creating data *with* the public, not *for* it. Communities are makers, not just consumers, of data. Hampel speaks of data as a tactic of engagement: co- or self-designing surveys involve community members and help build collective buy-in. Whether data is for community asset mapping, collaborative visioning, or other forms of participatory planning, increasingly accessible tools and technology—from mobile apps to online public forums—can educate residents and empower them to explore and visualize data themselves. But Alicia Rouault contends that it is not (yet) common for municipal governments to work directly with communities in the production of official datasets. Universities and community-based organizations have a role to play: by helping to legitimize and integrate community voices in data-collection processes, they can facilitate (and instrumentalize) the co-creation of data.

These ideas highlight the complicated relationship between expert and public ways of knowing when it comes to heritage. Preservationists bring disciplinary knowledge—and professional responsibility—to the heritage enterprise. At the same time, they are charged with helping to spatialize the narratives of diverse publics and realize community desires. These mandates are often in tension. As policy evolves and as participatory decision-making becomes more institutionalized, we may see a new generation of preservationists with expertise not only in heritage values (as defined by the field) but also in methods for better understanding how the public creates and values heritage. Jeremy C. Wells, Vanilson Burégio, and Rinaldo Lima explore how preservationists might develop new approaches to this charge. They propose a specialized web-based platform-cum-computational tool, the Social HEritage Machine (SHEM), to collect metadata on the language laypeople use to relate to heritage. A better understanding of public perceptions can help make heritage decision-making more responsive to community interests and help reconcile public and expert knowledge.

However, Eduardo Rojas reminds us that while data may be increasingly democratized, the decision-making processes they inform may not be. Different social actors have varying degrees of agency and leverage in preservation policy. In generically categorizing "communities" or "the public," we sacrifice a more nuanced understanding of these diverse stakeholders (whether individuals or institutions) and the relative influence each brings to the table. More than simply understanding public perceptions, we also need to understand who has power in decisions that affect heritage, what their motivations are, and how the creation and use of data may influence these dynamics. In this sense, it is important to remember that the new data landscape and civic engagement are not only about big data. Rouault outlines several tools that are helping to gather individualized, qualitative data. Marco Castro Cosio illustrates the importance of intimate, personal knowledge through his work incorporating visitor memories at the Queens Museum and taking community engagement beyond the walls of cultural institutions.

● BUILDING PRESERVATION POLICY-SPECIFIC DATA

Preservation has a long legacy of deep qualitative research into the formal arrangements and historical meaning of significant places. The new data landscape in many respects affords the possibility of transectional views of preservation policy decisions, across time and space and between people and places. But standardizing and scaling data to foster such views can, at times, be at odds with traditional heritage research methods and discipline-specific forms of data. Likewise, inaccuracies in existing data and disparate data types complicate both cross-sectional and longitudinal research. Andrew S. Dolkart raises the issue of bad legacy data, using "year built" information from New York City's PLUTO database as an example of how a single datum fails to represent or capture the relevance of time and longitudinal change. Amanda L. Webb likewise plumbs the "year built" polemic, arguing that date of construction can be a seminal piece of information for preservation decision-making but that it is nevertheless nonstatic and inexact.

Threaded throughout the volume is a call to collect, characterize, and manage data in ways that more effectively serve the preservation enterprise. Despite its long history of creating and managing inventories, and more than half a century of policy implementation in the United States, the preservation field has a poor track record of systematizing data. Stephanie Ryberg-Webster and Kelly L. Kinahan, in their research on federal historic tax credits, and Michael Powe, in his work with the National Trust's Research and Policy Lab, highlight the lack of baseline policy data, mismatched data repositories, and variable data quality endemic to preservation. These shortcomings impede robust policy research and underscore the fundamental role that government must play in ensuring effective data collection and management.

Douglas S. Noonan and Tetsuharu Oba argue that a great promise of new technology is the opportunities for "connecting previously disconnected datasets." And preservationists need not carry that burden alone. Rouault, Hampel, and other technology experts who have participated in this dialogue stressed the passion in the tech world for tackling these types of problems. Engaging "civic hacker types" and drawing on the ever-improving means of data collection—from crowdsourcing to crowd editing to data scraping—can open up new possibilities for preservation policy research. That said, there is still an essential role for what Rouault refers to as "translators," those with both tech knowledge and an understanding of the built environment and urban planning tools, who can mediate between these fields, help to optimize data, and spearhead research that is preservation policy-specific. Jennifer L. Most echoes this idea; she argues for better training of preservationists in GIS and other data-driven research methods and for empowering preservationists to work with quantitative data. There is an inextricable link between evidentiary data and the stories we seek to tell as preservationists; therefore, preservationists must be educated and professionally positioned to analyze their own data and to evaluate the outcomes of their own policies. While interdisciplinary collaboration may be warranted, the preservation community also needs its own data fluency to ensure that the preservation-specific data and policy research needs of the field are effectively addressed.

● CHALLENGING AND SUBSTANTIATING NARRATIVES

In the same way that legacy data can complicate contemporary research, there are legacy narratives that influence the discourse surrounding preservation policy and its effectiveness. Randall Mason argues that the new data landscape affords possibilities for new discoveries, new stories, and new connections. It may likewise challenge preservation's ways of knowing and doing by testing longstanding narratives. For example, the aforementioned SHEM platform specifically seeks to challenge expert knowledge—the "authorized heritage discourse"—by experimenting with new methods for probing public values and perceptions. Castro Cosio's work in interactive technologies supports community and individual storytelling, reinforcing the idea that heritage is more than just a set of resources to be preserved: it is also an open-ended, spatialized narrative of collective memory.

Heritage narratives relate not only to *what* and *how* we preserve but also to *why* we preserve. Emily Talen, through her study of mom-and-pop retail, and Powe, through his work showing why old buildings matter, analyze and find evidentiary support for a fundamental tenet of preservation first proffered by Jane Jacobs: that neighborhoods with a mix of old and new buildings have a positive influence on urban vitality. Both caution that the potential of such research can only be realized if there is a clear articulation of the ways in which preservation policy goals intersect with socioeconomic goals, such as supporting small businesses. Preservation policy's emphasis on regulating historic fabric cannot, in and of itself, plumb the dynamics of these social-spatial relationships, nor can it assure outcomes that engender broader social and economic benefits.

Similarly, climate change has given new voice to a preservation narrative dating back to the oil crisis of the 1970s, which asserts that old buildings are inherently more energy efficient. Webb makes a strong case for how increasingly sophisticated energy data and research may not support this claim. However, because policy research in the realm of preservation is often advocacy driven, it may focus too heavily on reinforcing the time-honored narratives. The energy narrative is underpinned by a preservation philosophy that strives to minimize physical change, and adherence to it misses the opportunity to maximize the potential benefits of energy efficiency in the historic built environment. More explicitly aligning the goals of energy efficiency and historic preservation could inform more sustainable heritage policies, and new energy data provides a rich foundation for exploring these intersections. In this sense, the field can operationalize data to evolve preservation narratives and update policies in response to contemporary needs.

● INFORMED DECISION-MAKING AND EVIDENCE-BUILDING

The primary tool in the municipal-level preservation policy toolbox has historically been the regulatory instrument of designation. The use of government action to physically protect a historic property from market forces and the specter of significant physical change—or the lack of such protection—has institutionalized a binary mind-set. One might argue that the overreliance on this one powerful tool has inhibited the development of other policy instruments that more deeply explore the broad spectrum of options between "saved" and "not saved."

Data in service of policy can provide critical feedback loops and insight into new avenues of policy development or governance reform. In their analysis of Kyoto, where datasets track the implementation of landscape and viewshed policy, Noonan and Oba argue that this kind of monitoring informs decisions about Kyoto's wider heritage resource portfolio and advances the "menu of policy tools." Hansen and Delgadillo Cruz emphasize that HistoricPlacesLA enables better management of heritage resources but also facilitates the integration of heritage interests within broader planning and land use decisions. Powe reaffirms the power of data to inform urban policy, especially when aggregated and evaluated across municipalities. Even beyond policy, both Ackerman and Mason underscore the potential of data to improve heritage management and governance structures and to connect preservation more substantively with other disciplines. Heritage data can help forge the channels needed for cross-policy research, interagency cooperation, and decision-making systems for the built environment and for communities. It can likewise unite governmental policy actors through mutual accountability.

Data, as Hampel maintains, imparts legitimacy and gets preservation a proverbial seat at the table. It is not only a building block of policy research; it is also a form of political currency. Data can leverage support and resources, build trust, speak truth to power, and engage "opponents" to negotiate solutions. But capitalizing on this potential requires preservation to actively engage in other urban agendas and embrace policy outcomes beyond the protection of architectural fabric. Economic vitality, social well-being, and environmental sustainability are all areas in which preservation claims a role, though largely to support the existing priorities of regulatory designation and design review. The new data landscape calls on the field to build a more evidence-based cadre of data and research that does not simply use these claims to justify its cause but instead thinks creatively and progressively about improving its policies in relation to the results they produce.

On the economic front, Main Street and small-business interests, as Talen suggests, constitute an area of common ground. Rojas sees untapped opportunities for preservation policy in urban investment and more holistic decision-making. Ryberg-Webster and Kinahan underscore how improved data can help us understand the role of incentive-based policy tools, like historic tax credits, and better position preservation to align with urban revitalization agendas. The environmental front offers a lot of low-hanging fruit with regard to data and research. By acknowledging energy efficiency as a means to preserve, rather than as a threat to historic fabric, Webb argues that research into better models and benchmarking could enhance the stewardship of heritage as an integral element of a sustainable built environment.

● TELLING BETTER STORIES, ASKING BETTER QUESTIONS

Will better data lead to better preservation? The rosters of heritage sites in the United States and around the world are growing. But quantity does not necessarily equate to quality. As a form of public policy, intended to serve all, there is an obligation on the part of preservation to tell better stories through the historic built environment—stories that represent the diversity of our communities, stories that redress spatial and social inequities, and stories that reflect our collective agency in promoting a sustainable environment. But to tell better stories, preservation must ask better questions.

Asking better questions means taking stock of the last half century of preservation policy implementation. It entails establishing a culture of self-reflection that counterbalances the impulse to keep identifying more and more heritage by critically evaluating the strengths and weaknesses of our work vis-à-vis society and the environment. Asking better questions also involves recasting preservation as a means of instrumentalizing heritage to align with and support related urban goals, rather than to serve as an end in and of itself. It means more evidence-based research that works toward socially inclusive processes, which in turn support a just and sustainable built environment, all to inform the next generation of preservation policy.

The new data landscape is fraught with challenges, and preservation's existing data deficiencies and limited policy-research infrastructure only compound these problems. But the opportunities for improved heritage management and policy reassessment far outweigh the potential difficulties. A new outlook on and orientation toward data can help modernize the preservation policy toolbox and enhance the benefits that heritage can create for society.

Big City, Big Data:
Los Angeles's Historic Resources

Janet Hansen
Sara Delgadillo Cruz

Institutionalizing Data

When most people think of Los Angeles, historic preservation does not come to mind. But Los Angeles's 1962 Cultural Heritage Ordinance, which established a program for the local designation of city monuments, makes the city's historic preservation program one of the oldest in the country—predating both the National Historic Preservation Act (NHPA) and the founding of the National Register of Historic Places. More recently, Los Angeles has been at the national forefront in its efforts to provide a comprehensive and up-to-date record of the city's important historic resources. The resultant dataset—the largest publicly accessible digital dataset on significant historic resources of any city in the nation—is the product of two parallel but related projects: SurveyLA and HistoricPlacesLA. SurveyLA, the citywide historic resources survey, was specifically designed to identify and document important resources in Los Angeles that are not designated under any local, state, or federal program and that cover a broad range of historic and cultural themes and property types. HistoricPlacesLA, the city's online historic resources inventory and management system, grew out of the need to keep data on all of the city's historic resources, including those documented through current and future survey work and designated properties, in a single location where it is fully accessible, mappable, and searchable.

● DOCUMENTING HISTORIC RESOURCES

In US cities large and small, there is a resurgence of interest in completing historic resources surveys, particularly at the citywide level. Some municipalities are updating and augmenting existing surveys, while others are pursuing surveys for the first time. Most survey work in American cities started in the late 1970s and the 1980s. After the passage of the NHPA in 1966, the National Park Service developed professional standards and guidelines for surveys including the 1977 *Guidelines for Local Surveys: A Basis for Preservation Planning* (revised in 1985) and the *Secretary of the Interior's Standards and Guidelines for Archaeology and Historic Preservation* (published in 1983 and since revised). These publications provide technical advice regarding the identification, evaluation, and registration of significant historic resources as well as a framework for using this information to inform preservation planning. Although more than thirty years old, these publications still serve as go-to sources for standards.

The NHPA also called for the establishment of state agencies to implement provisions of the law, including statewide surveys of historic resources. State preservation programs developed survey standards based on the federal standards. By the 1970s, a growing interest in municipal preservation programs led to the 1980 amendment of the NHPA, which established the Certified Local Government (CLG) program to offer federal grant funding for surveys and to encourage local government participation in the identification and preservation of historic properties in their jurisdictions. Early municipal survey work from this time generally focused on buildings of architectural significance and typically covered only resources dating from before World War II.

The information needed to complete standardized historic resource survey forms drove data-collection processes for early surveys. While some municipal agencies designed forms in-house at this time, state preservation agencies developed forms for statewide use. In either case, the forms were completed from handwritten field notes—first in hard copy and later as digital forms filled out on a computer. The reliance on paper forms limited thinking about the kinds of data that could be collected and what could be useful for planning and other purposes. Though some state and local agencies put survey data into a simple database to allow for rudimentary sorting and searching, in most instances these survey forms were shelved. Nevertheless, the result in Los Angeles, as elsewhere, is that this legacy data, available in a variety of digital and nondigital formats, often serves as the starting point for new surveys.

The reasons for the renewed interest in survey work are varied but are connected to technological advances that make data collection more efficient and economically feasible and that also make the data more usable. Urban centers such as Los Angeles are experiencing fast-paced growth, as well as pressure to create more housing, revitalize neighborhoods and downtowns, develop transit-oriented communities, and embrace diversity, all while dealing with issues including gentrification, displacement, and economic inequality. Usable information on historic resources is critical to meeting community objectives in planning for growth and change. New technologies allow for the collection of precise spatial data, the recording of a wider range of resource types, the incorporation of digital photography, and the inclusion of historic contexts, all of which contribute to an analytical framework for using the data to inform planning goals and policies.

Contemporary surveys also expand on the time frame covered to include postwar resources, which now make up a large percentage of the built environment in American cities. These surveys focus on associated topics including midcentury modern architecture, postwar suburbanization, and even the more recent past. Similarly, the field of preservation generally is experiencing a shift in terms of social inclusion and the identification and celebration of diverse places of ethnic, social, and cultural importance, which have been largely underrepresented in earlier surveys and historic preservation efforts. Along with this shift, the field encourages innovative outreach strategies to include all communities in historic preservation, especially as community members are expert sources of information on places that matter. These factors broaden the meaning of the term "historic resource" to now include resources not represented by earlier surveys. This shift in focus is concurrent with the now common use of more fluid terms such as "cultural resource" or "heritage resource."

● DOCUMENTING HISTORIC RESOURCES IN LOS ANGELES

The concept of a citywide historic resources survey and inventory for Los Angeles started in 2000 when the Getty Conservation Institute (GCI) undertook a study of the potential for a documentation effort of

1
The $2.5 million grant agreement called for a dollar-for-dollar match from the city.

2
Interestingly, the 1962 ordinance predates the passage of the National Historic Preservation Act and the establishment of the National Register of Historic Places.

FIG. 1: *The expansive city of Los Angeles, as seen from the Griffith Observatory. Image: Asim Bharwani/Moment/Getty Images.*

this magnitude—Los Angeles encompasses about 500 square miles and includes 880,000 legal parcels. *FIG. 1* The GCI's *Los Angeles Historic Resource Survey Assessment Project: Summary Report* (2001) revealed that only 15 percent of the city had previously been surveyed and that city government, neighborhoods, preservationists, and the business community supported the need for reliable and up-to-date information on the city's historic resources.

In 2005 the city entered into a multiyear grant agreement with the J. Paul Getty Foundation to complete the citywide survey.1 SurveyLA, as it came to be called, officially launched in 2006 with the establishment of the city's Office of Historic Resources (OHR) to manage the project. The inception phase relied heavily on the GCI's publication *The Los Angeles Historic Resource Survey Report* (2008), which provided a blueprint for the project and addressed such issues as technology, historic contexts, public engagement, use, dissemination, and long-term management of the resulting data.

SurveyLA is not the first large-scale survey of Los Angeles. Efforts to initiate a citywide survey began in the late 1960s, not long after the adoption of the Cultural Heritage Ordinance and establishment of the Historic-Cultural Monument designation program.2 With the passage of the NHPA came the implementation of the National Register of Historic Places and the associated federal Section 106 review process. City agencies receiving federal funds for projects and responsible for Section 106 review included the Community Redevelopment Agency (CRA) and the Bureau of Engineering (BOE). While the CRA began conducting small-scale surveys in areas under their jurisdiction, the Cultural Heritage Commission and BOE worked together to find funding for a citywide survey. The California Office of Historic Preservation (established in 1975) awarded Los Angeles a grant in 1979 to plan a survey and another grant in 1980 to implement it. While at the time it was referred to as a citywide survey, the project focused on a limited number of areas; after all, with a general fifty-year rule for National Register eligibility, the survey

3
City correspondence files are available in the OHR.

4
In general, SurveyLA considered resources constructed up to 1980. Surveyors had the discretion to record more recent resources, guided by historic contexts.

5
The GCI provided some funding for the application as part of its technical support for the project, but the customized application was not designed for longevity. The software is now outdated, and there are no plans to upgrade it as the field surveys are complete.

6
Pilot surveys were completed to test survey tools and methods before the official surveys began.

considered only resources dating from before 1930 and did not include the vast sections of Los Angeles largely developed after World War II, including the San Fernando Valley. 3 Twenty-five years later, plans for a citywide survey broadened to include all of Los Angeles and to cover the period up to 1980. 4

● DEVELOPING A METHODOLOGY FOR SURVEYLA

In this new era of survey work, Los Angeles was the first city in the nation to complete a citywide survey using digital technology. From its inception, the project followed best practices in historic preservation, including standards and guidelines developed by the California Office of Historic Preservation and the NPS. However, the project updated these practices to take advantage of new technologies and to fully digitize the data-collection process. Factors taken into account included the level and type of documentation required to satisfy the standards of the state survey forms, to provide the foundation for a comprehensive preservation program, and to serve as baseline data for planning purposes. Developing strategies for public participation in the survey came later.

The sheer geographic scale of the survey required some basic decisions about what resources would be recorded and how. Efficiencies of scale demanded that a new approach be applied to what is known as an intensive level survey, where in-depth research is conducted on every property in a survey area and the recording process includes detailed, narrative descriptions and significance statements. To do so in Los Angeles would have taken decades. The new methodology implemented efficiencies to accomplish the following:

- evaluate properties for local listing as well as for the National Register of Historic Places and the California Register to facilitate use of data for multiple purposes
- record only properties determined to meet criteria for designation
- not record properties and districts already designated
- guide identification and evaluation using a citywide historic context statement
- conduct limited research on properties to substantiate significance
- develop an outreach program focused on soliciting input from the community on places of social and cultural importance

Efficiencies in field survey work were also achieved through the use of a customized geographic information system (GIS) survey application loaded on portable tablet computers. 5 *FIG. 2* At the time SurveyLA pilot surveys began in 2008, no off-the-shelf software for historic resources data collection was available. 6 Most municipalities and agencies developed their own in-house systems, using simple databases and spreadsheets, as GIS software for historic resource surveys was in a nascent stage. To take advantage of the most updated technologies, city planning staff worked with consultants to develop SurveyLA's survey application with the ability to do the following:

- record precise spatial data in a widely accepted format
- record a variety of resource types (which, in addition to individual buildings, include structures, objects, cultural landscapes, and historic districts, including features within a district)
- use standardized vocabularies (which established data fields such as architectural style, property type, and architectural features and eliminated the need to write time-consuming narrative descriptions) and drop-down lists to minimize free text and ensure consistency in recording by surveyors
- record historic context and property significance
- incorporate a variety of GIS reference layers such as built dates, aerial photographs, subdivision and tract maps, annexation maps, previous survey data, information on designated resources, and address-based information collected through outreach efforts

Ultimately, the structure and content of the field application contributed to the consistency and quality of the data collected, and the GIS platform visualized this fully searchable dataset on a map. The ability to accurately map the data offered a great advantage over the creation of a customized, nongeographic database for the storage and long-term use of the resulting dataset.

Digitizing Historic Contexts
Standard No. 1 of the "Secretary of the Interior's Standards for Preservation Planning" is "Preservation Planning Establishes Historic Contexts." As stated in the standard:

Decisions about the identification, evaluation, registration, and treatment of historic properties are most reliably made when the relationship of individual properties to other similar properties is understood. Information about historic properties representing

FIG. 2: *Portable tablet computers expedite the surveying process. Image courtesy of the City of Los Angeles, Department of City Planning.*

7
"Secretary of the Interior's Standards for Preservation Planning" (National Park Service, 2001), https://www.nps.gov/history/local-law/arch_stnds_1.htm#guide.

aspects of history, architecture, archeology, engineering, and culture must be collected and organized to define these relationships. This organizational framework is called a "historic context." The historic context organizes information based on a cultural theme and its geographical and chronological limits. Contexts describe the significant broad patterns of development in an area that may be represented by historic properties. The development of historic contexts is the foundation for decisions about identification, evaluation, registration, and treatment of historic properties.[7]

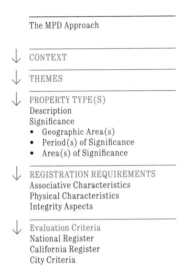

The MPD Approach

↓ CONTEXT

↓ THEMES

↓ PROPERTY TYPE(S)
Description
Significance
• Geographic Area(s)
• Period(s) of Significance
• Area(s) of Significance

↓ REGISTRATION REQUIREMENTS
Associative Characteristics
Physical Characteristics
Integrity Aspects

↓ Evaluation Criteria
National Register
California Register
City Criteria

FIG. 3: Diagram illustrating the Multiple Property Documentation approach applied in SurveyLA field surveys.

A historic context statement is a narrative, technical document that guides the survey and evaluation of historic resources. Historic contexts differ from other types of narrative histories in that they identify important themes in history and then relate those themes to extant historic resources or associated property types. Historic contexts establish the significance of themes and related topics and provide specific guidance regarding the physical and associative characteristics necessary to be a good example of a type. While narrative contexts have served as the foundation for best survey practice for decades, new technologies enable the development of contexts in digital formats to collect and use significance information in meaningful ways. Further, contexts—and survey work generally—have moved away from an emphasis on architectural significance to cover a broader range of topics, especially ethnic, gender, and cultural histories.

Los Angeles's citywide historic context statement (HCS), initiated as part of SurveyLA, is based on the Multiple Property Documentation (MPD) approach developed by the NPS. *FIG. 3* This approach organizes the trends and patterns of history shared by properties into themes, identifies and describes property types that represent those themes, and provides registration requirements to guide evaluation. Evaluating properties on a comparative basis within a given geographical area can help establish preservation priorities.

Although the intent of the MPD format is to streamline the nomination of properties related by theme to the National Register, it is also highly effective for survey work at any level. The format clearly defines the structure and content of contexts and establishes a narrative statement of significance applicable to all related property types. The registration requirements detail the physical and associative characteristics and integrity aspects a resource must have to be a good example of a type, making them usable for the National Register as well as local and state registration programs.[8] Importantly, the MPD format provides a consistent evaluation framework for use by all field surveyors and eliminates the need for customized narrative significance statements for every property surveyed.

SurveyLA's HCS is organized into nine broad contexts, listed below, which cover the period from about 1780 to 1980 and are specific to the city of Los Angeles.[9]

- Spanish Colonial and Mexican Era Settlement
- Pre-Consolidation Communities of Los Angeles
- Residential Development and Suburbanization
- Commercial Development
- Industrial Development
- The Entertainment Industry
- Public and Private Institutional Development
- Architecture and Engineering
- Cultural Landscapes

The contexts are further refined into a number of themes, over two hundred in all, associated with the architectural, social, ethnic, and cultural history of Los Angeles; the themes cover a wide range of topics and associated property types, such as Automobile Suburbanization, Water and Power, Labor History, Aviation and Aerospace, Los Angeles and the Automobile, and Women's Rights. The city has also developed themes relating to the histories of the LGBT, Jewish, Latino, Chinese, Japanese, Korean, Thai, Filipino, and African American communities of Los Angeles.

While the narrative historic contexts stand alone, the property types and evaluation components of the HCS have been formatted as drop-down lists during data collection. This format is highly replicable for survey work carried out by any agency at any scale and provides an analytical framework for studying survey results. Since context information is collected electronically, it gives immediate information on the citywide geographic distribution of property types by theme and by frequency, abundance, or rarity of a resource; it streamlines the evaluation of resources in accordance with national, state, and local designation criteria. Los Angeles's HCS is now being used by city and outside agencies so that all surveyors are using the same evaluation framework. Because the HCS format follows federal standards, it is usable by any US municipality conducting context-based surveys. The concept is even gaining interest worldwide.

Incorporating Community Outreach into Data Collection
Engaging the public in the process of data collection is critical to all survey work. For SurveyLA, the city developed a comprehensive outreach

8
Los Angeles's city historic context uses the term "eligibility standards" instead of "registration requirements."

9
Designing a citywide HCS from the ground up has the advantage of providing a structure that is both flexible and expandable over time. As new surveys are conducted, new themes can be added for topics not previously addressed or recognized. See a list of contexts currently in use at "Historic Contexts," SurveyLA, https://preservation. lacity.org/historic-context.

10
The GCI grant did not include funding for outreach. The city used Certified Local Government grants to fund production and translation costs of most of the materials used to inform and request input from the public.

11
Public outreach involved organizing a SurveyLA advisory committee, developing a website, and producing an Emmy award-winning video for the city's cable television channel. It also included programs designed to directly involve the public in various aspects of the project. This outreach helped build support and also supplemented the project budget in much-needed areas.

12
The questionnaire can be accessed at "Contribute Information to SurveyLA!," SurveyLA, https://preservation.lacity.org/survey/contribute.

13
The MyHistoricLA webpage on the SurveyLA website has been updated, and content has changed.

program that included various components. 10 Throughout SurveyLA, outreach focused on developing multilingual materials, reaching out to underrepresented communities, and broadening the public's concept of preservation beyond the protection of architecturally significant buildings. The program evolved over a number of years based on feedback from the public, lessons learned, and available funding. Ultimately, one of the main objectives of outreach was to directly engage the public in helping identify places of significance in communities throughout Los Angeles. 11 Particularly important were places whose social, ethnic, and cultural significance were not readily known from field surveys alone. This section focuses on components of the outreach program that directly informed the data-collection process.

Members of a public outreach advisory committee, organized early on for SurveyLA, underscored the need to help the public understand what type of information was valuable to SurveyLA and in what format it should be submitted. From this input, the OHR and a consultant team developed the MyHistoricLA program, which included three components. The MyHistoricLA questionnaire, a form with a series of ten short questions, was widely distributed in hard copy at outreach meetings, public libraries, city council offices, and other places. 12 The SurveyLA website also featured a form that could be submitted directly to the OHR.

The associated *Guide to Public Participation in SurveyLA* went further to collect information at a neighborhood level. A previous version of the guide explained:

There are a million stories in the "City of the Angels," and MyHistoricLA wants to know yours. Help us reveal the history of the people and places that make Los Angeles unique. Where do you live? What do you know about who lived there before you? How has your neighborhood grown or changed? What is your favorite historic building in your neighborhood or area? MyHistoricLA seeks to uncover the varied and multicultural heritage of the city, engage residents neighborhood by neighborhood, identify traditionally underrepresented groups, and gather information about resources of social and cultural significance. 13

Activities in the guide have been divided into themes to collect a wide range of historic information and insight; the guide includes a variety of activities to engage both individuals and groups.

The MyHistoricLA form allowed neighborhoods to take ownership of and manage their own contributions to SurveyLA, and the companion guide offered information up front, to inform surveys before fieldwork started. To make this method possible, the OHR designed a spreadsheet that indicated the type of data collected for SurveyLA and the associated data fields in the survey application. The OHR, primarily working with graduate student interns, undertook a large-scale effort to collect outreach information into GIS data for use during field surveys. For example, standing in front of an otherwise undistinguished single-family residence, a surveyor could quickly access the story of an important person who lived there.

While the form and the guide resulted in useful information, in reality this success was limited. In-person training meetings for the guide were generally not well attended, and the OHR had no dedicated staff and limited funding for outreach. The MyHistoricLA website (MyHistoricLA. org), launched in 2012, grew out of a need for public engagement with a broad-based audience and a desire to initiate online conversations. The OHR implemented MyHistoricLA during field surveys rather than ahead of them. As with the form and the guide, the website allowed a diverse audience of participants to provide information on historic resources. It also allowed the OHR to pose questions about resources in specific geographic areas to fill information gaps. For example, while surveying in the suburbs of the San Fernando Valley, MyHistoricLA asked participants about the now rare agricultural resources that remain, which may not be readily visible from the public right-of-way. FIG. 4

A feature of the system tracked demographic information on participants. FIG. 5 The MyHistoricLA website was short-lived because of its limited success in reaching all of its intended audiences. However, it is nevertheless helping to shape future plans to reinstate an online and ongoing forum for public participation.

FIG. 4: The MyHistoricLA web page.

FIG. 5: Gender and age of MyHistoricLA users. Courtesy of the City of Los Angeles, Department of City Planning.

14
In many cases, resources identified—regardless of age or property type—are the only tangible connection to the story or history they represent and with which they are associated.

15
Though the unrest spread throughout Los Angeles, this intersection and the location of the beating of King are the two locations most associated with the 1992 uprising.

16
Even though state and local designation programs may not have a fifty-year rule for significance, this National Register rule still guides most survey work in the United States.

Local efforts to identify places that matter in Los Angeles mirror national efforts to be more inclusive in the type of resources recorded and to develop programs that reflect the country's diverse communities. The shift in the way resources are recorded and the reasons resources should be considered important are underscored by SurveyLA's methodology. Guiding survey work with historic contexts leads to identifying and recording a wider range of property types than had been considered in earlier surveys. 14 Information received through outreach efforts greatly informed contexts and surveys associated with social, ethnic, and cultural significance. These associated property types and resources may have gone unnoticed without the community's input. Sites representing cultural histories and unique property types raise questions about how these places are taken into account in survey work and, more importantly, in the development of planning policies for the communities that value them.

One example is a street intersection significant for its association with the events of Los Angeles's 1992 uprising. *FIG. 6* The intersection is a flashpoint site and the location of the beating of Reginald Denny following the acquittal of police officers tried in the Rodney King case. 15 Despite the fact that no more than twenty years had passed, SurveyLA recorded this site based on a context-driven approach, rather than recording only resources that met the fifty-year age requirement established by the National Register. 16

FIG. 6: *Image of the intersection of Normandie and Florence Avenues, a flashpoint of the 1992 civil unrest in Los Angeles. Image courtesy of the City of Los Angeles, Department of City Planning.*

● DEVELOPMENT OF HISTORICPLACESLA

To accomplish the goal of improving access to historic resources data in Los Angeles, the city and the GCI further built upon the SurveyLA partnership. As SurveyLA field surveys progressed, the GCI and World Monuments Fund (WMF) had separately been developing Arches, an

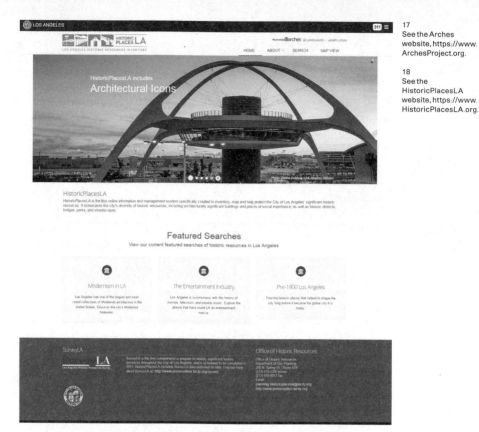

17
See the Arches website, https://www.ArchesProject.org.

18
See the HistoricPlacesLA website, https://www.HistoricPlacesLA.org.

FIG. 7: Home page for HistoricPlacesLA.

open-source, geospatial, and web-based software, to document and inventory cultural heritage sites worldwide. 17 The GCI chose Los Angeles as the first large-scale US implementation site for Arches. This customized system, named HistoricPlacesLA, premiered in 2015. 18

The Arches software was created in response to the substantial challenges in data management faced by heritage organizations globally. Recognizing the lack of software systems to address these challenges, the GCI and WMF set out to provide a user-friendly, low-cost, and accessible solution. The collection of heritage data often involves many different digital and nondigital formats, and datasets vary widely in both scale and complexity. Many organizations and communities that are engaged in protecting some of the world's most threatened heritage resources do not have access to sophisticated technology or substantial funding. Nevertheless, as in the case of Los Angeles and most heritage-based organizations, making relevant data easily accessible is a high priority.

First released for public use in 2013, Arches is a web-based inventory and management platform with GIS capabilities created specifically for cultural heritage data. Because Arches is open-source, heritage organizations worldwide can independently deploy and customize the system to fit the resources they manage while also meeting widely adopted international standards for heritage-resource inventories. *FIG. 7*

19
"Standards &
Interoperability,"
Arches Project,
https://www.arches
project.org/standards.

20
HistoricPlacesLA
currently holds
about 40 percent of
SurveyLA data and
also includes partial
data for the city's des-
ignated resources.

The use of international standards for information technology, heritage inventories, and heritage data management by Arches promotes data sharing; meanwhile, the format in which the data is stored safeguards its longevity.[19] For HistoricPlacesLA, Arches's carefully developed structure is merged with the federal- and state-standards framework of SurveyLA to support the data for surveyed and designated historic resources within the boundaries of the city.[20] *FIG. 8* As an online searchable database, HistoricPlacesLA is a valuable resource for the city and the public to conduct advanced queries using mapping, geographical buffers, time frames, and even combined searches. *FIG. 9*

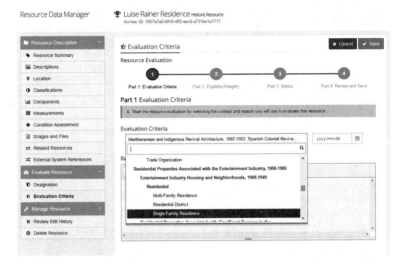

FIG. 8: Adding or editing a resource in HistoricPlacesLA is steered by the Multiple Property Documentation approach.

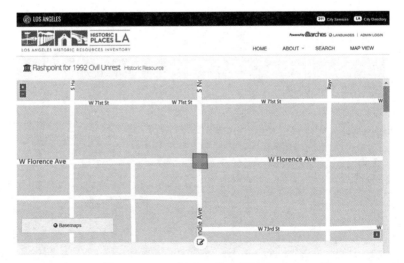

FIG. 9: Map of the intersection of Normandie and Florence Avenues. The resource was recorded as a polygon, encompassing the site.

● BIG DATA: WHAT'S IT FOR?

With big data comes big responsibility. Los Angeles now has the largest and most advanced dataset on historic resources of any municipality in the United States. This puts the city at the forefront of a new era in digital historic resources data, which can serve a range of purposes both within and outside urban planning. While on its own the dataset is impressive, it becomes more powerful when integrated into HistoricPlacesLA. At the most basic level, HistoricPlacesLA serves as a system to manage information on historic resources over time. *FIG. 11* But this information has broader uses: it can both inform and influence the shifting practice of historic preservation in Los Angeles and in the United States more widely.

The city's responsibilities lie not only in managing and maintaining the data but also in promoting its use. As the first step in this process, the Department of City Planning hired a data manager, signaling its long-term commitment to HistoricPlacesLA and making historic resources data available. The ultimate goal is to have HistoricPlacesLA serve as the one-stop source of information for the city's significant historic resources. 21 With SurveyLA now complete, work is underway in the OHR to fully integrate the data into HistoricPlacesLA. As well, data integration includes adding further survey data, revising and expanding the historic context statement, and providing up-to-date and complete records of the city's designated historic resources. 22 While this data integration continues,

21
The Department of City Planning manages an online GIS-based database that is currently incompatible with HistoricPlacesLA. This parcel-based database does not support more than minimal information on historic resources. As it remains well used, the ultimate goal is to have the definitive records in HistoricPlacesLA connect to the city's parcel-based database in real time.

22
The Community Redevelopment Agency of Los Angeles completed surveys in some parts of the city concurrent with SurveyLA. Data from these surveys needs to be reformatted before being merged into HistoricPlacesLA.

FIG. 11: Evaluation and significance of the site associated with the 1992 civil unrest in Los Angeles, as seen in HistoricPlacesLA.

23
"Put Her on the Map,"
https://putheron
themap.com.

new features for Arches are in development. Most notable is the forth-coming mobile data-collection application, which allows for the remote addition of new survey records, both small and large, directly into the system, eliminating the need for data conversion. When this feature is implemented, HistoricPlacesLA will be a single system to collect, manage, use, and query data.

The OHR also plans to add capabilities that facilitate administration of the city's historic preservation programs, in parallel with the development of the casework/workflow module in development for Arches. For the city, this feature could provide a much-needed system to track processes associated with formal historic designation and financial incentive programs. In addition, because it is an open-source platform, improvements to the Arches software will become available to other heritage organizations as they implement and customize Arches for their use. The city will benefit from contributions made by other organizations in the Arches open-source community.

Opportunities for the dataset are still evolving and will accelerate as data integration into HistoricPlacesLA is completed. Consistent with the earlier goals and objectives of SurveyLA, uses of the data now focus largely on shaping preservation planning in Los Angeles. The Department of City Planning is, in fact, the primary user of the data. Most often, the data informs day-to-day case processing and decision-making regarding development projects affecting historic resources. In this era of rapid growth and change, tracking development activities in specific areas helps assess cumulative impacts to resources geographically. The data is also informing updates to the city's community plan program. These local-use plans guide future growth and development in neighborhoods throughout Los Angeles. Comprehensive historic resources information helps planners and community members work together to develop goals and policies that recognize and protect important historic and cultural resources.

While HistoricPlacesLA serves as the city's internal historic resources inventory and management system, it is also the public portal for the data. This means that other departments and agencies, both within and outside of the city can and are using HistoricPlacesLA, oftentimes to obtain information regarding properties under their management. Property types include city parks, fire stations, libraries, schools, hospitals, and bridges, and knowing which properties are significant helps in the development of long-range plans regarding properties that may need updating as well as those that may be decommissioned. Recently, the Office of the Mayor, the OHR, and Mount Saint Mary's University collaborated in planning and hosting a community research event for Women's History Month to establish a list of influential women connected to the history of Los Angeles. Volunteers searched through SurveyLA data for notable women, ultimately aiding in the development of the Los Angeles Women's Rights theme, underway at the time, and launching a Los Angeles–based "Put Her on the Map" initiative that aims to increase the number of streets, landmarks, and monuments named after women.[23]

As we look forward, perhaps one of the greatest opportunities for HistoricPlacesLA is as a tool to promote greater inclusivity in historic preservation. Using data for analytical purposes, particularly through mapping, can indicate where the city's important ethnic and cultural resources are located and can serve both as an indicator of changing demographics and an identifier of places that are largely unrecognized in designation programs. The data can also help expand public perceptions of historic preservation to include a wide range of historical themes and types of cultural resources.

In the coming years, as both HistoricPlacesLA and Arches mature, uses of the data will grow. From the city's perspective, promoting full use of historic preservation data requires a greater level of interdepartmental and intradepartmental collaboration and information sharing. And to accomplish the goal of reaching a wider preservation audience in a more advanced digital age, a crowdsourcing feature to enhance public outreach can draw upon the successes and failures of the MyHistoricPlacesLA program implemented for SurveyLA. The city's big and growing heritage dataset brings with it challenges, responsibilities, and opportunities. As Los Angeles moves forward, and as big data continues to inform the city's preservation practices, the lessons learned can influence the heritage field internationally.

An interview with Lisa Ackerman

Institutionalizing Data

ERICA AVRAMI
From the 1980s to the present, through positions at the International Foundation for Art Research and the Samuel H. Kress Foundation and now as the acting CEO of World Monuments Fund, you have had a privileged view of the role of data collection in the conservation of heritage, both movable (objects) and immovable (such as the built environment). Can you share some insight into how the field has evolved in the last thirty years?

1
Lisa Ackerman, "Modern Museology: 108,000 Images per Disk," *Art Research News* 2, no. 4 (1983).

2
Laura Corti and Marilyn Schmitt, eds., *Automatic Processing of Art History Data and Documents: Pisa, Scuola Normale Superiore, September 24–27, 1984: Proceedings, Second International Conference on Automatic Processing of Art History Data and Documents* (Florence: Regione Toscana, 1985).

LISA ACKERMAN

The impetus to categorize information is clearly something that evolved early in the history of scholarship. Whether it is the desire to map the world, document species, or identify genetic material, human resilience is linked to a quest for knowledge and the ability to organize and retrieve it. In the humanities, this is clear in the formation of encyclopedic collections of art, the creation of catalogues, and the many other examples of inventories related to the arts and cultural activity.

At the International Foundation for Art Research, one of our main projects in the late 1970s and early 1980s was the publication of a monthly newsletter, *Stolen Art Alert*. This was an attempt to alert museums, art dealers, auction houses, and collectors to works of art that might appear illegally on the art market. It was a valiant effort to use a printed newsletter to circulate critical information. Today, such information can be made public nearly simultaneously with the report of a theft, looting, or other criminal act.

At the same time, museums were beginning to create digital resources documenting their collections. After writing about the virtues of digitizing collections and the unparalleled new access to information that would be available because of this resource for *Art Research News*, in 1984 I had the privilege of attending the Second International Conference on Automatic Processing of Art History Data and Documents in Pisa, hosted by the J. Paul Getty Trust and the Scuola Normale Superiore.[1] This was truly a groundbreaking event, dedicated to developing standards by which museums, art historians, and research centers would agree upon methodologies, lexicons, and iconography to advance the idea of universal access to collection catalogues, archival information, and resources in the field.[2] Today, it is hard to imagine there was life before the Internet and global searches. In those early days of the 1980s, however, this conference opened a new world to many of those assembled.

The Samuel H. Kress Foundation is the former owner of a renowned art collection and a significant supporter of heritage conservation projects. In what ways did the foundation's history of managing an actual collection influence its early funding for systematic heritage documentation?

Since its founding in 1929, the work of the Samuel H. Kress Foundation in many ways established a history of caring about academic resources and access to that data. When the foundation amassed the Samuel H. Kress Collection, one of the first acts was to create a catalogue and assemble a dossier for each work of art. A number was assigned to each work acquired, quaintly called "K" numbers by staff members. But the process was far from quaint or ad hoc. Each work was photographed, described, its conditions noted, and later an X-ray was taken of each work of art. Even later, when the collection was well over two thousand objects, the foundation hired Fern Rusk Shapley to create a nine-volume catalogue of the collection. Each work was thoroughly researched, and the publication offered a brief biography of the artist, a description of the work of art, and then a thorough explanation of every instance in which the work had been publicly displayed and published. Assembling data of this nature from 1929 until 1968, the date of the Phaidon catalogues, was painstaking research—especially without the help of rapid Internet searches or indexed online reference libraries. It remains a remarkable addition to our knowledge of European old master paintings, particularly those in US public collections.

Similarly, for decades the foundation's grant giving sought to develop scholarly resources and improve access to that information. These initiatives ranged from requiring grant recipients that produced new images of works of art or historic architecture to provide copies to the National Gallery of Art photographic archives or to make those images available in ways that benefit the field or contribute to the research of other scholars—for example, creating a database on historic stained glass in America, or contributing to the work of Corpus Vitrearum. For every area of specialization in art historical study, there is undoubtedly an inventory that has been carefully crafted. The foundation sought to encourage the growth of such databases and make them available to a wider audience. It was also an early supporter of the Index of Christian Art and paid for the digitization of the Cicognara Library of the Vatican's collection so that scholars could remotely access its more than five thousand volumes, which are considered an important foundation for art historical study.

Most importantly, it provided access to scholars and students who might not have access to rare book collections or specialized archives, which might contain only a selection of the volumes in the Cicognara Library. These projects may seem unremarkable today, but in the predigital age, and even in the early days of digitization, these were extraordinary undertakings in democratizing access to scholarly resources.

In addition to artworks, you mentioned documenting stained glass and historic architecture. Do you see connections between the fields of movable and immovable heritage growing stronger as data collection and digitization have progressed?

Architectural preservation has been closely allied with art and art history for centuries. Raphael was charged with cataloguing Roman ruins; Palladio wrote what is considered the first modern guidebook to the architecture of Rome; Thomas Ashby of the British School at Rome created an incredible collection of guidebooks to Rome, chronicling the evolution of the city through the sites visitors were encouraged to see.

It is no surprise, then, that many of the early tools for preservation were inspired by the ideas of art historians: encyclopedic inventories of the built environment, portfolios of works by particular architects, the categorization of building types, and physical descriptions that were very similar to descriptions of art. Before long, there were calls for national inventories of heritage sites and all manner of lists and itineraries were created.

As the field of historic preservation progressed, it began to inventory threats and risks to heritage sites—problems that ranged from the physical, such as typologies of deterioration, to the more philosophical, such as rapid urbanization, climate change, shifts in population, and natural or man-made disaster. As the notion of heritage evolved, so did the desire to create databases that could help identify important places, changes to them, their risks, and in many cases the opportunity for sustainable solutions to a mounting range of challenges in the field.

At World Monuments Fund, you deal almost exclusively with immovable heritage. What have been some of the biggest challenges for systematic data collection about the historic built environment and its management?

Looking at this challenge through the lens of World Monuments Fund's work has been illuminating and frustrating in equal measure. There is an astonishing array of information collected through site-based conservation projects, national heritage inventories, university collections, and field research. At the same time, there is the difficulty of accessing the information, fear of what ills might befall some sites if data were readily available, and the reality that much of the work is driven by limited budgets. Thus data is regularly trapped on outdated hardware and software.

In 1989, World Monuments Fund issued a report, *The Razing of Romania's Past*, written by Dinu Giurescu, a Romanian scholar who chronicled the systematic destruction of historic architecture and towns throughout the country. This was followed in the 1990s by a series of publications with titles such as *Survey of Jewish Monuments in Poland and Inventory and Survey of America's Heritage Abroad: Sites of Jewish Heritage in Czechoslovakia*. This collection of information was groundbreaking in that decade of discovery of what remained of Jewish heritage in former East Bloc countries after the fall of Communist rule. By the time I arrived at World Monuments Fund at the end of 2007, these publications were nearly forgotten—and yet they contained a wealth of interesting data about heritage sites. More powerful tools had been developed in the ensuing decade, and new datasets were being collected and were available in ever more practical ways on the Internet. But there was still a sense that information was not reaching a wide audience. You still needed to be involved in these projects to know the datasets were available.

Similar to the Automatic Processing of Art History Data and Documents conferences and the efforts to develop standards for and universal access to collections data, how has the architectural heritage field attempted to standardize its digital inventory data, and what challenges does it face?

As news reports of the US-led invasion of Iraq covered the looting of archaeological sites and museums, in the cultural heritage sector there was a call to do more to protect vulnerable heritage. In the aftermath of the invasion, as war and sectarian violence continued to rage, World

3
Arches Project,
https://www.
archesproject.org.

Monuments Fund and the Getty Conservation Institute began the development of an open-access software program known as MEGA, Middle Eastern Geodatabase for Antiquities. The idea was to develop a model for creating a digital, national inventory that would improve knowledge of and access to sites in any country. As it was not possible to mount such an effort in Iraq as conflict raged, the program was implemented in Jordan, which had developed an inventory system a decade earlier known as JADIS. MEGA then transformed into Arches, an open-source heritage management tool.[3] Thanks to the work of the Getty Conservation Institute, it has become a compelling digital tool driven by the needs of the field and augmented by contributions from an active online community.

Yet it is those early years and the transformation from MEGA into Arches that are most interesting when trying to understand the challenges in the field of historic preservation. The biggest breakthrough was recognizing that heritage sites are not dots on a map but polygons that need to be drawn correctly to understand the boundaries of a site. This may or may not concern the average person looking for a site, but it has vast implications for those managing a site. Qusayr 'Amra in Jordan provides a prime example of what happens when you see a dot on a map. It can result in a road being created through the middle of an archaeological site. A polygon illustrating boundaries makes clear where a site is actually located, pushing the road around the edges of the site. From a planning perspective, understanding shape and dimensions can make a dramatic difference in decisions that affect the well-being of a heritage asset. There are many technological advancements in the software, but at the most basic level, simply moving toward a more integrated approach to mapping sites advances the management dialogue and integrates heritage into larger planning objectives.

JADIS and MEGA also demonstrated that an investment in software and hardware was not sufficient. Leaders in the field also needed to invest more substantially in training for those charged with maintaining digital inventories. Information on cards may become outdated, ink may fade, and cards are vulnerable in times of crisis. Transferring data to digital technology eliminates one set of problems but can also create new challenges, like ensuring enough people are trained to maintain the systems, to migrate the data to the next iteration of hardware and software, and to understand how and when to upgrade systems. The learning curve was substantial, which explains why some of the problems persist and why, indeed, integrated national heritage inventories are still being developed. There is no question that heritage inventories are essential tools for monitoring heritage. What we are lacking as a field is cohesive, integrated access to that data. The way in which JSTOR bundles access to scholarly texts and Artstor provides access to millions of images demonstrates that it is possible to find ways to standardize access to materials for the benefit of the scholarly community. Many universities now regularly provide open access to significant archival and library resources.

Arches is closing the gap for the heritage field in terms of easing the collection of data and the migration of information from older systems. There of course remain other obstacles, such as knowledge of the software, funds to maintain systems, and, in some countries, access to reliable Internet connections. Time, hopefully, will provide the means to overcome these challenges.

What issues do you see on the horizon as data creates more robust tools for heritage management?

The breadth and depth of information presented at the Urban Heritage and Data in the 21st Century symposium held in February 2018 was astonishing. The efforts that have been mounted and the powerful results demonstrate how much information is harnessed regularly in the field. With a few exceptions, most of the presentations were a first-time look at the information for many assembled in the room. So the question arose once again of when will that information be pushed out into a more public arena so that planning, preservation, and research all benefit from the tremendous work that is being done.

We've come a long way from Raphael recording descriptions of ancient ruins in Rome. GIS, laser scanning, remote sensing, satellite imagery, and numerous other digital tools are employed daily in the field. Our documentation standards are high. Our challenge for the twenty-first century is to employ data in ever more powerful ways: to elevate preservation discussions beyond inventories, landmark designations, and recording losses through demolition, neglect, and disaster. As we move through this next era, we need to think critically about preservation and livability. How will preservation data shape our decisions and visions for the communities in which we live and visit? How will data help us understand the narratives that are not being told through our built heritage?

In 1995, when the World Monuments Watch was launched, the goal was to provide a conduit for learning about heritage sites in peril around the world. A large net was cast by soliciting nominations from anyone who wished to submit a dossier. Announced as the 100 Most Endangered Monuments in the World, it was a powerful message that across the globe, people could reach out to WMF and describe the places that they cherished. Today, the program has included more than eight hundred sites and brought attention to places that were previously unknown to many or that people are surprised to learn are considered heritage. The 2018 Watch contained twenty-five sites, and the "Most Endangered" label was dropped a decade ago. But the message remains the same. People from around the world have taken the time to tell WMF about the places that matter to them and what threats, challenges, and opportunities exist to maintain these sites as beacons in their communities.

World Monuments Fund is, in many ways, struggling today to improve its own ability to harness data: how to move from compelling anecdotes to more data-driven decisions that can help the World Monuments Watch for the betterment of the field—and by extension society. It's easy to fall in love with historic sites, their values, and the strong narratives that Watch sites convey. Even the simplest description of a few of the sites evokes strong reactions. Explaining why the bridges of the Merritt Parkway, the Taj Mahal, Great Zimbabwe, the historic skyline of St. Petersburg, the Mortuary Temple of Amenhotep III, and the Chankillo archaeological site have all been on the World Monuments Watch and how they represent an extraordinary journey through human achievement can provoke so many discussions. The challenge as we contemplate the future of the program is how to apply greater rigor to the inherently emotional process of researching highly significant places, presenting them to the public, and building upon the success of past Watch sites and defining measurable outcomes as each cycle launches. In essence, how do we move away from thinking about historic preservation research and data as linear and instead move toward a more relational model that thinks about outcomes before they happen?

Managing Historic Complexity: Practical Lessons from Tech-Forward Historic Resource Surveys

Matthew Hampel

Institutionalizing Data

Surveying is the key to the collection—and thus the use—of data in cataloguing, managing, and promoting urban heritage. From surveying the condition of every property in Detroit to helping the Office of Historic Preservation in Austin collect data on the city's historic inventory to working with preservation consultants to prove the market viability of historic neighborhoods, the range of survey and data-collection projects is wide. For us at Loveland Technologies, a survey is defined as a coordinated effort to collect data on a significant set of properties in a target class or area. This coordinated effort includes marshaling resources, planning consistent questions, and organizing the data collection. A significant set of properties can be either a statistically significant number or a survey or an entire population of homes. These surveys typically have a target area (such as a whole city or neighborhood) or class of property (such as every home on the city's historic register). For example, a citywide effort to identify potentially historic commercial buildings meets our definition of a survey. Collecting notes on a few properties of interest or doing an in-depth study of a single building or block is out of scope.

We divide the goals of surveying into three categories: baseline data collection, operational management, and social change. This list certainly is non-exhaustive, but it is useful for classifying survey management. The first category, collecting baseline data, is the fundamental goal of many surveys: acquiring the data necessary to understand an issue. The second, managing operations, typically comes after a baseline survey and helps practitioners achieve outcomes by extending the operational impact and life of data. Influencing the built and social environment through policy and community change is the highest-level goal of many projects.

1
City of Detroit, "Detroit Hardest Hit Fund Strategic Plan," http://www.detroitmi.gov/Portals/0/docs/EM/Reports/Hardest Hit Funds Strategic Plan.pdf. The Hardest Hit Fund was established in 2010 to provide funding for a range of programs focused on foreclosure prevention and neighborhood stabilization in states hit hard by the 2008 financial crisis.

2
"Motor City Mapping," https://motorcitymapping.org.

3
"The Historic Resource Survey: Community Data Collection in Action," Data Driven Detroit, July 9, 2014, http://datadrivendetroit.org/blog/2014/07/09/2613.

● BASELINE DATA

In 2014, the City of Detroit received a large infusion of money from the Hardest Hit Fund targeted at demolishing vacant and abandoned homes in poor condition. 1 At the same time, the city, along with Loveland Technologies, was running Motor City Mapping, an extensive project to survey the condition of every property in the city. 2 Residents were paid to drive every street and record basic information, including occupancy status, for each residential structure in order to help prioritize investment and demolition. Because of the speed of the survey and the baseline nature of the data, the survey included no questions about historic character.

Recognizing the potential impact of this work on the city's historic inventory, the Michigan Historic Preservation Network, in partnership with the National Trust for Historic Preservation and Data Driven Detroit, used the tool kit provided by LocalData (now a part of Loveland) to run a parallel survey on targeted neighborhoods. Volunteers trained in recognizing historic characteristics were sent out with a mobile app and a limited list of questions about the properties. In just a few weeks, they collected data on over seventeen thousand properties. 3 This project offers three lessons on baseline surveying:

Keep the Surveys Short

One operational need for the Detroit project was to keep the survey short. Because the time to complete the survey work was limited, managers could not add every question that might be useful to the survey form—and that was a good thing. Surveying is often seen as a rare event that requires maximum output. Asking a broad set of questions can be appealing; after all, surveyors will be in the field anyway, and the cost of each single additional question can seem small. This situation gives organizers the temptation to bundle in as many questions as possible.

The time adds up, though. Even if there is a budget for surveying, brevity both saves resources and means that surveyors can be less likely to rush through questions in order to hit targets. Keeping the list of questions short keeps surveyors engaged, not exhausted. To achieve brevity, we advise that organizations focus only on the questions that will have an immediate impact. A simple test is to ask what each question will be used for: if the answer to any proposed question is "It'll be useful sometime" or "I don't know," strongly consider removing it from the survey.

Use Data to Bring Preservation to the Table

Organizations can use data to bring their issues to the table. In the case of the Detroit survey, the discussion of demolition and investment was highly politicized. At the city level, it was a technocratic process driven by numbers-focused teams. The citywide survey timeline didn't allow room for questions not related to the core issues of housing condition and occupancy, and preservationists were not included in the conversation.

By building a survey, owning the data, and managing the process independently, the preservation advocates were able to demonstrate their seriousness and gather evidence. Preservation always has strong voices; data helps to amplify those voices and, if nothing else, wrap the discourse in the evidence-focused vocabulary of today.

Use Data as an Engagement Tactic

Through our work, we have found that data is an effective engagement and organizing tool. The process of collecting data itself can be useful for organizing. It is a strong way to call for participation from volunteers, to bring in people who haven't participated before, to create media-ready moments (for example, the kickoff and the close of the process), and to grow your rolls of interested participants. While we don't suggest setting up a survey simply as a way to activate volunteers or get press, we do find that there are important benefits to engaging preservation-interested networks, and these collateral benefits should be managed strategically.

Two common concerns in working with volunteers are work quality and training. A well-designed survey can be communicated to a group of lay supporters in a reasonable amount of time, like a short workshop, meaning that quality can be fairly consistent. By keeping the survey short, you reduce chances for misunderstanding and the time needed for training. The quality-assurance process also becomes easier.

The immediacy of survey work can have a positive impact on participants. With modern mapping tools, data can fill maps as surveyors work. Data entered on a phone or a tablet in the field is instantly visible to organizers in the office. When surveyors return to base, they can see the collective impact of their workday, and the results can be shared quickly. This immediacy is rewarding, in contrast to both paper processes, where there is a time-consuming transcription step, and political and policy organizing, which requires drawn-out processes with less frequent opportunities to celebrate success.

● MANAGING OPERATIONS

After some baseline surveys, the data languishes, bundled into a report never to be seen again. For many organizations, though, a survey is only the start of a longer process. This fact allows them to keep the data fresh while serving the organization's mid-term goals.

In Pittsburgh, Grounded (formerly GTech Strategies) uses surveys to track the work of contractors who maintain vacant lots. The Detroit Riverfront Conservancy has been keeping an inventory of properties that are available for adaptive reuse. In Chicago, the Southwest Organizing Project used our surveying tools to track the status of single-family homes across several years. When a staffer observed a change in the condition of the home—for example, a For Sale sign appearing or visible construction—they would note the change, using the survey tool to track the home's status over time. This allowed the organization to see trends and patterns in neighborhood development and to target homes and owners to support.

These projects reveal several best practices. First, the work done in a baseline survey should transition into an ongoing project to extend the value of the data. Second, the ability to react quickly is enhanced by switching to operational surveys. Finally, despite apparent cost and logistical barriers, simply starting the process with an easily available tool can avoid the risk of "analysis paralysis" and reduce project delays.

Track Constantly, Not Just Once
Many surveys are set up as one-time processes. Every ten years, or whenever funding can be wrangled, an organization does a baseline survey of its target areas. However, large data-collection efforts are increasingly only the start of an ongoing process in heritage work. After the large survey, an organization may shift to collecting updates either on an ad hoc basis (e.g., as inspectors or volunteers go out in the field), or on a regular but slower rotation. To make the work more manageable, the set of variables tracked can also be reduced to just those that are more likely to change.

There are multiple benefits to this kind of shift. Smaller real-time updates allow the results of time- and cash-intensive baseline survey-ing to have a longer shelf life; costs for maintaining data can be lower when this work is included in existing staff time; and when the benefits of the data are realized over a longer time frame, they can have a more direct impact on an organization's mid-term goals, like managing a successful project.

4
Chris Whong,
"Whong's Law,"
Twitter, March 22,
2018, https://twitter.
com/chris_whong/
status/9768166
80256135169.

Have Shovel-Ready Projects

By keeping data up to date over time rather than focusing on occasional large pushes, an organization can react more quickly to funding opportunities. We saw the inverse of such readiness around the American Recovery and Reinvestment Act and Hardest Hit Fund investment in Detroit. When large amounts of funding became available to tackle local projects, organizations in Detroit had to rush to put together a working coalition. They needed to quickly find the capital and do the work to record the conditions across 370,000 properties.

When a dataset is maintained over time, this kind of large outlay may be less necessary. Groups have the information at hand to make the case for funding a specific project. When data is up to date, groups also avoid the need for potentially costly large-scale surveys undertaken just for a specific grant, which may not be received.

Value Process Over Tools

Finally, for organizations considering a more operational style of surveying, a lack of familiarity with available tools or a perceived lack of technological knowledge can lead to paralysis. It's easy to lose focus on the core work and instead divert attention to selecting the right tool. "Whong's Law," coined by Chris Whong of the NYC Planning Labs, cheekily explains the danger: "Every government agency, everywhere is working on a 'new system'; it will solve *all* of their data problems and will be ready to use in 18–24 months."[4]

Picking a good tool is critical, but picking any tool is more so. We see groups that are successful when they pick a tool (even if it's as simple as a spreadsheet), understanding that it can be changed later, and simply use it to accomplish their goals. Inexpensive tools, like shared Google spreadsheets and off-the-shelf mapping products, can fulfill most needs and avoid a lengthy procurement process or costly custom development time. Lessons from using an off-the-shelf tool can also define needs for the next version of the tool (itself potentially a shovel-ready project for funders).

● POLICY ADVOCACY AND ACTIVISM

Many organizations have a difficult relationship with policy advocacy and activism. Distinct from managing a project (handling day-to-day processes, ensuring milestones are met), with advocacy and activism data is deployed to push for a (possibly divisive) outcome. While most nonprofits cannot campaign for candidates, many do have a focused policy agenda directly connected with their mission. Government-housed preservation agencies are also charged with interpreting and occasionally lobbying to improve policy that affects preservation.

In concrete terms, action-focused data collection in this area can take many forms. First, this kind of data collection can help to shape the narrative: data is a tool that can frame conversations about the built environment, as in the way data brings preservation to the table. Second, expanding beyond physical resource surveys to speak with residents can increase the power of surveys. Finally, data can be used to broaden an organization's base of support among otherwise loosely affiliated groups.

5
Conor Dougherty, "The Great American Single-Family Home Problem," *New York Times*, December 1, 2017.

Fighting Against NIMBYism and Parochialism

The discourse around preservation is changing. The YIMBY, or "Yes In My Back Yard," movement is gaining awareness as a reaction to opposition to new development. Spurred by rising rents and a lack of affordable or inclusive housing options, this narrative positions anti-development (NIMBY) activism as classist and shows it in an unfavorable social light.[5] Supporters see a need for increasing housing stock on a large scale, and they typically favor upzoning and urban density. Preservation runs the risk of being caught up and vilified (fairly or unfairly) by this pro-development narrative, but using data and tools in new ways to show the power of preservation can help reduce this risk.

Organizations like PlaceEconomics do a good job of finding data that supports a pro-preservation agenda. Framing survey work in the context of development is key to addressing the narrative. For example, large-scale identification of buildings suitable for adaptive reuse could provide a menu of options for new projects with character that is not available in new construction. Comparing market values and change in historic versus new communities can demonstrate how preserving urban heritage can have positive impacts like growing wealth in minority communities and reducing inequality.

Focusing on People, Not Just Places

Many surveys focus purely on the built environment—the condition of a home or the occupancy status of a building—but perhaps more important and immediately impactful are efforts that lead to direct contact with residents. Several recent surveys by the Detroit nonprofit United Community Housing Coalition have focused on combating the region's long-running foreclosure crisis. Coalition surveyors have been canvassing homes that may be foreclosed in the Detroit area to get in touch with the occupants, understand their situation, and offer connections to support. While not strictly preservation surveys, these efforts are highly interconnected with preservation. By working to keep people in their homes, such efforts also preserve places. There are a wide range of services and incentives available for preservation, and we believe policy goals are best achieved with more proactive, survey-based outreach. A baseline survey can be used to identify properties for targeted follow-up and in-person contact from organizers.

Broadening the Base of Allies to Include Nontraditional Supporters

Bringing more data into policy can also help to widen the discussion to include organizations that might not traditionally ally or work with historic preservation groups. By partnering with groups that are fighting discrimination, poverty, and related issues, preservationists can increase their shared capacity to collect data as well as grow the pool of allies. For example, a data-collection effort is an opportunity to document neighborhoods of underrepresented communities and the

6
For more information
on the Arches project,
see http://www.arches
project.org.

unrecognized historical patterns that shape a place. Care does need to be taken to work *in partnership with* and not *for*. On a tactical level, foregrounding survey work can also engage new audiences. Through volunteer days and publicized events, you can attract participants who might not otherwise be excited about the project or know much about the preservation field. Events are also excellent opportunities to engage local college and high school students, who often are required to do volunteer work to graduate.

● PERSISTENT CHALLENGES

Organizations face a series of common challenges when implementing heritage-related data projects. Many are quite persistent and likely will never be completely solved. But there are some powerful approaches to tackling these challenges that are made easier or even necessary by the changing data and technical landscape.

Funding
The biggest challenge for most groups is finding the funding to plan and execute a survey. Surveys can quickly get expensive, even when using volunteer labor and off-the-shelf software. Some cost-reducing measures are simple, like picking an off-the-shelf tool rather than building software from scratch, but funding is nevertheless a challenge for most projects.

We see collective action as the best strategy for sustainable funding. By working across local organizations or regions, groups can pool resources and afford tools that otherwise would be out of reach for any one community or organization. There are several patterns to follow. First, a regional funder can take the lead in buying a tool and providing it to constituents. In this case, care must be taken by the funder and the vendor to ensure that the tool meets real needs, not just perceived needs. Second, organizations can come together without an intermediary funder to procure tools; this strategy also supports regional collaboration, rewarding groups that share knowledge and resources. In this model, though, there is a risk that surveys bloat with each additional partner; each organization must be free to do its own implementation and fieldwork (the *keep it simple* principle). Finally, disparate groups can come together to independently invest in a more general framework and then separately adapt it to their own needs.

In Cincinnati, Cleveland, and Columbus, local groups have partnered with Loveland and the JPMorgan Chase Foundation to provide surveying and data-management tools to any nonprofit that needs them, citywide. In this case, smaller organizations that might not otherwise be able to justify the cost of software access can freely use the tools. Arches is another excellent example: as an open-source platform, Arches is freely available to anyone who wants to implement the software.[6] It works out of the box with a generally useful default configuration, and it also can be customized at local expense to meet specific needs. This model means that groups that have special requirements can leverage the existing structure and do not need to build software from scratch.

Complexity

There are thousands of start-ups competing with big players like Google and Amazon in the ecosystem of modern data systems. It's hard to know what tools to use and when to use them. In addition, finding skilled technologists to build custom solutions is costly and time consuming.

In addition to focusing on process over tools, there are other avenues for help. Local groups of civic-minded technologists are emerging throughout the United States. These "civic hackers" are programmers, visual designers, service designers, and engineers by trade, and they volunteer their efforts on community projects. Many are organized under the auspices of a Code for America Brigade, currently operating in dozens of cities.[7] In addition, many metro areas have either a regional data-focused nonprofit that can provide consulting help (many organized in the National Neighborhood Indicators Partnership) or general technical assistance.[8] Reaching out to these organizations can help build heritage data capacity.

Hype

There is a great deal of hype in the data space. We've moved on from dashboards and visualizations to big data, machine learning, and Bitcoin. Free and paid apps abound. It is a wonderful world—but it can be hard to navigate the marketing, even with volunteers from a local civic tech group or technical assistance provider. Which of these solutions are really workable? Which technologies will persist?

There are several clear warning signs that something new hasn't been built to last. Any app that locks you into a corner and won't let you take your data back out with you is suspect. Free is also a big warning sign. As the modern adage goes, "If you aren't paying, you're the product." At the same time, the open-source community has made huge contributions to the public domain in the form of tools like Arches. A simple heuristic is the "robot test": does the tool help the organization do less tedious work by hand, or just add more work? The tools we feel most confident about are the ones that automate routine work. If a task (transcribing reports, hand-copying data, searching old records) feels like it could be done by a robot, it probably should be. These are the technologies that are highly worth organizational investment. At the same time, sometimes implementing a new tool might take more time than it's worth. If a project is tedious but only happens once and only takes an hour, it's not worth spending a day automating it, no matter how popular the tool.

Future Challenges and Strategies

While the technical landscape is always changing, these general strategies work today and have been relevant in previous generations of surveys. Even with the rise of machine learning and automated classification, baseline surveys will always be needed to create a solid foundation for future work. Program implementation will continue to be driven more and more by data and quantifiable outcomes, and despite national trends, data-based advocacy and activism will be key to local decisions. Perhaps most importantly, the social contexts that urban heritage programs are rooted in will drive the creation of new tools, strategies, and outcomes.

7
The Brigade Network, Code for America, https:// brigade.code foramerica.org.

8
National Neighborhood Indicators Partnership, https://www.neighbor hoodindicators.org.

○ Institutionalizing Data
● Co-Producing Knowledge
○ Building Evidence-Based Narratives
○ Informing Policy Agendas

Urban Planning and Technology Practice:
A Heritage Opportunity

An interview with Alicia Rouault

Co-Producing Knowledge

JACQUELINE KLOPP
You have spent the last decade working between urban planning and technology development. Tell us how you came to work for Boston's Metropolitan Area Planning Council (MAPC) and about the nature of your work leading their Digital Services Group.

ALICIA ROUAULT
I began my career in New York City, where I was deeply inspired by early data visualization work by Laura Kurgan and Sarah Williams at Columbia University's Spatial Information Design Lab (founded in 2004 and now known as the Center for Spatial Research) and by the work of the now-defunct nonprofit OpenPlans (founded in 1999). At the time, the field of planning and technology was just beginning to play with information design and not very formalized in terms of pedagogy or professional practice. I worked for the Architectural League of New York as the assistant editor of their online publication, *Urban Omnibus*, where I found myself reporting on technology in architecture and planning. In 2010 much of that conversation was devoted to how technology could benefit or influence community engagement. How could we use technology and data to better involve residents in decision-making processes at the local level?

In 2012 I moved to California to try my hand at ideas I had only written about: bringing technology and interaction design to municipal government. At Code for America, I worked with a small team of programmers on municipal innovation for the City of Detroit Mayor's Office. Under the leadership of Karla Henderson, a veteran government executive, we used data and technology to solve problems with transportation, blight, land use, and open data. In particular, one problem we focused on was the lack of reliable property data in Detroit. We designed and built a solution, called LocalData, to help governments and community groups collect new geospatial data about cities.

After a very successful pilot in Detroit, we were funded as a software company by the Knight Foundation to scale the idea to nearly fifty more cities across the country. The tool was used for a myriad of applications: historic preservation, economic development, and urban design. Eventually our company merged with a similar firm called Loveland Technologies, which operates out of Detroit and continues to help municipalities gather and use urban data.

Just prior to MAPC, I worked as senior advisor to Jennifer Pahlka of Code for America. Much of my role there involved thinking about the future of government and how technology can change the services governments deliver to citizens. Primarily, we worked with large municipalities: places like San Francisco, Chicago, or New York City. While that was tremendously rewarding, I decided to return to urban planning in Boston to join the Metropolitan Area Planning Council and build out an embedded digital services group within a state-level government agency.

This was, in some ways, an experiment: could we take the ideas that had been tested and refined within large urban bureaucracies and have the same level of impact in small communities (some with populations under twenty thousand)? Could technology and data support less prosperous, midsized cities with the same degree of success we found in much larger places? I now lead a small team of programmers and designers who create technology to solve various problems within municipal and state governments across the 101 cities and towns that make up metropolitan Boston.

You note that you work in these interdisciplinary teams with programmers, designers, and policy experts. Could you describe how that works?

I am a firm believer that creative problem-solving is done best with a diversity of opinions and perspectives. Typically, in the technology sector, teams are structured to include programmers, designers, and domain experts. In my experience, teams comprised of diverse roles provide a natural configuration for success.

If you think about creative problem-solving—and in the work we do, that typically involves really big, intractable problems that do not have clear solutions—having a difference of opinion improves the end result. Approaching problems from different angles yields more generative discourse—there are all sorts of reasons why a diverse team works. It works for what we are trying to do, which is, by nature, cross-sector.

Working in this interdisciplinary way must also have its challenges. What do you think are the biggest challenges when you try to build this creative problem-solving space?

One challenge is the need to bridge two rather well-defined vocations (technology and urban planning), each with their own unique professional culture, vocabulary, roles, and expectations. Anytime you are working in an interdisciplinary manner, you may need a bridge.

I tend to play the role of translator. I weave back and forth between traditional urban planning practice and technology practice; I speak both languages. I bridge the gap between the goals, the priorities, and the literal words of each profession. If you were to just plop a technology team into the middle of any planning firm, university department, or public sector agency, it would be challenging to bridge that gulf without a dedicated role or institutional practice.

Another challenge involves the logistics of financing and supporting a new technology team within a public sector agency. As a new team, we must constantly demonstrate value. Like any new thing, we are still testing and proving our contributions to a time-honored profession. As emergent practitioners, we have to justify why we are in the room, because we have not been in the room for decades. So that is certainly something that we struggle with.

The last challenge we tackle is that of change agency. In many ways, we are introducing new ideas, new concepts, and new ways of working. With this comes the enormous task of developing social capital and educating our partners, to "grease the wheels" of innovation within a government bureaucracy.

I am interested in how you do this work of building up technology with smaller towns, which probably have less capacity than cities like New York

On the whole, one thing we have to do in smaller communities that we do less of with a partner like the City of Boston is to educate our partners about what it is that we are doing and why it is important. I think one good way of doing that is to demonstrate that technology is not an end in itself but rather a tool and a catalyst. Data and technology are ways to enhance or push planning practice forward. Technology suffers a bit from magical thinking—because so few in the planning field understand how it is created or how it works, tech can be slated as a sort of magical elixir. It is important to remember that no one tool or dataset will solve all of our problems. Often technology works best alongside process and operational innovations that have nothing to do with writing code.

One way we successfully partner with communities is to prioritize quick wins early on. If we can fix something at very low cost to our team, even if it has absolutely nothing to do with the project at hand, we can very quickly demonstrate value to the people we are trying to help (who, at times, can be hostile to change or innovation). This is an exercise in building trust and a shared sense of purpose. We are in the room to help. We are not here to take away your job, or data, or value. There is a great deal of fear that comes along with municipal innovation. Fear of change, fear of loss, fear of irrelevance. That is a dynamic that we have to grapple with. By making sure that we build solid relationships and emphasize mutual benefit, we demonstrate that we have no interest in taking away power. We are not building you solutions in an isolated chamber; rather, we are designing and building technology in collaboration to make things work better.

Can you give us a concrete example of something you might do to build this kind of trust and demonstrate value even before you start the actual project?

The anatomy of a good partnership while working with *government* (distinct from working with a nonprofit or university) is highly contingent on the health of the relationships you build and the ability to manage power effectively. One of the most important strategies I use is to identify a champion of our work. Any technology project will fail if you do not have someone at a sufficiently high level who will provide the political cover or social capital required for success. This is particularly the case if you are trying to introduce a completely new type of work into whatever agency or department you are entering. Having the buy-in and the support of a person at the highest level possible proves effective when you are trying to make big changes. That may sound like a no-brainer, but it is quite important.

The second strategy is having a champion at a much lower level, which means making sure to involve people who are actually going to be impacted by the project on a day-to-day basis. This actor is important on a number of levels. They can be a key provider of information on how things actually happen (or don't) and, in many ways, hold more soft power than a champion at the head of an organization.

In most projects that involve government partners, we often have to do things like get an endorsement from the mayor's office, which provides the space and the permission to simply be in the room and do the work. We also need to make sure that the person responsible for actually managing that work is on our side too. That is done by simply practicing good relationship-building—by upholding the notion of "meeting people where they are" through small but meaningful acts, like holding meetings in the partner's office instead of ours. We develop dialogue and a human relationship. And ultimately the project is successful because we had buy-in from the person at the desk level as well as the higher authority buy-in that gives us permission to make big, sweeping changes.

In the past, you have worked with universities, and you have described how anchor institutions can be important to a successful partnership. Can you talk a little bit about how these collaborations between institutions and community organizations work in practice? Do you have insights on how to make these collaborations successful?

At my time with LocalData, we focused on a number of projects that served multiple audiences, typically pursuing better data about the condition of blighted properties or creating data where none existed. We saw some patterns repeat among the partners we worked with: governments that wanted to build reliable administrative datasets to be used for policy-making and budgeting; community-based organizations that were motivated to close information gaps on quality-of-life issues to fuel activism and fundraising activities; and universities (anchor institutions) that sought to provide graduate students with an opportunity to apply social science research methods to real-world scenarios.

In working toward these related but distinct goals, we formed partnerships across all three stakeholder groups. They represented users or consumers of the data/technology, the power brokers (those with the power to use the data and technology in an official capacity), and a third party, the university or anchor institution (in some cases a museum or library), which lent a sense of legitimacy and neutrality to otherwise politically charged groups.

This partnership model—a university, a community-based organization, and a government body—proved highly effective in building a lasting community around data and technology.

In 2012, Detroit was scattered with thousands of vacant properties. Many of these abandoned homes negatively impacted quality of life for remaining residents, especially for reasons of arson and public safety. Community groups were feeling frustrated with the lack of public response to this crisis of vacancies. People were mobilizing locally to save their neighborhoods by collecting their own data in low-fidelity ways. Neighborhood associations would do walking tours and write down information that they thought was important to foundations that fund neighborhood cleanups or safety patrols. They might use this data as evidence to bring to police departments or to point to public health concerns at specific intersections. As neighborhood organizations were collecting data, government agencies (local and federal) were also collecting data, typically for regulatory purposes: The tax collector gathers information about condition of properties because they have to by law. The Census Bureau (relatively) infrequently gathers information about property vacancy for regulatory reporting.

Detroit was also under a great deal of political pressure to respond to the major public health problem impacting the community. There was a sense that something needed to be done, but there was little reliable data available to work with. Local universities were also active—these are institutions that provide a great deal of historical context and research capacity to understand complex problems from many different angles, and they are connected to groups of willing young novices in the field. We typically partnered with university planning departments because they had graduate students eager to practice what they were learning. This trio all had unique motivations for collecting data, but LocalData was a tool and a process to do that work together—something we dubbed "productive engagement."

I will also say this was not and is not the norm. Governments do not usually work with communities to collect or produce administrative datasets in an official capacity. Universities may partner with a community-based organization or a nonprofit on a capstone, but rarely do they work with governments to produce datasets with any authority. The inclusion of community-based organizations allowed for the voices of residents to be embedded within the information itself. Sometimes datasets that nonprofits produce independently can be considered "fringe" special-interest data (depending on the size and the perceived legitimacy of the nonprofit). They are not typically considered legitimate or "official." Working together provided inclusion and legitimacy to the dataset. Even more so, universities actually do provide the rigor that is rooted in social science research. Universities know how to design a survey well, and they will enforce quality standards in the process.

The final benefit of this partnership model is community-building. When we observed graduate students teaming up with police departments, or mayor's offices and university planning departments teaming up with the community-based organizations, even for a weekend or two, the experience created a united coalition engaged in a productive, volunteer-based activity that could actually help all of them.

You are describing data collection almost as a democratic practice, reinforcing accountability politics and shared dialogue about what the problems are, which does this beautiful thing of melding local and expert knowledge into a kind of shared vision.

There is a lot that can go wrong when you are involving multiple stakeholders in a really complicated task like collecting information about every single building in Detroit. That is a lot of complexity. I think it works because it is productive. People want to work on things that actually have an impact. Nobody wants to spend their time volunteering or providing input for something that is not going to go anywhere. There is a magnitude associated with forms of collective action that surpass individual actions like 311 complaints and town hall attendance. We closed the time and space between input and outcomes so that everyone could very quickly see the impact of their volunteerism. There is an immediacy to it that makes it feel really good to all parties.

You use the word "literacy." A lot of planners and citizens may not have facility with technology and data, but one of the most powerful ways to build that data literacy is to really involve people in these kinds of data-collecting efforts. Are there other ways to support this kind of data and tech literacy for civic engagement?

Absolutely. Data and technology literacy has a great deal of potential even for those new to the field. If we look at the history of how technology and data analysis has evolved within urban planning, we can see one of the greatest success stories in pedagogy itself. In the spring of 2018, MIT created a new field of study called "urban science," which is a blending of urban planning and computer science. UC Berkeley's and Harvard's planning departments now offer urban informatics or urban analytics courses. We are now training new and professional urban planners about how data and technology are best applied in the field and, more importantly, how to create new tools instead of just how to use them. Today, we see graduating master's students leaving universities with a basic literacy in programming languages and databases that just wasn't taught five or ten years ago. This is becoming as common as learning GIS.

While this is occurring in academic departments, there is also a great opportunity to blend urban data science and technology in fields outside of planning. An easy path to doing so is to go back to this theme of working across disciplines. Within a university setting, this can be done by leveraging adjacent departments in computer science and information science. There are whole pools of talented engineers looking for ways to apply their skills to real-world problems. Working across departments is a great way to introduce technology and data into your practice.

A lot of developers and programmers are also reaching out, so it's kind of a two-way, or multidimensional, interdisciplinary movement that is really exciting.

Another resource available to professionals or academics are volunteer networks of programmers and data scientists who want to give back to their communities. These are groups like the Code for America Brigade, which are decentralized networks of volunteer programmers all over the country just looking for ways to support nonprofits or government agencies.

There are also emergent internship and fellowship programs for civic engagement, urban planning, architecture, and more. Brick-and-mortar coworking and innovation spaces are growing—places like New York City's Civic Hall, which has created a physical space and an annual conference to bring technology, public policy, and civic engagement into the twenty-first century in a local way. There are a lot of exciting things happening, and it's just about tapping into those networks as they are beginning to grow.

Now just a fun question about tools: what are some of your favorite tools for citizens and cities, and how might they be applied to the urban preservation agenda?

I get asked this question a lot, and it's a tricky one because there are so many amazing tools out there that solve so many different kinds of problems. So when I talk to people in planning who ask me this, I tend to respond with "What problem are you trying to solve?" or "What outcome are you trying to achieve?" or "What context are you operating in?" Once we have a clear idea of the problem and the context, it is an easier endeavor to find the right tool. So I will home in on a few problems I think might be appropriate and some of the associated tools for the urban heritage space.

One problem could be about collecting qualitative information: gathering public input in a meaningful but structured way. Oftentimes, when qualitative data is generated, it is done in a way that is not useful for analysis or policy-making. So if we host a town meeting, and we get people to talk about what their preferences or priorities are or what they hold dear, how that information is captured and then used really matters. Over the last few years, there have been quite a few applications that have been designed to gather and structure this type of qualitative information.

One, called Textizen, is designed around SMS-based surveying. This company spun off from Code for America, and the idea was to break out of the confines of the traditional town hall structure to survey the public through advertisements in the built environment. This could involve messaging on a poster to reach people while they are waiting for a bus or doing something else that does not occupy all of their attention. The idea is to meet people where they are and ask them about a particular policy, proposed change, planning decision, et cetera. That is one tool that many planning agencies use.

Another tool that is novel in terms of qualitative data collection is CityVoice. This is an open-source project that is, in many ways, similar to Textizen: it provides public polls and surveys, but through voice message as a primary medium. For example, you could be sitting in a park and see a sign that says "Call 1-800-CITY-PARKS and tell us what you think about this playground. What should be here that is not? How should we improve this space for children to play in?" Instead of texting a multiple-choice response, you can actually leave a message.

Hearing a human voice is powerful. A recorded memo lends itself well to sticky qualitative information. Using technology to gather this input opens up demographics that wouldn't feel comfortable texting, whether they are elderly or people who just don't want to text. Hearing a voicemail is a really easy way to engage immediately and naturally. The compelling technical advantage is that CityVoice then structures that data. You receive a transcript and useful quantitative analytics on very qualitative information.

Another area that may be of interest is regulation. Historic preservationists may be motivated to protect or stop certain policies or regulations that might impact the preservation of places that citizens care about. Madison is a really useful tool for public comment on proposed legislation. This tool invites the public to comment on proposed legal language. It is an open forum used primarily to draft open data policies. It is free to use and allows users to publish and get a record of the public's beliefs around proposed legislation.

Another important part of this work may be around storytelling and discovery. There are all sorts of ways to do that well, and there is plenty of out-of-the-box software that can help to tell a story. Much of how urban planners tell stories is through the use of GIS and online maps. I have been pleased to see the field move into the development of narrative and context, placed strategically near and around data and maps. One tool many planners use is called Story Maps (an Esri product). They have made it really easy to build a website that involves data-driven maps and charts that offer narrative.

It is easier than ever to publish data online and visualize that information in a chart or map. Besides Esri (the incumbent GIS software provider), there is CARTO, which is an emergent mapping platform and something that a relative novice can use and get up to speed really quickly on. Mapbox is a little bit more geared toward the expert cartographer or programmer; however, it is really sophisticated mapping software and relatively easy to learn.

The last opportunity is emergent data sources. Though we have discussed tools available to us in June 2018, I want to emphasize that the landscape of new and existing tools will only continue to change and change rapidly. The real opportunity is to find and use emergent datasets. With the creation of new industries and with our economy changing, we are beginning to see how things like the gig economy and on-demand services like Uber, Airbnb, or Instacart are not only changing the way that the public uses the city but changing the information that we have to make decisions about the city.

Suddenly we have proprietary companies that are producing an immense amount of data that could be really powerful in shaping decisions about the places where we live. So whether it is using new sensors that are installed by municipal parks departments or historic preservation alliances to understand use or disuse of certain places, or simply using Google Street View to capture and archive what is there today that might not be there tomorrow, there is an enormous amount of opportunity in emergent data sources. I would highly encourage preservationists to be comfortable with, be curious about, and try to anticipate what those data sources are that may be meaningful. Get comfortable using APIs and using data so that we can extract meaning and value from new information feeds and use it for the goals that we have in urban heritage.

Is there any other advice you would give to those working in urban heritage who want to start using these powerful tools and possible collaborations?

In planning there is a natural avenue to get excited about technology: mapping and geospatial data. With technology-savvy planners, one common progression I see is people who learned GIS in planning school and then later become comfortable with databases. GIS is a visualization layer on top of a database. Now there is a growing group of urban planners who are comfortable doing basic Structured Query Language commands.

Many researchers are also comfortable using SQL commands because if you store a lot of data, you likely need to query it.

As planners build a competency around SQL or other basic database commands, they may begin to store those as functions that they want to run over and over again. Often this is just to save time. When logic is introduced, suddenly it's programming territory. Planners get more curious about building a competency and an interest in programming.

I would not say that every urban planner or every preservationist should become a programmer. I don't think that is a realistic expectation, nor do I think it would be valuable. But what I would advise, and what pedagogy is starting to encourage, is to develop a basic literacy so that if preservationists want to start using data in a serious way or need to use technology, they are literate enough to hire experts and embed them into their practice, whether that is at a university, in a private firm, or in the public sector.

The second bit of advice is to not be afraid of technology. I often hear people say, "I'm just not a techie." Sometimes this is generational, and sometimes it is just the fear of new things. Learning something new can be intimidating, but I would invite folks who feel that way to understand that this was once all new to us as well. There is an enormous amount that anyone can learn and that is accessible to everyone. That is the power of the Internet. All of this information is available and accessible online for free. That is how the Internet was designed. It is our Library of Alexandria.

So we should be excited and engaged and not fearful.

Not fearful. Consider this an invitation. The technologists who work in pursuit of the public interest are very invested in helping and in building your capacity, and we are excited about that. We want you to learn, and we need you to make sure our work is relevant and rooted in the expertise you bring to the table.

And you're actively seeking out domain experts, so urban heritage experts could be collaborators in these interdisciplinary teams that are so powerful for the future of our cities.

Absolutely.

Democratizing Data: Pratt Center's Neighborhood Data Portal

Vicki Weiner

Co-Producing Knowledge

To many who work in the field of historic preservation or who study its concerns, it is a challenge to find and tap data sources in order to reexamine long-sought and protected building conservation programs and policies. We need data to examine what these policies have achieved, to identify and measure their outcomes or face their failings. But the data we need—while in some cases not so easy to acquire—is out there.

To others in preservation and allied fields, however, the issue of the need for data takes on another dimension. Access to essential and accurate information about people and their neighborhoods is critical to community-based preservation, planning, and policy activities that advance a more equitable and sustainable city. Without the ability to gather and understand some of the most basic data—from datasets that inform on land use questions to demographic information—community residents and other local stakeholders are at a major disadvantage when it comes to understanding the potential impacts of city-led plans for their communities. Data is crucial to a broad range of community issues, including the denigration of community character and aesthetics due to new development and the loss of urban heritage due to other changes in the neighborhood.

Despite the current proliferation of public data outlets and open data initiatives—and their potential to help communities assess their needs and assets and advocate for change—the reality is that resource-strapped, grassroots, community-based organizations often lack the capacity to collect, manage, analyze, and portray data. Many are only on the receiving end of selective information about their own neighborhoods, rather than positioned to access and interpret that information—and propose ways to act on it—for themselves. The imbalance in *who* has the ability to assess a community asset or need is cause for concern. This imbalance is a significant factor in a number of inequities that rob communities of self-determination: government agencies and professionals feel—and therefore typically act out of—a sense of ownership over the information that is used in developing programs that will have an impact, whether positive or negative, on communities.

What, if anything, is being done to democratize data? One example may be found in an initiative of the Pratt Center for Community Development, based in Brooklyn, New York.[1] In 2016 the Pratt Center created the Neighborhood Data Portal (NDP), a free online application that allows nonspecialists to visualize and analyze key citywide and local data, including demographics, school capacity, housing conditions, infrastructure assets, and more.[2] *FIG. 1* The NDP addresses the challenge of data inaccessibility by removing the expensive barriers of proprietary software, hardware, and datasets and by minimizing the educational and training requirements often needed to master and use data. The NDP also supports community groups in making evidence-based claims about inequality in New York City. By placing the tools of participatory and equitable planning directly into the hands of community members, the NDP empowers them to plan for the future they want to see.

New York City's low-income communities and communities of color face enormous challenges in their efforts to achieve racial, economic, and environmental justice, especially given the growing impacts of climate

1
The Pratt Center for Community Development—of which I am the deputy director—has worked to enhance the value of meaningful community participation in public decision-making for over fifty years. As part of Pratt Institute, the Pratt Center is the only university-based community development organization that operates both on the ground and at the policy level.

2
See http://prattcenter.net/neighborhood-data-portal.

FIG. 1: *Screen shot of the Neighborhood Data Portal showing libraries and school districts around Pratt Institute.*

change, regressive federal immigration and housing policies, increasing displacement caused by gentrification and speculation, and deteriorating public housing. In thinking through these difficult issues, community advocates need greater access to information and resources in order to build their capacity and address the growing inequality observable in our city. As a well-established, respected, and trusted technical assistance provider, the Pratt Center is able to provide data-gathering, analysis, and visualization services, traditionally in the form of finished products such as illustrated reports and static maps. But these services are still limited by the financial constraints of grassroots organizations and the diminishing role played by philanthropy in highly localized community advocacy efforts. The "give them a fish" model is somewhat problematic for an organization such as the Pratt Center, which has long believed in community empowerment and self-determination.

What is unique about the NDP effort is that it includes a free community training series and online training videos that provide community groups and individual NDP users with skills to interpret and incorporate data as they develop responsive, impactful community-serving programs, design advocacy campaigns, and share critical narratives from their community. Pratt Center trainings teach grassroots organizations how to access key datasets and how to visualize the data in maps for use in everything from funding proposals to community plans to public testimonies.

In addition to empowering citizens to use public data, we are exploring ways to gather or create data on community assets to add to the portal. In planning parlance, the term "community asset" typically refers to institutions such as nonprofit service providers, houses of worship, and nonprofit cultural organizations. In addition to these important community assets, every New York City neighborhood has hundreds, if not thousands, of places of importance and value to neighborhood residents: cultural hubs like arts spaces, green markets, and ethnic grocery stores and restaurants; economic resources like nonprofit workforce centers and local businesses that extend credit to residents; historic and aesthetic assets such as locations of significant community events and architecturally

67

distinguished buildings. City agencies do not typically collect or provide data on either the more traditional or the more expansively defined community assets. If they do—as in the case of religious institutions, for example—the data is limited to location and does not offer vital information such as the capacity the institution adds or the services it provides to its community. Essentially, public data on such assets does not speak to why they are assets; further, publicly accessible data for less traditional community assets simply does not exist. That lack handicaps the ability of communities to paint a full picture of the strengths and weaknesses of their neighborhoods and to accurately identify and evaluate the local resources they can marshal to support problem-solving and planning.

In our work with community-based organizations to gather community feedback about housing, environmental, or economic issues, intercept surveys have both engaged residents in conversations about the community and uncovered the lived experience that often defines and describes the strengths, challenges, and opportunities within a community as well as or better than public datasets can. When the data created by on-the-street surveys is digitized and analyzed, findings often illuminate local conditions in revealing and surprising ways. While this data is useful for bringing locally generated facts to bear on city plans and for assisting communities to assess problems and identify their own solutions, it is both difficult to gather and seriously underutilized—the data is captured in spreadsheets and reports and perhaps is essential for negotiation with city agencies, but it is stored in formats that do not lend themselves to deeper or comparative analyses. At the Pratt Center, we are starting to explore methods for layering this type of data into the NDP so that it can be shared among community groups struggling with the same issues. The NDP could also serve as a platform for comparative analyses over time so that Pratt and other citywide advocates can view conditions across the city when developing policy solutions.

This aspect of the NDP effort may have the most relevance for heritage conservation. Dozens of communities in New York City have conducted surveys of their historic and cultural built assets, and local, community-based historic preservation advocacy organizations are repositories of the data. Professional preservation researchers and consultants have assisted in the gathering of archival information, historical maps, and images and in the documenting of historic blocks and buildings. But much, if not all, of this information is static: contained in privately held digital files or paper archives. Even when published in reports, the data gathered by groups across the city is not easily shared or updated, hampering its usefulness and in some cases its validity. Citizen preservation advocates would also benefit from tools and training that make it easier for them to research a broader range of physical conditions in their communities, beyond the basics of what was built and when.

As currently configured, the NDP is an important resource, but with additional effort, we are hopeful that it can provide access to community-generated data that speaks both to the unique features and the shared challenges of neighborhoods citywide. Can a tool like NDP help to democratize data in the historic preservation field in New York City?

The Case for Data Analytics in Preservation Education and Practice

Jennifer L. Most

Co-Producing Knowledge

The twenty-first century has, so far, proven to be a data-obsessed age. More data than ever is being generated, whether passively, through our cell phone use and online presence, or actively, through our academic research and workplace tasks. As data, and access to it, continues to expand, those of us engaged in managing the historic built environment have to ask whether all of the key players involved with policy planning and decision-making in our field have the necessary tools and training to engage with data in meaningful ways. I posit that the answer is a resounding no: those working in historic preservation lag far behind their colleagues in related fields such as urban planning, environmental engineering, or policy administration.

When preservationists engage in discussions of data, it is largely in a reactive way, defending themselves against specific claims or defending the field more broadly.[1] Preservationists instead need to participate in the generation, collection, analysis, and visualization of data about our historic built heritage. In order to do so, data analytics (including geospatial data analytics) must be brought into the classrooms where preservationists are trained, and we must overcome the latent gender disparities that may well be the reason data analytics have thus far been left out.[2] Fluency in data analytics will augment the field's standing in public discourse and empower preservationists to engage with those who challenge the field. It will also lead to the creation of data that is directly relevant for more than just responding to these challenges—it will proactively generate data for new and interesting preservation-related analyses.

● WHO IS ANALYZING DATA FOR PRESERVATION?

To understand the disparities in who is presently executing analyses related to historic preservation, it is important to understand what training is (and has been) available to preservation students, as well as the traditional composition of those student bodies. In April 2018, I reviewed thirty master's in historic preservation programs in the United States to determine the availability of data analysis (or geospatial data analysis) courses to students enrolled in the programs for the 2017–2018 academic year.[3] By consulting the course requirements, course catalogues, and other program listings on the website of each school, I was able to determine which schools offered a data analysis (or geospatial data analysis) course specifically for students of historic preservation and whether this course was a requirement or an elective.[4]

The results were rather shocking. While three of the institutions appear to offer some data analytics training as sections of larger courses (at two of those institutions, the larger courses are program require-ments), not a single historic preservation program appeared to offer a semester-long course of this type, let alone one that is required or that is specifically tailored for preservation students.[5] Though Columbia University's Graduate School for Architecture, Planning, and Preservation offered a semester-long geographic information systems (GIS) course titled GIS for Preservation, a course I developed and taught from 2012 to 2017, this course was not offered during the 2017–2018 academic year.

1
A notable example is the preserva-tion community's response to the 2013 report "Landmarking, Housing Production and Demographics in NYC," published by the Real Estate Board of New York (REBNY). The report analyzed land-mark, demographic, and housing data and con-cluded that landmark designation was imped-ing affordable housing production in New York City. Few preservation groups, if any, took the highly questionable methodologies of the report to task. Typical responses from the preservation commu-nity either defended landmark designation as a public good or aimed to discredit REBNY, for example, "Check the Facts & Consider the Source," published by the Greenwich Village Society for Historic Preservation, http://www.gvshp.org/_gvshp/preservation/rebny/doc/rebnyfinal.pdf.

2
Preservation has long been perceived as a female-dominated pro-fession, whereas data analytics falls under the STEM umbrella, putting it in a field long dominated by men.

3
The thirty master's programs analyzed were identified using PreservationDirectory.com's "Graduate Programs in Historic Preservation," http://www.preservationdirectory.com/preservationorganizations resources/Organization Listings.aspx?catid=8.

4
The websites for each program were accessed between March 23 and April 1, 2018.

5
The three universities that offer data analysis or geospatial data analysis as sections of larger courses are the University of Colorado–Denver, the University of Kentucky, and the University of Maryland. The courses are required only at the latter two institutions.

6
Amanda L. Webb, "Examining the Use of Municipal Energy Benchmarking Data in Historic Preservation Planning and Policy" (lecture, Urban Heritage and Data in the 21st Century conference, New York City, February 9, 2018); the other presentations at the conference mentioned are Eduardo Rojas, "Social Actors and the Financing of Urban Heritage Conservation" and Stephanie Ryberg-Webster, "The Possibilities and Perils of Data-Driven Preservation Research: Lessons from a Multi-year Study of Federal Historic Tax Credits." Amanda L. Webb is an assistant professor in the Department of Civil and Architectural Engineering and Construction Management at the University of Cincinnati; Eduardo Rojas is an architect and an independent consultant and lecturer at the University of Pennsylvania School of Design; and Stephanie Ryberg-Webster is an associate professor in the Department of Urban Studies at Cleveland State University.

7
Two examples of presentations at the Historical GIS session were "Grave Situations: Dislocated Memorialization at the Blue Grass Army Depot Cemetery, Richmond, Kentucky" by Margaret Gripshover and "Historical Administrative Maps of the Czech Republic: A Case Study of the Conceptual and Quantitative Merit of Historical GIS" by Kelly Measom, Association of American Geographers Annual Meeting, New Orleans, LA, April 10–14, 2018, http://www.aag.org/galleries/conference-files/AAG_2018 AnnualMeeting Program_Final.pdf.

8
Darrell Huff, How to Lie with Statistics (New York: Norton, 1954).

Additionally, while about half of the schools note elective data or geospatial data analysis courses offered by other departments, there is typically no guarantee that preservation students can successfully cross-enroll. It stands to reason, then, that the majority of preservation students are graduating without this training.

The scarcity of preservationists trained in data analytics does not mean that quantitative preservation research is not taking place; it just means that those conducting the research are more likely to come from other disciplines—like civil engineering, city planning, and even architecture. For example, presentations at the February 2018 symposium that served as the foundation for this volume ranged from how municipal energy benchmarking data can inform energy policies for historic buildings (Amanda L. Webb, engineer) to a study of who is actually shouldering the financial burden of heritage conservation projects in Latin America (Eduardo Rojas, architect) to whether federal historic rehabilitation tax credits have had the positive impact on communities that has long been assumed (Stephanie Ryberg-Webster, urban planner).[6] Similarly, the 2018 Association of American Geographers annual meeting devoted an entire poster session to uses for GIS in historical studies, with preservation-related topics and site-based cases.[7]

The breadth of preservation-related data analyses is unquestionably valuable and has the potential to result in significant findings and insights. However, one has to wonder whether it matters that such studies are generally not performed by either academic or professional preservationists. Are there consequences of so little parallel quantitative research being conducted by those within the field? Ultimately, the question is whether it matters who is deciding what subjects are being researched, who is designing the methodology, and who is drawing the conclusions. It is reminiscent of the argument in How to Lie with Statistics, by Darrell Huff, that data can be manipulated to anyone's, or any group's, advantage.[8] The author refers not to actual lies but rather to all the tweaks that go into devising calculations and that can, unconsciously or not, lead to dramatically different outcomes, always to the benefit of a specific constituency.

Another analogy can be extracted from a March 2018 CityLab article titled "Who Maps the World?," which discusses the impacts of the gender imbalance among contributors to the OpenStreetMap (OSM) project, a crowd-sourced cartographic project dedicated to mapping parts of the world that have not previously been mapped digitally. The author notes that only 2 to 5 percent of contributors to the OSM project are female, though this number can leap as high as 48 percent for projects focused on humanitarian efforts. The author states:

> When it comes to increasing access to health services, safety, and education—things women in many developing countries disproportionately lack—equitable cartographic representation matters. It's the people who make the map who shape what shows up... If two to five percent of our mappers are women, that means only a subset of that gets to decide what tags are important, and what tags get our attention...[9]

The article goes on to note that while sports arenas, bars, and entertainment venues are well represented within OSM, childcare centers, health clinics, and specialty clinics that deal with women's health are vastly underrepresented. In fact, from 2011 to 2013 the OSM community hotly debated whether childcare facilities were altogether appropriate to tag on the map. [10] This raises the question of whether major areas of significance to preservationists are similarly unexamined because of preservationists' reliance on those outside the field to determine which quantitative and geospatial analyses ought to be performed.

As a profession, preservation has long been seen as female dominated, though there do not appear to be verified statistics about this gender breakdown. As a means of testing this perception, I conducted another analysis based on information available online. I identified three master's in historic preservation programs that comprehensively list the titles and authors of master's theses for at least the past ten years (2008–2017), including Columbia University, the University of Pennsylvania, and Clemson University. Analyzing the names of the authors and verifying gender to the extent possible, I was able to determine that the gender composition at each of the three schools over the last ten years has ranged from 61.5 to 100 percent female, with the average across all the schools being 77.3 percent. [11] Narrowing the scope of my analysis to the last five years indicates no significant change. These statistics are relevant precisely because, as the CityLab article continues:

> The concentration of women mappers in humanitarian projects [as opposed to general mapping projects] is partly due to the framing of cartography [in humanitarian projects] as a service-driven skill… rather than a technical one. That perception reflects the broader dynamics that alienate women from STEM fields—the idea that women should work as nurturers, not coders… [12]

Perhaps the lack of emphasis on data analytics training in graduate preservation programs is derivative of the same gender bias evident throughout the American education system, the result being fewer women involved in STEM research or careers. Regardless of the reason for the relative absence of data analytics training in preservation education, the effect has been clear: there is an extremely low number of preservationists with the skills required to carry out quantitative explorations of subjects important to the field.

● WHY IS DATA ANALYTICS TRAINING IMPORTANT?

At minimum, it should be reasonable to expect that preservationists are knowledgeable about datasets that pertain to the built environment. Take, for example, PLUTO (Primary Land Use Tax Lot Output), a massive dataset containing more than seventy fields of information about New York City tax lots that is managed and disseminated by the New York City Department of City Planning. [13] One of the preservation-related attributes in this dataset is the "Year Built" field, which purports to

9
Sarah Holder, "Who Maps the World?," *CityLab*, March 14, 2018, https://www.citylab.com/equity/2018/03/who-maps-the-world/555272.

10
Those in opposition to listing childcare facilities cited too much overlap with an existing tag for kindergarten, while proponents argued that kindergarten is a limited term with various definitions but mostly representing an educational facility ("Tag:amenity= childcare," *OpenStreetMap*, https://wiki.openstreetmap.org/wiki/Tag:amenity=childcare). A post-mortem that followed a 2012 vote against the childcare tag noted "there is an inherent problem when discussing this concept stemming partly from the linguistic divide between German and English, and partly from an inadvertent ignorance or dismissal of childcare stemming from most OSM contributers [sic] and voters being male and thus being on average tasked less with childcare duties. Fundamentally, school-age children would not attend a kindergarten for day care and it is unhelpful to map child daycare facilities using the tag." "Proposed features/childcare," *OpenStreetMap*, January 17, 2018, https://wiki.openstreetmap.org/wiki/Proposed_features/childcare.

11
Gender was determined by using authors' names and did not take into account an individual's actual gender identity, which may be different. Further research was conducted via LinkedIn. Authors not identified as either male or female were recorded as "unknown." A separate review by Columbia University's Historic Preservation Program of more than fifty years of master's of science in historic preservation graduates produced a similar gender ratio of 70.2 percent female.

19
Fei Teng, "People
Distribution Patterns
for Historic Districts in
the City of Los Angeles
and New York City"
(final project, GIS for
Preservation, Spring
2017).

Demographic analysis is another important tool that becomes available with adequate data analytics training. Demographic studies are a good way to understand who is impacted by preservation policy. The US Census, though not a perfect fit, is still an incredibly useful and accessible tool for this kind of research, with data readily downloadable and easily imported into database and GIS software programs. One student sought to answer whether there are demographic differences inside and outside historic districts in New York City and the city of Los Angeles. [19] She looked at factors including educational attainment, household income, and population diversity. Augmenting her research with charts and maps of each demographic category, she presented some compelling findings. She found that in Los Angeles, historic districts exhibit higher population diversity than the city as a whole; conversely, she found that inside New York City's historic districts, population diversity was, on average, lower than for the city as a whole. Another finding was that median household incomes in New York City historic districts were more than 10 percent higher than in the city as a whole, while in Los Angeles, median household incomes within historic districts averaged nearly 15 percent lower than in the city as a whole. A major limitation of her study is that US Census boundaries are rarely coterminous with those of historic districts, which demands significant methodological compromises when accounting for census districts that fall both inside and outside historic districts. This does not render an analysis invalid; it just means that conclusions must be more carefully measured.

● THE POWER OF DATA

It is time for data analysis (and geospatial analysis) to become more integrated into the professional practice of historic preservation. Data-based preservation research is being done, but little of it is conducted by those within the profession, weakening the standing of preservationists in public discourse about the built environment. Quantitative and geospatial preservation research can help preservationists become empowered as actors in policy-planning and decision-making about the urban environment, and it can help them do so in a proactive way. Training and exposure to data analytics will also enable preservationists to more authoritatively critique analyses put forth by others and to build data repositories that can assist future preservationists. Preservation professionals need not devote all their time and efforts to devising metrics and analyzing data about our historic built heritage, but the ability to use data should be one of the many tools available in the preservationist's arsenal. Until quantitative analysis, including geospatial analysis, becomes standard training in the preservation classroom, however, the possibilities for what can be achieved will remain unknown.

The Challenges of Legacy Data in Preserving the Historic Built Environment

Andrew S. Dolkart

Co-Producing Knowledge

There is great potential in the collection of big data by municipalities and institutions. For those of us who research the history of cities, particularly the history of the built environment, and use this research as a tool for preservation advocacy, the promise of having the basic data about buildings and neighborhoods at our fingertips is extremely exciting, saving days, weeks, or even months of basic research in dusty government documents and other sources. However, unless special care is taken at the start to assure that the historical information is correct, the data available is, at worst, useless and, at best, unreliable. Sometimes it perpetuates false history.

A key feature of data on the built environment is the date when individual buildings were erected. Making sure that dates are correct may seem like a precise exercise of interest only to historians, but dating is often the basis for deciding whether or not a building or an area is historic. Only "historic" buildings are deemed deserving of official preservation—or some other sort of recognition—and of intervention by government agencies or local advocates for architecture and history. Dating is also a tool for historians and activists who want to understand how their community evolved over time. Correct dating is a guide for many kinds of decisions that impact both buildings and the people who own and use them. Historians are generally savvy enough to know when the data they are finding online is incorrect, but this data is also available and used by members of the public who may not have the background knowledge to see that there is a problem when a block of 1840s row houses is dated to 1920.

The New York City dataset known as PLUTO is especially problematic when used to find the date of buildings. PLUTO, or the Property Land Use Tax Lot Output, is a vast database for the more than one million lots in New York City. It was first amassed by the City Planning Commission in the early 2000s, drawing from data compiled by a range of city government agencies, and was made freely available to the public in 2013. PLUTO enables research by borough, block, and lot, and includes such useful data as lot area, use, owner's name, size of building, tax assessment, floor area ratio, and more. It also includes year built. Here is where the problem arises. Historian Ward Dennis succinctly noted, "The data for building age (Year Built) is so flawed that you really should just delete that column from your dataset." 1 Neither the City Planning Commission nor any other city agency has ever collected information about the year of construction for every building in the city, but each lot in the dataset does include such a date. For buildings erected before the mid-twentieth century, these dates are usually wrong. In Greenwich Village, with its large concentration of row houses from the early and mid-nineteenth century, most of these buildings are dated 1899 or 1900, and similar dates can be found throughout Brooklyn's nineteenth-century row house neighborhoods. Indeed, Dennis has found that PLUTO records only 671 buildings erected in all of Brooklyn before 1895! 2 Shortly after the PLUTO dataset became publicly available, Thomas Rhiel used the building date information to create a color-coded map, available online, that ostensibly showed the evolution of Brooklyn's built fabric. Unfortunately, almost all of the lots in southern Brooklyn Heights and Cobble Hill, where the

1
Ward Dennis, "Older Than You Think," *Brooklyn 11211* blog, August 13, 2013, http://brooklyn11211. com/2013/08/pluto-old.

2
Dennis, "Older Than You Think."

3
Thomas Rhiel, "Block by Block, Brooklyn's Past and Present," *Bklynr* blog, August 1, 2013, https://www.bklynr. com/block-by-block-brooklyns-past-and-present.

4
"Urban Layers," Morphocode, http:// io.morphocode.com/ urban-layers.

5
"Discover New York City Landmarks," New York City Landmarks Preservation Commission, https:// nyclpc.maps.arcgis. com/apps/webap-pviewer/index. html?id=93a88691 cace4067828 b1eede432022b.

6
New York City Landmarks Preservation Commission, *Brooklyn Heights Historic District Designation Report* (New York, 1965).

7
These designation reports include, for example, those for the Charlton-King-Vandam Historic District (designated in 1966), Gramercy Park Historic District (1966), Treadwell Farm Historic District (1967), Cobble Hill Historic District (1969), and Mount Morris Park Historic District (1971).

streets are lined with pre-Civil War row houses, are dated around 1900.[3] And similar results appear on Manhattan maps that use PLUTO building dates. Urban Layers's interactive map of Manhattan shows (incorrectly) that Greenwich Village was built up almost entirely in 1899 and 1900.[4]

Many in New York City government acknowledge the lack of accuracy in the year-built data, but there has been no corrective action. This "official city data" keeps on being used. Once the data is out there with the official imprimatur of the city, it is assumed to be correct. It then creeps into student papers, into newspaper articles, onto blogs, and into official reports. These documents then become the basis for the regulation of the built environment as well as for policy-level land use decisions that rely on an understanding of the significance and vulnerability of neighborhoods.

The buildings in Brooklyn Heights, Cobble Hill, and Greenwich Village are all located within the boundaries of historic districts designated by the New York City Landmarks Preservation Commission (LPC). The commission has undertaken extensive research on the age of individual landmarks and buildings erected in most of the historic districts, but LPC data is not part of PLUTO, and the PLUTO dataset misidentifies the age of many designated landmarks. In 2018, the LPC completed its own dataset, called Discover New York City Landmarks, which is completely independent of PLUTO.[5] Discover New York City Landmarks "provides detailed building-by-building information" for all individual, interior, and scenic landmarks, as well as an entry for every building in designated historic districts throughout the five boroughs of New York City. Each entry in the database provides construction date, architect/builder, owner/ developer, major alteration(s), alteration architect(s), style(s), material(s), building type, original use, and the block and lot number. This is, in many ways, an excellent database: it is easy to use, with maps, graphics, search parameters, and basic information presented in a clear manner, and it includes links to the original reports that the LPC prepared for every designation.

The LPC's designation reports are the source for much of the infor- mation that appears in the Discover dataset. As required by law, every individual landmark and every historic district designation is accom- panied by a designation report. These reports are then submitted to the New York City Council (or, before 1990, to the Board of Estimate) for review and approval. Thus, they become legal documents. Many of these designation reports are scholarly works prepared by well-trained architectural historians and preservationists, providing context and detailed background information on dates, architects, builders, styles, residents, and history of every building in the district. However, early designation reports, dating from the years following the creation of the Landmarks Preservation Commission in 1965, vary in their quality. The designation report for the Brooklyn Heights Historic District, the city's first designated district, for example, consists of approximately two pages of general background information and no discussion of any of the buildings in the district.[6] Other early designation reports discuss selected buildings but are far from complete discussions of the buildings that comprise the district.[7]

Of course, the data in any dataset is only as good as the information available for input. In this regard, the LPC project is not always a success. According to the Discover website, "Data for each building was directly transcribed from building entries in historic district designation reports, or in some cases, designation report supplements. No new research was conducted during the development of the dataset." 8 There are two problems with this statement. First, it is not true; some data comes from sources other than the designation reports. For example, most Brooklyn Heights entries include dates of construction and the name of the owner/developer. Each website entry for Brooklyn Heights clearly states that "all building data and notes [come] from the Brooklyn Heights Historic District designation report," despite the fact that this information is not provided in the abbreviated designation report. Although not referenced, this information appears to have been culled from Clay Lancaster's *Old Brooklyn Heights: New York's First Suburb*, which includes detailed research on the neighborhood's pre-Civil War houses. 9

The second problem is that—especially in early designation reports—the information can be incomplete or, in some cases, has been superseded by later research, resulting in incomplete or inaccurate data that could have serious consequences for the landmark building. For example, in 2009 I published a book titled *The Row House Reborn: Architecture and Neighborhoods in New York City, 1908–1929*, which argues that the row houses that we revere today were completely out of fashion in the early twentieth century; they were seen as "dreary," "characterless," "lugubrious," and

8
"Methodology and Credits," Discover New York City Landmarks, New York City Landmarks Preservation Commission, https://nyclpc.maps.arcgis.com/apps/webap-pviewer/index.html?id=93a88691cace4067828b1eede432022b.

9
Clay Lancaster, *Old Brooklyn Heights: New York's First Suburb* (Rutland, VT: Charles E. Tuttle, 1961).

FIG. 1: *Frederick Sterner House, 139 East 19th Street, Gramercy Park, New York City. Originally published in "House at No. 139 E. 19th Street, New York,"* American Architect *95 (February 24, 1909).*

10
Andrew S. Dolkart,
*The Row House Reborn:
Architecture and
Neighborhoods in New
York City, 1908–1929*
(Baltimore: Johns
Hopkins University
Press, 2009), 12–15.

11
Dolkart, *Row House
Reborn*, 26–37.

12
New York City
Landmarks
Preservation
Commission, *Gramercy
Park Historic District
Designation Report*
(New York, 1966), 4.

"a blight," and, it was assumed, all would eventually be demolished and replaced by more modern structures. 10 Instead, these old houses were renovated with new interior plans, with utilitarian yards converted into gardens, and, most significantly from the point of view of the LPC, with redesigned facades. This movement, which created a new type of urban residence, was widely chronicled in professional and popular magazines and newspapers. Many of these buildings are located within the boundaries of designated historic districts. These houses are significant examples of early twentieth-century design, and I argue that they should be preserved as such—not restored to their nineteenth-century character, as has occurred in some designated historic districts.

The most important building in the development of the movement to rethink the row house is 139 East 19th Street, in the Gramercy Park Historic District. *FIG. 1* The house was originally built in 1842–1843 and was redesigned in 1908 by the architect Frederick Sterner for his own use. At the time of its completion, it was widely hailed as a new type of urban dwelling, and it was soon understood as the progenitor of a movement. 11 With its light-colored stucco facade, stoop replaced by a basement entrance, colorful Moravian tile entry trim, and Spanish tile roof, it was the antithesis of the reviled brownstone front or the aged brick facade. The brief historical text in the Gramercy Park Historic District designation report does mention the remodeling of the early houses on 19th Street into what was widely called the "Block Beautiful," although it mistakenly dates these changes to the 1920s. 12 However, the LPC's database does not indicate these changes at all—not for this house and not for any of the similarly remodeled houses that give East 19th Street its unique character. Instead, the data states that the house dates from 1842–1843 (although this date cannot be found anywhere in the designation report) and that there are no major alterations. *FIG. 2* This, even though the only visible details on the exterior that survive from the 1840s are the window lintels and sills.

Accordingly, pursuant to the provisions of Chapter 8-A of the Charter of the City of New York and Chapter 8-A of the Administrative Code of the City of New York, the Landmarks Preservation Commission designates as an Historic District the Gramercy Park Historic District, Borough of Manhattan, consisting of the property bounded by Park Avenue South from East 21st Street to the northern property line of 273-277 Park Avenue South, the northern property line of 273-277 Park Avenue South, the eastern property line of 273-277 Park Avenue South, East 21st Street, Gramercy Park North, Gramercy Park East, the northern property line of 34 Gramercy Park East, the western property line of the northern extension of 34 Gramercy Park East, the northern property line of the northern extension of 34 Gramercy Park East, the entire eastern property line of 34 Gramercy Park East, East 20th Street, the eastern property line of 31 Gramercy Park South (148 East 20th Street), a portion of the eastern property line of 145 East 19th Street, the rear lot lines of 147 and 149 East 19th Street, the eastern property line of 149 East 19th Street, East 19th Street, the eastern property line of 146 East 19th Street, the rear lot lines of 146 and 144 East 19th Street, the eastern property line of 153-155 East 18th Street, East 18th Street, Irving Place, the rear lot lines of 18 through 16 Gramercy Park South, a portion of the eastern property line of 119-121 East 19th Street, East 19th Street, a portion of the western property line of 119-121 East 19th Street, the rear lot line of 13 Gramercy Park South, a portion of the western property line of 13 Gramercy Park South, the rear lot lines of 12 and 11 Gramercy Park South, a portion of the western property line of 11 Gramercy Park South, the rear lot lines of 10 and 9 Gramercy Park South, the western property line of 9 Gramercy Park South, East 20th Street, the rear lot lines of 7 through 1 Gramercy Park West, East 21st Street to Park Avenue South.

FIG. 2: New York City Landmarks Preservation Commission, "Discover New York City Landmarks," 139 East 19th Street, https://nyclpc.maps.arcgis.com/apps/ webappviewer/index.html?id=93a88691cace4067828b1eede432022b.

FIG. 3: Aymar Embury II House, 230 East 62nd Street, Treadwell Farm, New York City. Image courtesy of the author.

FIG. 4: 93 Perry Street, Greenwich Village, New York City. Image courtesy of the Museum of the City of New York, J. Clarence Davies Collection.

FIG. 5: 235 East 62nd Street, Treadwell Farm, New York City. Image courtesy of the author.

Similarly, 230 East 62nd Street in the Treadwell Farm Historic District is cited as an 1868 house in the database, but its facade was completely redesigned in 1927 by prominent architect Aymar Embury II for his own household. FIG. 3 Again, the LPC database states that there have been no major alterations. Many houses in Greenwich Village were remodeled in the 1910s and 1920s, including 122 Waverly Place, one of a significant group of row houses defined by the artist's studio windows that transform their facades. The LPC database dates 122 Waverly as an 1834 house, despite the

13
Meenakshi Srinivasan,
Lisa Kersavage,
and Daniel Watts,
"NYC Landmarks
Preservation
Commission's Historic
Building Data Project"
(PowerPoint presen-
tation, Urban Heritage
and Data in the 21st
Century Symposium,
New York, NY,
February 8, 2018).

14
Andrew S. Dolkart,
Guide to New York
City Landmarks
(Washington, DC:
Preservation Press,
1992) and Andrew S.
Dolkart and Matthew
A. Postal, Guide to New
York City Landmarks,
4th ed. (Hoboken, NJ:
John Wiley & Sons,
2009).

fact that it was largely redesigned in 1919. And 93 Perry Street is identified as a house from 1828, not from 1927, although there is absolutely nothing nineteenth-century on the exterior of the building. FIG. 4 In none of these cases is the date of the major alteration provided, even though there is a place to enter such information. If a property owner was seeking a permit to alter 93 Perry Street or one of the other houses with important alterations that are not recorded in the LPC database, an LPC staff member, relying on the database, might approve the removal of the 1927 facade to rebuild the house in its original Federal style. The same situation applies for 235 East Sixty-Second Street, which is identified as a house dating from 1874–1875 in the LPC database, when in reality its facade dates from 1919. FIG. 5 In 2018 this house, with its somewhat deteriorated facade, stands on a very expensive residential block in the Treadwell Farm Historic District. Someone will undoubtedly purchase this building and invest in improving it. Given the information in the database, they could easily assume that it would be acceptable to recreate its 1874 brownstone front, and there is nothing in the given information to prevent the issuing of a permit to do just that. These are not far-fetched scenarios: many of the redesigned row houses in Treadwell Farm have already been destroyed with permits to "restore" them to their nineteenth-century character; indeed, one such change is what prompted me to write The Row House Reborn.

My purpose is not to condemn the LPC's database; it is a wonderful project, and most of the data is correct and quite useful. But I do want to raise a cautionary flag. The LPC insists that it must use the data from the designation reports because these are legal documents and the LPC cannot correct information that is wrong. 13 The reports are, indeed, legal documents, but the dataset is not. Over time, new information comes to light, and additional research is undertaken. One would expect that the LPC would incorporate this new information into its data. In a sense, the Discovery database is the twenty-first-century version of the LPC's Guide to New York City Landmarks, first published in 1992 and updated in three additional editions through 2009. 14 All entries in the guidebook are based on material in the designation reports but also include new information, including construction and alteration dates. Changes were also made to building names in accordance with modern thinking about how landmarks should be characterized. For example, all houses commissioned by individuals for their own home, and designated as individual landmarks, have been renamed for both the husband and the wife who built them, rather than named just for the husband, as had been the custom. Thus, for example, the building designated as the James B. Duke House, at 1 East 78th Street, became the James B. and Nanaline Duke House. The LPC is certainly aware that new information has become available. Indeed, some entries in the Discovery database note that the information provided comes from the designation report "supplemented by the LPC's Guide to New York City Landmarks (2009)." This approach should be expanded to include other reliable sources, duly cited in the database entries. The Discovery website does allow the public to submit corrections through the Data and Mapping Feedback Portal, but it is not clear where this corrected information will appear, and the incorrect information remains official data.

Beyond the validity of basic information in databases, another concern for preservation advocates is that big data projects generally lack any "human" content. These databases miss issues of cultural and historical significance and tend to perpetuate the notion that preservation is only about the physicality of old buildings. There is often no evidence of people and their impact on the built environment and no way to categorize intangible heritage. 15 About two years ago, two colleagues and I founded the NYC LGBT Historic Sites Project. Our project seeks "to make invisible history visible," to find, interpret, and publicize sites throughout New York City that relate to LGBT history and people. 16 The project's website includes more than 125 entries on the more than 400 sites that we have already identified; we have also completed new or reinterpreted National Register nominations for significant sites. A few of these buildings are works of architectural importance such as Carnegie Hall, Earl Hall at Columbia University, and set designer Oliver Smith's Greek Revival-style home in Brooklyn Heights, where author Truman Capote rented the basement apartment. But in many cases, the sites are not works of architectural interest. Instead, they are places of cultural import that would never be picked up in an architectural survey: for example, the house in Flushing, Queens, where the organization PFLAG (Parents, Families, and Friends of Lesbians and Gays) was founded by the Manford family in 1973, or the modest commercial building in Crown Heights, Brooklyn, that was home to the Starlite Lounge, which billed itself as "the oldest black-owned, non-discriminating club" from 1962 to 2010. *FIG. 6, 7*

15
The LPC's Discover database does mention people of importance when a landmark, such as the Langston Hughes House at 20 East 127th Street, was specifically designated for its historical or cultural significance.

16
NYC LGBT Historic Sites Project, https://www.nyclgbtsites.org.

FIG. 6: 235 East 62nd Street, Treadwell Farm, New York City. Image courtesy of Christopher D. Brazee/NYC LGBT Historic Sites Project, 2016.

FIG. 7: *Starlite Lounge, 1084 Bergen Street, Crown Heights, Brooklyn. Video still from* We Came to Sweat: The Legend of Starlite, *a documentary film directed by Kate Kunath (2014).*

The point is not that we should stop undertaking big data projects. These projects are crucial. But we need to demand data of the highest, most reliable quality, and we need to always be aware of the risks of these projects—just because information is in a database does not mean that it is correct. But even when the data is correct, it is still only a foundation on which to build an understanding of communities and their physical and historical development. Data that fails to acknowledge the human history of buildings can only ever be a skeleton on which we flesh out history and significance. All of this data should not be used to reach broad conclusions about buildings and communities until we have confirmed its accuracy and until we have done good, old-fashioned archival and community research to give the data—and its associated buildings and communities—life.

Mapping Experiences onto the Digital and Physical Landscapes

An interview with Marco Castro Cosio

Co-Producing Knowledge

ERICA AVRAMI

As an artist exploring the frontiers of technology, how did you come to work with cultural organizations and with the visitor experience as a form of qualitative data?

1
See Queens Memory, http://queensmemory.org.

MARCO CASTRO COSIO

Cultural organizations that care for objects and stories from the past serve as time machines for visitors. Museums, libraries, and cities serve as hubs in which the past, present, and future share the same space in time. Spaces like these are crucial for the healthy development of our communities; they allow designers and technologists to reflect on the past and to come up with real-world solutions to improve our society.

In my work as an artist and cultural strategist, I have been honored to work at major museums and institutions, such as the Queens Museum and the Metropolitan Museum of Art. I'm interested in mapping and connecting the various innovative, cultural, and creative labs around the city and in resurfacing the connective tissue that brings them together —in making the content more engaging for the average visitor without watering down the important research and content produced by curators and experts. I am fascinated by the potential of two-way communication, by the possible routes and destinations to which a conversation can take its participants. The aim is to contextualize how these conversations develop and to illuminate the different ways that citizens and cultural institutions can go about gathering and making sense of stories relating to our urban and natural heritage.

Can you tell us about your work at the Queens Museum? While there, you were part of a fascinating project that involved the New York State Pavilion in Flushing Meadows, which has long been a focus of preservation advocacy. How did your work collecting visitor memories add new layers of contemporary meaning to our understanding of this historic place and the stories associated with it?

The Queens Museum provided for me a great platform for learning how to establish conversations. The director at the time, Tom Finkelpearl, advocated for openness as the museum's one-word guiding mission, and he would act on this mission by having open-ended conversations with our visitors in the lobby while they played Ping-Pong. Managing visitor experience at the Queens Museum, I worked with a team of welcoming visitor experience agents (VEAs). The team of VEAs helped our visitors understand the pioneering contemporary art exhibitions presented at the museum and also connected the museum to the visions of the future captured in the mementos from the 1939 and 1964 World's Fairs. VEAs were part of the education department and were also an integral part of the security and visitor services department. These trained listeners were on the lookout for visitor stories relating to the museum, which they ultimately recorded and shared as part of the Queens Library Memory Project.[1] The Queens Library project helped our team at the museum map stories to a digital space in a process I refer to as "story mapping." It helped us pinpoint the cultural provenance of the stories behind the objects in the museum.

2

For additional information, see "New York State Pavilion," NYC LGBT Historic Sites Project, https://www.nyclgbtsites.org/site/new-york-state-pavilion, and *13 Most Wanted Men: Andy Warhol and the 1964 World's Fair*, exhibition brochure, http://www.queensmuseum.org/wp-content/uploads/2015/06/Andy%20Warhol_13%20Most%20Wanted%20Men.pdf.

Next to the Queens Museum lie the remnants of the New York State Pavilion, designed by Philip Johnson for the 1964 World's Fair. At the time of its opening, works were commissioned for the curved walls of the building from up-and-coming artists of the day, including Robert Indiana, Ellsworth Kelly, Roy Lichtenstein, Robert Rauschenberg, Andy Warhol, and others.

Warhol's installation was titled *13 Most Wanted Men*, and he used the mug shots of the New York City Police Department's thirteen most wanted criminals of 1962 to create a large silk-screen grid tableau. The piece was immediately controversial, in part because Warhol's content and use of the term "wanted" had homoerotic undertones. Within days, Warhol granted permission for it to be painted over, resulting in a silver monochrome square that remained during the 1964 and 1965 seasons of the fair, and which itself became a Warholian statement. 2 *FIG. 1*

FIG. 1: *Andy Warhol*, 13 Most Wanted Men.

In the spring of 2014, fifty years later, the Queens Museum celebrated this historical moment by exhibiting the original thirteen wanted men in reproductions made by Warhol alongside other works by the artist, including a portrait of Jacqueline Kennedy. The VEAs, with their training and curiosity for stories, asked the curators if any of the wanted men or their descendants had ever been found or identified. The curators explained that, given their criminal status, they were not identified, and their families would probably not want to be associated with them.

Our VEAs had learned to give attention to first-time visitors, to gain their trust by listening to and engaging with them, and to answer questions that would help the visitors understand and improve their museum-going experience. The *New York Times* reviewed the exhibit opening, after which a VEA called over the two-way radio for me to come down to the galleries to meet a visitor. I came down as soon as I could, since calls on the walkie-talkie usually meant something was going wrong. I learned that this particular visitor had heard about the exhibition through the newspaper and wanted to see the portrait of Thomas Francis (Duke) Connelly, one of the thirteen most wanted men, who happened to be his biological father.

FIG. 2: *George Lawler and the image of his father. Image: Sara Krulwich/ New York Times/Redux.*

3
"Oral History: A Hidden Past," August 21, 2014, Queens Memory, http:// classic.queensmemory. org/index.php/Detail/ Object/Show/object_ id/1964.

4
Tatiana Schlossberg, "Son Discovers His Father's Life of Crime Is Now a Work of Art by Warhol," *New York Times*, August 21, 2014.

Our oral history intern, Abigail Banks, worked with the VEAs to capture the story from the visitor, George Lawler, for the Queens Memory Project. 3 The museum's curatorial and communications department then contacted the *New York Times*, hoping the story would be picked up. George Lawler came back to the gallery to talk to an up-and-coming reporter just starting her internship in the Metro section of the *New York Times*, Tatiana Schlossberg. As they met and had a conversation for the article, I once again realized the museum was housing not only artworks and artifacts but living stories connected across generations. 4 Surrounded by Andy Warhol's work, Mr. Lawler stood in front of his father's portrait while the reporter asked her questions in front of a portrait of her grandmother, Jackie Kennedy. Just like a Polaroid, Warhol's tableau of characters censored at the World's Fair went from a silver square in 1964 to a fully exposed snapshot of New York City fifty years later. Thanks in part to the subtle work of the VEAs, this snapshot helped me understand the role that museums can play in activating our histories and making them relevant to our communities in the present day. *FIG. 2*

FIG. 3: *Projection of colors onto the Temple of Dendur, Metropolitan Museum of Art. Image: Brian Harkin/New York Times/Redux.*

5
See "The Temple of
Dendur," Metropolitan
Museum of Art,
https://www.met
museum.org/art/
collection/search/
547802.

How did your experience at the Queens Museum influence the next avenues of your work, dealing more directly with interactive technologies for heritage?

After the Queens Museum, I started work at the MediaLab within the Metropolitan Museum of Art. Our task was to imagine the futures of museums and culture and envision the use of art and technologies to improve the visitor experience. We looked at the museum as a narrative ecosystem to be experienced, remixed, and approached through different angles in both the physical and digital space.

While manager of the Met MediaLab, I found that the best way to work and collaborate with the institution and with my colleagues in other departments was to be open and to be a good listener. Once a trusting relationship was developed, common goals were achieved. My predecessor, Don Undeen, started the MediaLab and different experimental projects within it. Our main collaborators were other departments in the museum, but also universities and research organizations. Following various conversations between the lead curator of Egyptian art, Diana Patch, and the MediaLab, we began crafting a collaboration. Two interns from the MediaLab, Matt Felsen and Maria Paula Saba, worked with then-research fellow Erin Peters to help illuminate the original colors of the Temple of Dendur. 5 This project took approximately six months, and it used a technique called projection mapping, where the digital projection gets mapped to a specific architectural structure to highlight certain content or stories using the built environment as a canvas. It allowed the researchers to show, using a digital tablet, the different theories and evidence of how the Temple of Dendur was originally decorated in full color and with different color patterns throughout time. *FIG. 3*

FIG. 4: Bus Root VRV.

In the spring of 2016, the museum launched a semipermanent installation of this project for sixteen weeks, where it was finally shown to the public during the later hours of the day. It received wide acclaim from the public, the press, and academia. The 2016 summer interns worked on a manual and instructions for the project to be easily shown. Even though the MediaLab closed down in October 2016, the projections were lit up again in the spring of 2017 for the fiftieth anniversary of the awarding of the temple to the Metropolitan Museum of Art.[6]

The museum's mission states that it "collects, studies, conserves, and presents significant works of art across all times and cultures in order to connect people to creativity, knowledge, and ideas."[7] Through this application of projection mapping, the museum and its researchers used data and technology in innovative ways to bring humanity's heritage back to life and create a new experience of this ancient vestige.

The ways in which we engage with heritage in a museum setting can be very different from how we experience it in the broader built environment. Can you tell us how your work with creative installations and community engagement is pushing beyond the walls of cultural institutions to explore other forms of urban heritage?

Our urban heritage isn't simply composed of historic elements of the built environment; it's about how we create spaces of living and meaning within the environment as a whole—built and natural.

As part of my artistic practice, I have come to think of the city as a canvas upon which different layers are placed, allowing us to live inside a living, ever-changing artwork every day. In a quest to set a more ecologically friendly footprint and find ways to adapt to climate change, I have proposed installing gardens on city buses. The project I have been working with the longest, Bus Roots, is a platform for people to imagine a new, greener version of their city. I hope people feel encouraged to imagine new ways to adapt to climate change and make our lives better at the same time.

With Bus Roots—the proposal to install lightweight gardens on top of city buses and other vehicles—I talked to different designers, engineers, architects, artists, and gardeners to arrive at the latest design. *FIG. 4, 5* This past year, when I was designing the Bus Roots VRV, a food truck with a garden on its roof and a virtual reality studio, I went through the same process and talked to game designers, technologists, and developers to get feedback on the project. Once we launched the prototype in New York

6
For more information, see "April Events to Mark 50th Anniversary of Presidential Award of Temple of Dendur to the Met," Metropolitan Museum of Art, https://www.metmuseum.org/press/news/2017/dendur-at-50.

7
For more information, see "About the Met," Metropolitan Museum of Art, https://www.metmuseum.org/about-the-met.

FIG. 5: Bus Root VRV.

and Guadalajara, Mexico, we learned a lot about what users reacted to and how the experience could be improved. Now with a virtual reality component, Bus Roots VRV allows visitors to virtually draw a greener city. In Central Park in New York and in public spaces across Guadalajara, Mexico, Bus Roots VRV reached 1,500 visitors in 2017 with the support of public and private art organizations and municipal, state, and federal institutions.

The truck went out into the streets and asked users ranging in age and disciplinary background to draw their favorite plant, both on paper and in virtual reality. The result is a collection of 1,200 plants that could be the seeds of a future distributed botanical garden, but hopefully they also become the seeds for us to imagine our neighborhoods as fertile ground for innovation.

Bringing the tools of creation outside the institutional walls and meeting people where they are can be very helpful in our missions as cultural advocates. These practices allow us to enhance and make more effective the ways we capture stories and information from multiple publics. The three projects I've discussed here have allowed me to understand our communities better and develop tools and strategies to engage in two-way communication. I hope we can find other ways to remix culture and bring about new solutions to improve our cities and communities.

○ Institutionalizing Data
○ Co-Producing Knowledge
● Building Evidence-Based Narratives
○ Informing Policy Agendas

The Possibilities and Perils of
Data-Driven Preservation Research:
Lessons from a Multiyear Study of
Federal Historic Rehabilitation Tax Credits

Stephanie Ryberg-Webster
Kelly L. Kinahan

Building Evidence-Based Narratives

Federal historic rehabilitation tax credits (HTCs) motivate thousands of historic preservation projects around the nation. Wide-ranging arguments praise the power of HTCs to underpin urban revitalization—for example, the National Park Service, which oversees the program, claims that it is "the nation's most effective program to promote historic preservation and community revitalization through historic rehabilitation" and that it "generates much needed jobs, enhances property values in older communities, creates affordable housing, and augments revenue for federal, state, and local governments." [1] Others argue that "the most significant program involving historic preservation and the production of housing (including affordable units)... is the historic rehabilitation tax credit," [2] and, after the housing crisis in 2008, the National Park Service claimed that the HTC "continues to be a major stimulus for economic recovery in older communities throughout the nation." [3] Descriptive statistics and highly aggregated data underpin these compelling arguments. Recent studies quantify the program's economic impact at the federal level, yet minimal scholarship examines the use and effects of HTCs in cities, neighborhoods, and downtowns. [4] Urban policy makers have a limited understanding of where the private sector invests in historic buildings, how these projects shape cities and neighborhoods, and if and how HTCs interact with other urban revitalization efforts.

To better understand the spatial dynamics, change over time, and subnational effects of the HTC, we conducted a multiyear study of the federal HTC using a limited dataset provided by the Technical Preservation Services division of the National Park Service. The broad question underpinning this research was, what is the impact of HTC activity on urban places? We then further explored methods for evaluating and analyzing community and economic development effects, spatial distribution and patterns of investment, and variations across different market contexts.

Federal tax incentives to support historic preservation have existed in some form since 1976, when Congress sought to bring some balance to a tax code that encouraged demolition, to alleviate urban decline, and to repurpose outmoded commercial and industrial facilities. [5] Modified in 1978, 1981, 1986, and 2017, the current HTC is a 20 percent income tax credit on rehabilitation expenses for income-producing properties listed in the National Register of Historic Places. There is no cap on the amount of credit or the number of credits awarded each year, and state historic preservation offices (SHPOs) and the National Park Service review applications on a rolling basis, making it both a functional and an attractive incentive for developers of historic buildings. Using the HTC comes with a steep learning curve and significant costs; users often require the assistance of preservation consultants, accountants, and tax attorneys. There is a three-part application process to obtain the credit that involves state offices, the National Park Service, and the Internal Revenue Service. Part 1 certifies that the building is listed in or eligible for listing in the National Register of Historic Places. If eligible but not already listed, a full National Register nomination must proceed alongside the rehabilitation. Part 2 details the proposed rehabilitation work, which must comply with the Secretary of the Interior's Standards for Rehabilitation. Finally, Part 3 certifies that the completed project complied with federal preservation

1
National Park Service, *Federal Tax Incentives for Rehabilitating Historic Buildings: Annual Report for Fiscal Year 2017* (Washington, DC: US Department of the Interior, National Park Service, Technical Preservation Services, 2018).

2
David Listokin, Barbara Listokin, and Michael Lahr, "The Contributions of Historic Preservation to Housing and Economic Development," *Housing Policy Debate* 9 (March 1998): 431–478.

3
National Park Service, *Federal Tax Incentives for Rehabilitating Historic Buildings: Statistical Report and Analysis for Fiscal Year 2011* (Washington, DC: US Department of the Interior, National Park Service, Technical Preservation Services, 2011).

4
Center for Urban Policy Research, *Annual Report on the Economic Impact of the Federal Historic Tax Credit for FY 2016* (Washington, DC: US Department of the Interior, National Park Service, 2017).

5
Stephanie Ryberg-Webster, "Urban Policy in Disguise: A History of the Federal Historic Rehabilitation Tax Credit," *Journal of Planning History* 14, no. 3 (August 2015): 204–223.

standards and details the final rehabilitation expenditures. The Internal Revenue Service releases the credit at the end of the project, thus minimizing program abuse and fraud. The tax reform law in 2017 modified the 20 percent HTC so that recipients must take the credit over a five-year period beginning when the building goes into service.6

Using aggregated data, the National Park Service reports 43,328 certified rehabilitation projects involving an estimated investment of $89.97 billion from 1977 through 2017. Developers have used the HTC to rehabilitate 278,270 housing units and create 289,933 new units. The HTC has helped to preserve or create 160,058 affordable housing units and, according to the National Park Service, create 2.54 million jobs. In 2017, there were 1,035 completed projects, totaling $5.82 billion in qualified rehabilitation costs; in the same year, the HTC helped fund the rehabilitation and/or creation of more than 19,000 housing units, of which approximately 35 percent (6,803) were low- or moderate-income units. While the average rehabilitation expense per project was more than $5.6 million, in half of all projects the expense was less than $1 million, suggesting that the HTC supports the rehabilitation of a range of building scales.7

To further encourage investment in historic buildings, thirty-four states offer their own HTC. State policies vary, with differing credit percentages, requirements for geographic dispersion, annual caps on number and/or total value of credits awarded, annual caps on the amount of credit awarded to each project, and availability for owner-occupants. While state HTCs play a crucial role in preserving and rehabilitating historic buildings, our research focused on the federal incentives.

● HTC DATA

Within the National Park Service, Technical Preservation Services retains data on HTC applications but does not have an open data portal. Technical Preservation Services provides a "check project status" tool on its website with extremely limited information. Novogradac & Company, however, has a "Historic Tax Credit Mapping Tool" on its website, where users can download data as a .csv file.8 This data is limited to projects that received a Part 3 approval between 2001 and 2015, and it provides projects' address, total cost, project description (end use), and Part 3 approval date. The Novogradac tool provides useful overlays including federal Low Income Housing Tax Credit qualified census tracts, New Markets Tax Credits eligible census tracts, and Community Reinvestment Act eligibility.9

Given the dearth of publicly available information on HTCs, we worked directly with staff at Technical Preservation Services to obtain data for twelve cities, strategically selected to represent a cross-section of states, regional geography, city size, market conditions (growing/declining), and the presence of state-level HTCs. The data included all federal HTCs with an approved Part 1 submitted between January 1, 1997 and June 30, 2010. Each entry was a unique HTC project and included project address; Parts 1, 2, and 3 application dates, decisions (approved/conditionally approved/denied), and decision dates; estimated and final costs; land use (before and after); total housing units (before and after); affordable housing units (before and after); building square footage (before and after); age of building; and building count. The dataset had 3,514 unique entries across the twelve cities. FIG. 1

City	State HTC (date adopted)	Population (2010)	# of Federal HTCs	Total Estimated Cost	Housing Units (Before)	Housing Units (After)	Net Housing Units Produced	Affordable Units (Before)	Affordable Units (After)	Net Affordable Units Produced
Atlanta	Y (2002)	420,003	49	$153 M	292	763	471	0	144	144
Baltimore	Y (1997)	620,961	494	$1.37 B	1,314	4,243	2,929	416	623	207
Cleveland	Y (2007)	396,815	224	$1.20 B	1,805	4,854	3,049	1,158	1,215	57
Denver	Y (1991)	600,158	76	$325 M	294	1,670	1,376	240	738	498
Dubuque	Y (2000)	57,637	25	$172 M	40	206	166	0	106	106
Omaha	N	408,958	65	$278 M	652	1,990	1,338	247	714	467
Philadelphia	N	1,526,006	343	$2.10 B	2,080	7,680	5,600	916	1,873	957
Portland	N	583,776	84	$475 M	553	827	274	413	635	222
Providence	Y (2002-8)	178,042	117	$521 M	435	1,501	1,066	255	342	87
Richmond	Y (1997)	204,214	742	$1.30 B	2,779	8,743	5,964	896	1,637	741
Seattle	N	608,660	41	$317 M	1,008	1,165	157	776	1,020	244
St. Louis	Y (1998)	319,294	1,032	$2.66 B	6,182	11,976	5,794	1,294	4,478	3,184

FIG. 1: *Summary of HTC data for twelve cities, 1997–2010.*

As a result of how the National Park Service managed the HTC program before 1997, all data from that period is essentially lost at the federal level. In order to gather information on earlier projects, Technical Preservation Services staff directed us to the SHPOs. While nine of the SHPOs provided this data, it was highly inconsistent in terms of organization and information included. 10 We found it nearly impossible to merge the state-provided data with the federal data, a problem that impedes robust, cross-city longitudinal studies. Only two of the eight SHPOs with state-level HTCs provided state HTC data, again effectively preventing us from taking state HTCs into account and/or completing any cross-city/context studies using longitudinal state and federal HTC data. 11

● DATA-DRIVEN HTC RESEARCH

While the Technical Preservation Services data had severe limitations, it was more robust in recording recent HTC activity in the twelve cities. After geocoding the data, we studied HTC activity and trends, explored the use and effects of HTC investments in downtown areas, and analyzed neighborhood-level HTC activity. Overall, data-driven HTC research illustrated that these projects occur across a range of places and are especially crucial in legacy cities with weak market conditions—HTCs facilitate transformative land use change in postindustrial spaces. Empirical studies also show that HTC clustering is common and that local (neighborhood) saturation points spur diffusion over time. The data confirms that HTCs encourage market-rate and affordable urban housing, with little evidence of direct displacement. Particularly in legacy cities, there is no evidence of HTCs inducing widespread gentrification. But even with robust data, the effects of HTCs are difficult to isolate amid highly complex urban development processes.

10
For example, not all SHPOs provided information on housing or land use.

11
While we have not completed a comprehensive search, we have not found SHPOs that provide publicly available HTC data.

12
The hot-spot analysis used CrimeStat III, with a random nearest neighbor distance and a minimum of thirteen HTCs per cluster. The spatial autocorrelation calculated the global univariate Moran's I for individual HTC investments and block groups with HTCs. For the purposes of this study, the Herfindahl-Hirschman Index calculates the level of market concentration for HTC investment at the block group.

13
Stephanie Ryberg-Webster, "The Landscape of Urban Preservation: A Spatial Analysis of Federal Rehabilitation Tax Credits in Richmond, Virginia," *Journal of Urban Affairs* 37, no. 4 (October 2015): 410–435.

Robust data on HTC activity in any given city can account for the spatial distribution of these investments, patterns of clustering and dispersion, effects on urban housing and land use patterns, and changes in local HTC activity over time. Exploring these aspects of HTC activity in Richmond, Virginia, there are three primary questions: What are the spatial patterns of HTC activity? What housing and land use changes are associated with HTC investments? Is there spatial interaction between HTCs and locally based, targeted urban revitalization initiatives? With geocoded, longitudinal data on individual HTC projects, spatial analysis and other quantitative methodologies can illuminate HTC trends and patterns. Hot-spot analysis can identify spatial clusters, spatial autocorrelation clarifies the level of interdependence between HTC locations, and the Herfindahl-Hirschman Index analyzes market concentration. 12 These methods of analysis are widely used in urban research, yet their application to historic preservation remains underdeveloped. Used in combination, these three methods provided a robust and detailed portrait of Richmond's HTC geography. 13

HTC activity was resilient in Richmond through the recession, and by 2009 investment activity had surpassed 2007 levels. HTC projects were most concentrated in the center of the city but diffused over

FIG. 2: 16 North 22nd Street in Richmond. The Poythress Building was built in 1870 and adapted in 2001 to create thirty new housing units. The rehabilitation cost $1.94 million. Photograph by Kelly L. Kinahan.

time. Throughout the study time period (1997–2010), about one-third of Richmond's neighborhoods had some level of HTC activity, and the locations with the most investment in any given year changed over time. This data indicates that there is a saturation point of HTC projects, forcing developers to seek new opportunities, typically in adjacent neighborhoods or areas with a similar building stock. Analyzing the data on HTC buildings' land use (before and after) demonstrated that these investments contribute to Richmond's postindustrial transformation through the conversion of formerly industrial and vacant buildings into housing and mixed-use space. *FIG. 2* An analysis of the housing data (both total units and affordable units) illustrated that the HTC incentivizes housing production *without* directly displacing low-income residents. In Richmond, most neighborhoods actually gained affordable housing through HTC projects, and most increases in market-rate housing occurred via adaptive reuse. Analyzing the interaction between HTC investments and locally driven revitalization initiatives (in this case, Richmond's Neighborhoods in Bloom program) revealed that to an extent, activities aligned, suggesting that local strategies may have the potential to catalyze and capitalize on HTC projects. Still, more research is needed with detailed data on both HTC activity and local revitalization programs (investments, strategies, policies, etc.). [14]

HTCs' Contribution to Downtown Transformation

Analyzing HTC activity in each of the twelve cities clearly indicated a concentration of investment in downtown areas. Recently, scholars have documented the rise of so-called "new downtowns" as vibrant, mixed-use neighborhoods driven by demographic and generational change and reflecting a revived interest in high-density, transit-friendly lifestyles. [15] Yet there was a dearth of research on preservation's role in this transformation, and nearly zero attention was given to HTC investments. How are HTC projects contributing to downtown revitalization? What role has the federal HTC played in the postindustrial transformation of US downtowns? [16] Data provided by Technical Preservation Services can show how much local HTC activity downtowns captured (both in terms of number of projects and total investment); the resiliency (or lack thereof) of downtown HTC projects through the recession; the role of HTCs in facilitating downtown land use changes, specifically via the conversion of former office or industrial space into housing and mixed-use projects; and the direct impact of HTC projects on affordability and gentrification. In total, the downtowns of ten cities benefited from $3.6 billion (adjusted to 2010 dollars) in HTC investment between 2001 and 2010. [17] *FIG. 3*

[14] Ryberg-Webster, "Landscape of Urban Preservation."

[15] See Rebecca Sohmer and Robert Lang, *Downtown Rebound* (Washington, DC: Fannie Mae Foundation and Brookings Institution, 2001) and Eugénie L. Birch, "Downtown in the 'New American City,'" *Annals of the American Academy of Political and Social Science* 626 (Fall 2009): 134–153.

[16] Stephanie Ryberg-Webster, "Preserving Downtown America: Federal Rehabilitation Tax Credits and the Transformation of US Cities," *Journal of the American Planning Association* 79, no. 4 (Fall 2013): 266–279. Omaha and Dubuque were not included in this analysis.

[17] Ryberg-Webster, "Preserving Downtown America," 267.

	Increase in downtown housing units [US Census]	% new housing accounted for in HTC buildings	% of HTC units reported as affordable	Net affordable units in HTC projects
Atlanta	1,583	0%	0%	0
Baltimore	1,863	40%	1%	6
Cleveland	1,573	91%	18%	-10
Denver	1,374	3%	41%	16
Philadelphia	5,446	33%	8%	42
Portland	886	21%	84%	136
Providence	569	36%	8%	16
Richmond	1,329	47%	6%	3
Seattle	1,388	16%	38%	89
St. Louis	4,065	65%	13%	99

FIG. 3: *Summary of downtown HTC activity across ten cities, 1997–2010. Adapted from Ryberg-Webster, "Preserving Downtown America."*

Downtowns typically captured a minority of total projects in each city, but a majority (or near majority) of total investment. Thus, perhaps

18
Ryberg-Webster,
"Preserving Downtown
America," 276.

19
American Assembly,
Reinventing America's
Legacy Cities:
Strategies for Cities
Losing Population
(New York: American
Assembly, 2011).

unsurprisingly, downtown HTC projects tend to be larger and high-er-value investments than HTC projects in other neighborhoods. For these ten cities, HTC activity was fairly resilient through the recession, stabilizing or exceeding prerecession levels within one to two years. The data confirmed that the HTC helped finance land use changes at the core of recent downtown transformations. In all cities, developers used the HTC to convert outmoded and oversupplied office and industrial buildings into mixed-use spaces and housing. Reinforcing the findings for Richmond, downtown HTC projects produced market-rate and afford-able housing with no evidence of direct displacement. In other words, the downtowns of these ten cities did not directly lose any affordable units via HTC projects. The research concluded that federal HTCs play a key role in the postindustrial transformation of US downtowns and, perhaps most notably, that HTCs were a prominent force driving rein-vestment in declining cities such as Cleveland and St. Louis. [18] The study, though, is only so generalizable, due to the small sample size and lack of true longitudinal data. Additional research is imperative to confirm (or counter) these initial findings, provide a more robust and nuanced understanding of downtown HTC activity, and understand the time frame for this transformation as it is likely that many downtowns began their postindustrial transformation prior to 2001.

HTCs in Weak-Market, Legacy City Neighborhoods
The study of downtown HTC activity indicated that HTCs were especially important to the six legacy cities in the dataset (Baltimore, Cleveland, Philadelphia, Providence, Richmond, and St. Louis). When looking at projects in our dataset with a Part 3 completion, these six cities accounted for the majority of all projects (87 percent), total investment (83 percent), and housing units (83 percent). Legacy cities, also known as shrinking cities, are "a group of American cities that have rich histories and assets, and yet have struggled to stay relevant in an ever-changing global economy."[19] These cities contain a vast array of historic resources reflecting their booms in the early twentieth century. Yet they suffer from decades of population decline and economic distress that have left a landscape of vacant and abandoned buildings, vacant land, and oversupplied infrastructure. A lack of market viability and a surplus of buildings often leads policy makers to prioritize demolition, raising questions about the future of the historic built environment and the role of preservation in legacy city planning and development.

Considering these circumstances, we analyzed all neighborhood HTC projects in the six legacy cities. Neighborhoods are the primary spaces facing market distress in these cities, and thus they are the pri-mary location where city leaders struggle to decide what to demolish and/or where to direct limited reinvestment resources. Our research questioned if and how the federal HTC is a policy lever that spurs rein-vestment in distressed communities and/or supports affordable housing in areas of high need. Using this data, we were able to address three key research questions: Do HTC investments occur in legacy cities, and, if so, what are the characteristics of these projects? What is the distribution of HTC activity across legacy cities? What are the income characteristics of neighborhoods where developers use the HTC? The final question expands our understanding of where developers choose to undertake projects. We were able to begin to explore the question of who benefits from the incentive by looking at the range of places, based on socioeconomic conditions, where investments occurred. To answer these questions, we combined the HTC data with US Census 2000 tract-level data. The use of Census 2000 data provided a proxy snapshot of neighborhood conditions *prior* to the HTC investment. Using the Herfindahl-Hirschman Index, we explored the market concentration of HTC activity over time. 20

This research empirically demonstrated that HTCs occurred across a wide range of places. Especially important was the finding that HTCs were fairly prevalent in low- and very low-income neighborhoods, which captured a majority (57 percent) of the total neighborhood HTC activity in these six cities. The data also revealed that HTC projects occur in only a few neighborhoods in any given year but are more dispersed when looking at ten years' worth of activity. This pattern of HTC activity shifting across neighborhoods reinforces the idea of a saturation point of HTC activity at the neighborhood scale. In legacy city neighborhoods, HTC investments produced both market-rate and affordable housing across all of these cities' neighborhoods. *FIG. 4*

20
Stephanie Ryberg-Webster and Kelly L. Kinahan, "Historic Preservation in Declining City Neighbourhoods: Analysing Rehabilitation Tax Credit Investments in Six US Cities," *Urban Studies* 54, no. 7 (May 2017): 1673–1691. Neighborhoods included all tracts except downtown, as identified in Ryberg-Webster, "Preserving Downtown America."

21
Ryberg-Webster and Kinahan, "Historic Preservation in Declining City Neighbourhoods," 1685.

22
For more on legacy cities, see the Legacy Cities Partnership at http://www.legacy cities.org.

23
Kelly L. Kinahan, "Neighborhood Revitalization and Historic Preservation in US Legacy Cities" (PhD diss., Cleveland State University, 2016); Kelly Kinahan, "The Neighborhood Effects of Federal Historic Tax Credits in Six Legacy Cities," *Housing Policy Debate* (forthcoming); Kelly Kinahan, "Legacy City Historic Preservation: Neighborhood Patterns," in *The Legacies of Legacy Cities: Continuity and Change amid Decline and Revival*, ed. J. Rosie Tighe and Stephanie Ryberg-Webster (Pittsburgh: University of Pittsburgh Press, forthcoming).

24
Kinahan, "Neighborhood Revitalization," 28.

25
Kinahan, "Neighborhood Revitalization," 88; Kinahan, "Legacy City Historic Preservation."

FIG. 4: *East Fourth Street in downtown Cleveland. The development included ten HTC projects, completed between 2003 and 2008, at a total cost of more than $10 million. In total, the project created ninety-five new units of market-rate housing through the adaptive reuse of commercial buildings; vacant upper stories were used for residences, with commercial, retail, or entertainment spaces on the ground level. Photograph by Stephanie Ryberg-Webster.*

These findings contradict the popular notion that weak-market conditions in legacy cities impede development. 21 The study remains limited, though, by a lack of generalizability as it included only six of at least forty-eight legacy cities, as defined by the Legacy Cities Partnership. 22 Furthermore, the six cities were not selected strategically, nor

26
Kinahan, "Neighborhood Revitalization," 92; Kinahan, "Legacy City Historic Preservation." These findings differ from Ryberg-Webster and Kinahan, "Historic Preservation in Declining City Neighbourhoods," thus illustrating the need for continued analyses and refined metrics to understand the geography of HTC activity.

27
Kinahan, "Neighborhood Revitalization," 115; Kinahan, "Neighborhood Effects."

28
Kinahan, "Neighborhood Revitalization," 119.

29
Kinahan, "Neighborhood Effects."

did they reflect a random sample; rather, they were a sample chosen for convenience. Given the relatively small number of legacy cities, future studies would ideally look at HTC activity in all forty-eight cities to elicit patterns, trends, and outlier situations.

HTCs and Neighborhood Change in Legacy Cities

Finally, the HTC data facilitated an exploration of the effects these investments have on neighborhoods. Using advanced quantitative methods, we asked: Are HTC projects spurring revitalization and/or gentrification? What is the relationship between HTC activity and changes in a neighborhood's racial, socioeconomic, and housing characteristics? [23] A cluster analysis revealed eight neighborhood types within legacy cities, which can be grouped into two higher-order clusters, stable and high distress. [24] Overlaying HTC activity with the neighborhood typology and US Census data demonstrated that HTC investments occurred across all legacy city neighborhood types, further showing that developers undertake HTC projects in even the most distressed neighborhood contexts. [25] Nevertheless, stable neighborhoods captured more investment (80 percent of the total) and more projects (60 percent of the total) compared to high-distress areas. [26]

	Model 1: HTCs in Stable Tracts	Model 2: HTCs in High Distress Tracts	Model 3: High Level of HTCs in Stable Tracts	Model 4: High Level of HTCs in High Distress Tracts	Model 5: HTCs that Resulted in Housing	Model 6: HTCs that Resulted in Affordable Housing
Race/Ethnicity	No significance	No significance	No significance	No significance	No significance	No significance
Median Household Income (MHI)	No significance	No significance	No significance	No significance	Significant	No significance
Low-Income (31-50% MHI)	Small (-) effect*	No significance	No significance	Some (+) effect*	No significance	Significant (+) effect
All other income groups	No significance	No significance	No significance	No significance	No significance	No significance
Poverty rate	No significance	No significance	No significance	No significance	n/a	n/a
Percent Bachelor's or more	No significance	No significance	No significance	No significance	No significance (+) effect	No significance
Median Housing Value	No significance	Some (+) effect*	No significance	No significance	n/a	n/a
Median Rent	Some (+) effect*	No significance	Some (+) effect*	No significance	No significance	No significance

FIG. 5: Summary of regression results, HTC effect on indicators of neighborhood change. . Data from Kinahan's three studies, "Neighborhood Revitalization," "Neighborhood Effects," and "Legacy City Historic Preservation."

The effect of HTC activity on revitalization and gentrification was explored using a difference-in-difference regression model that compared outcomes in tracts with and without HTC activity. [27] The HTC spurred no significant revitalization or gentrification in legacy city neighborhoods, even when tracts with high HTC investment were isolated. [28] Further refinement of this analysis looked at changes in neighborhoods between 2000 and 2015 to better capture the lag effect of HTC investments and limited the independent variable to only those HTCs that produced housing units. [29] There were still only minimal changes in socioeconomic characteristics and no significant changes in racial or housing composition. Importantly, though, housing-based HTC investments were related to increases in median household income and, perhaps

30
Kinahan, "Neighborhood
Effects."

31
A possible model is
the US Department of
Housing and Urban
Development's
database: https://www.
huduser.gov.

FIG. 6: *1200 Allen Market Lane in the Soulard neighborhood of St. Louis. Formerly the Brown Shoe Company, the building was rehabilitated into senior housing and provides one hundred units of affordable housing. In addition to federal and state historic tax credits, the project also relied on the federal Section 8 Substantial Rehabilitation program. Photograph by Kelly L. Kinahan.*

unsurprisingly, there were significant increases in the share of low-income households in places where the HTC created or rehabilitated affordable units. 30 *FIG. 6* This finding of minimal, if any, significant effect on neighborhood change tempers sweeping claims that preservation—and the HTC specifically—spurs revitalization. It also helps to debunk popular critiques that preservation is a precursor, or even a signal, of gentrification.

● THE FUTURE OF DATA-DRIVEN HTC RESEARCH

There are immense possibilities for additional data-driven research on HTCs. The key is simple: more data! The National Park Service should gather more robust data on HTC activity and make this data publicly available and easily accessible. 31 While we were able to obtain a limited dataset, and while it may be possible for researchers to obtain similar information for different or more cities through the Freedom of Information Act, these approaches require researchers to resubmit requests each year for updated data—a cumbersome process for both researchers and National Park Service staff. Ideally, the National Park Service would make all information collected on the HTC application (which we recommend expanding) available online in a downloadable format. Data should already be geocoded and available in common formats such as shapefiles (for GIS applications), .csv files, or other database-friendly formats. By improving HTC data with an overall eye to building a rigorous body of knowledge about this popular historic preservation incentive, we can expand the overall understanding of preservation's role in community revitalization.

Going beyond the Preservation Silo and Economic Impacts
Professionally gathered and managed data that is available to the public would better inform public policy decisions, facilitate a range of policy studies, and provide the basis for a much-needed body of

32
Stephanie Ryberg-
Webster and Kelly L.
Kinahan, "Historic
Preservation and Urban
Revitalization in the
Twenty-First Century,"
*Journal of Planning
Literature* 29, no. 2
(May 2014): 119–139.

peer-reviewed scholarship on HTCs. Public data would allow scholars with advanced quantitative methodological skills to significantly
broaden our understanding of the use, spatial dynamics, and impacts
of the HTC. This would also help break preservation out of its silo and
better connect the field to related areas of social science, urban studies,
and public policy. 32 Continued research on the use and effects of HTCs
is necessary, in particular as it encourages a shift from economic impact
studies—which are essential policy documents—to rigorous evaluations
of neighborhood impacts. Even further, research across a variety of contexts and locations would be readily possible with an open data policy
on the part of the National Park Service.

Collecting, Compiling, and Releasing Pre-1997 HTC Data

Data on HTC investments before 1997 is imperative, and it is nearly
impossible to access in any comprehensive format, particularly across
states. This data is essential for rigorous longitudinal studies, which are
essential for understanding impacts on long-term processes of neighborhood change. Longitudinal studies are also key to analyzing HTC activity
as the program changed, including the 1981, 1986, and 2017 revisions.
Robust longitudinal studies could have better informed decision-making
in fall 2017 and should be developed to inform likely future debates about
expanding, contracting, and/or eliminating the HTC. Moving forward,
publicly available and comprehensive longitudinal data could support a
natural experiment that evaluates the effects of the most recent changes to
the HTC program and provides a strong, social science-based framework
for future policy decisions. We recommend that the National Park Service
or another preservation-focused entity seek funding for a data recovery
project. It may be possible for a coordinating entity to obtain HTC data
stored at all SHPOs and merge these datasets into a usable and consistent
format. A more difficult project would entail attempting to recover the
older data from the National Park Service's regional office computers; this
data would be better but perhaps more technically challenging to obtain.

Merging Federal and State HTC Data to Explore Interactions

Additional data on incentives and programs commonly paired with
the HTC is essential for a more rigorous understanding of the federal
historic tax credit. Where state-level HTCs exist, we recommend similar
open data portals for accessible, user-friendly, and up-to-date information
on projects. With specific geographic identifiers (accurate coordinates are
ideal, but addresses can also work most of the time), it would be a relatively
easy task for someone skilled in database management to merge these
datasets. With both federal and state HTC data, scholars could conduct
more in-depth and comparative analyses. Ideally, these analyses would
facilitate continual efforts to improve state- and federal-level incentives.

Aligning Spatial HTC Data with Common Partner Incentives and Programs

Data on federal New Markets and Low-Income Housing Tax Credits
that are used in conjunction with the HTC would offer a more detailed
view of how these popular federal incentives work (or do not work)
together. Pairing the HTC data with local building permit data would help

accumulate knowledge about how HTC projects are related to other, non-HTC investments, including what types of public or private investments precede and follow HTC activity. This, along with a clear understanding of the total costs of HTC projects and qualified rehabilitation expenditures, would facilitate studies evaluating catalytic impacts and spillover effects. In addition, future work should try to align HTC data with other unique state and/or local programs such as Richmond's Neighborhoods in Bloom, Philadelphia's Neighborhood Transformation Initiative, or Cleveland's Strategic Investment Initiative. This would give preservationists, planners, policy makers, and scholars a more well-rounded perspective on the intersections of HTCs with other urban reinvestment strategies.

Expanding the HTC Application to Collect Data on Other Funding Sources and Housing Provision

There is also significant overlap between HTC activity and the production of housing, including affordable housing. Currently, the federal HTC application asks how many affordable units will be in the completed project, but does not require applicants to list other sources of funding. While the US Department of Housing and Urban Development (HUD) provides data on its various programs via the HUD User online portal, it is difficult to identify which specific federal funding source (if any) is supporting the creation of affordable housing within an HTC project. While combining the HTC and Low Income Housing Tax Credit is common, developers could also use Section 8 funds, HOME, Section 202, and other programs. There are also state- and local-level housing incentives, in addition to many local affordable housing mandates.[33] In nearly every study we have published, peer reviewers questioned the lack of specificity about the affordable units in HTC projects.

To make that information more readily available, the National Park Service should expand the HTC application to include specific sources of funding and requirements for units reported as affordable. There are significant differences between housing for people making 80 percent of area median income and housing for the formerly homeless. Knowing how, exactly, units are affordable and for whom they are affordable is central to a deep understanding of HTCs and urban development. This additional section on the HTC application would generate robust data that would certainly be useful for future projects. Still, a data generation project is necessary to fill in the lack of specificity on affordability for past HTCs. This effort would dig into the affordable housing numbers reported for past HTC projects to identify source(s) of funds and/or the regulatory mandates driving those numbers. The results would facilitate better understanding of the intersection between preservation and affordability, a key concern in nearly all communities spanning high-growth areas, neighborhoods facing gentrification pressure, and communities where affordable housing is abundant yet of extremely poor quality.

Improving Consistency in Land Use Data

HTCs play a key role in postindustrial urban land use change. They support adaptive reuse of industrial and office space into housing and mixed uses. While the National Park Service collects fairly detailed

33 For example, inclusionary approaches that require a certain number of units to be affordable to people making less than a specified percentage of area median income.

34
For example, funding
the conversion of
schools into housing
but not funding the
rehabilitation of
schools as schools.

land use information, questions remain about consistency and reliability for applicant-reported information. For example, many buildings were listed as "vacant" before the HTC investment, but that is a vague category—was the building a vacant warehouse, an apartment building, offices, a theater, or something else? Additional research into the effects of HTCs on land use is particularly important for understanding broader patterns of neighborhood change and the ways in which HTCs do and do not support comprehensive neighborhood development.[34]

Providing Data on HTC Applicants

Although we requested information on individual HTC applicants, the National Park Service resisted including this information out of concern for privacy. While we respect the need to keep certain information confidential, we believe that names of applicants, LLCs, preservation consultants, and others working on a project are public information. Without this information, comprehensive data on who is completing projects is nonexistent. Questions related to who invests in historic buildings are important for understanding broader social and political contexts surrounding these projects. For instance, who are the key actors involved in HTC projects? What are the politics of HTC-supported development? What types of conflicts, collaborations, and/or partnerships arise from these projects? What types of developers spearhead these projects (e.g., local or national firms, private or nonprofit entities)? Do cities have many HTC developers or only a handful? Do the number and the mix of HTC developers differ among cities and/or within cities (i.e., neighborhood to neighborhood)? How do HTC developers relate to and/or intersect with other segments of the local real estate sector? Furthermore, knowing who is behind an HTC project is an essential first step for any qualitative study that questions how and why projects are undertaken.

Studying Failure, Not Just Success

While the increase in public data on the Novogradac portal is important, limiting available data to completed HTC projects with a Part 3 approval reduces the possibilities for HTC research. It is imperative to make information available on rejected applications and stalled projects as well as successful projects. The study of failure is essential, particularly for policy analyses that aim to improve programs and incentives. With this data, scholars can explore where and why developers initiated projects but did not complete them and what happened, in the long run, to those buildings. This data would also provide a starting point for more in-depth, qualitative studies exploring questions like: Why do some projects never make it to completion? How do applicants proceed after the National Park Service rejects their HTC application? Does the building languish or get demolished? Are developers able to find other incentives or financing mechanisms?

Continuing to Tell Stories of People, Communities, Heritage, and Buildings

While there are tremendous possibilities for future data-driven quantitative research on historic tax credits, we caution against an over-reliance on quantitative data to tell the HTC story. Mixed-methods and

109

qualitative studies offer context, narratives, and meaning that can get lost in big data analyses and high-level statistical and spatial studies. The stories of HTC projects—the communities, buildings, histories, developers, motivations for undertaking complex rehabilitations, and impacts of these projects on neighborhood quality of life and other difficult-to-quantify outcomes—are essential both to building a rigorous body of scholarly research and to crafting compelling policies aimed at retaining and even expanding the HTC. It is also clear that the HTC is an important policy in many cities and that HTC research, along with research on other aspects of preservation, needs to engage a wide audience. It remains imperative for preservationists and others to use quantitative data wisely, to explore this and other preservation policies through a critical lens, and to break down the silo in which preservation traditionally operates.

Historic Preservation in a New Era of Building Energy Data

Amanda L. Webb

Building Evidence-Based Narratives

Data has shaped our enduring narrative about the energy consumption of older and historic buildings for nearly forty years. Recent developments in the collection and use of data on building energy performance have opened a fresh set of possibilities for considering the relationship between historic preservation and energy efficiency. By better understanding the history of preservation and energy data and by recognizing the problems with the standard approach, the ways in which preservationists can become active stakeholders in conversations around energy efficiency begin to become clear.

● PRESERVATION AND ENERGY DATA:
   A LONG, CONNECTED HISTORY

Historic preservation and building energy performance data have a long, connected history. Since the development of the first energy conservation standards for buildings in the mid-1970s, energy performance data has been central to the preservation community's approach to energy efficiency.

ASHRAE Standard 90–1975 and New Energy from Old Buildings
The first energy conservation standard for buildings, ASHRAE Standard 90, was published in 1975, in the wake of the 1973 oil crisis. This and other early energy conservation efforts were largely prescriptive, specifying requirements for the design of building envelopes, lighting, and heating, ventilation, and air-conditioning (HVAC) systems. Older and historic buildings—typically constructed from locally available materials, using vernacular construction techniques, and designed before the widespread use of HVAC systems—did not necessarily meet these prescriptive requirements, forcing immediate questions about how these buildings fit into the nationwide concern for energy conservation.

Data played a central role in the preservation community's initial response to these questions. Early efforts to understand the impacts of preservation on energy use included quantifying a building's *embodied energy* (i.e., the energy used to extract, produce, deliver, and install a building's materials), as well as the *operational energy* used by the building's heating, cooling, lighting, and other systems. Research on embodied energy showed that, after accounting for both embodied energy and operational

Construction date	Number of buildings	Percentage of buildings	Percentage of area	Energy consumption range (MBtu/ft2)	Average consumption (MBtu/ft2)
Before 1900	3	6.8	1.1	83–115	95
1901–19	8	18.2	12.8	76–135	105
1920–40	18	40.9	28.3	68–223	109
1941–62	12	27.3	36.2	66–198	126
1962–70	3	6.8	21.6	78–163	115

FIG. 1: *Energy consumption in New York City office buildings. Data from* Energy Conservation in Existing Office Buildings *by Syska & Hennessy and Tishman Research Corporation, 1977. Data shown as presented in Baird M. Smith, "Making Buildings Work As They Were Intended," in* New Energy from Old Buildings, *64.*

1
Michael L. Ainslie,
foreword to New Energy
from Old Buildings,
ed. National Trust for
Historic Preservation
(Washington, DC:
Preservation Press,
1981), 16.

2
Syska & Hennessy and
Tishman Research
Corporation, Energy
Conservation in
Existing Office
Buildings, Volume 1,
Phase 1 (Washington,
DC: US Department
of Energy, 1977),
III-20, http://www.
osti.gov/scitech/
biblio/5663250-
energy-conservation-
existing-office-
buildings-volume-
phase; Baird M. Smith,
"Making Buildings
Work As They Were
Intended," in New
Energy from Old
Buildings, 64.

3
Ainslie, foreword to
New Energy from Old
Buildings, 16.

4
Ainslie, foreword to
New Energy from Old
Buildings, 16.

5
Ann Webster Smith,
"Saving Energy in
Old Buildings," in
New Energy from Old
Buildings, 47.

6
Baird M. Smith, "Making
Buildings Work As They
Were Intended," in
New Energy from Old
Buildings, 71.

7
Baird M. Smith,
Conserving Energy
in Historic Buildings,
Preservation Briefs 3
(Washington, DC: Office
of Archeology and
Historic Preservation,
US Department of the
Interior, 1978).

8
Smith, "Making
Buildings Work As They
Were Intended," 71.

energy, preserving an old building is often more energy efficient than demolishing it and constructing a new one.[1] A 1977 study examining energy consumption data from a sample of forty-four office buildings in New York City showed that the oldest buildings had the lowest operational energy consumption on a per square foot basis (this is known as energy use intensity, or EUI).[2] *FIG. 1* These early findings, which seemed to advocate for preservation, were highlighted in the National Trust for Historic Preservation's 1981 symposium, *New Energy from Old Buildings*, and were succinctly summarized as "preservation conserves energy."[3]

The operational energy data, in particular, seemed to confirm what the preservation community intuitively knew to be true. Preservationists knew "empirically that older buildings were more energy efficient than the post-World War II generation of structures," but until this data was available, they lacked "broad statistical proof."[4] Preservationists attributed the better energy performance of older buildings to what were termed "inherent energy-saving features." As one preservationist put it at the time: "The reasons seem rather simple: most old buildings have a ratio of 20 percent or less between glass and walls, providing only adequate light and ventilation; they use interior and exterior shutters, blinds, curtains, draperies, and awnings to minimize heat gain or loss and they use such architectural features as balconies, porches and overhangs and such landscape features as shade trees and plantings around foundations to minimize heat gain."[5]

This initial data formed the core of a broader narrative about older buildings and energy performance: older buildings have better energy performance than newer ones; the reason for this is their inherent energy-saving features; we should therefore preserve these features and avoid altering (and potentially damaging) older and historic buildings in the name of energy efficiency. It was noted early on that "the application of these modern [energy conservation] standards to old buildings produces sometimes disturbing implications"; the installation of dropped ceilings in spaces with high ceilings and the replacement of historic windows were cited as examples.[6]

This narrative became the basis for the approach to energy efficiency in historic buildings in the United States and was embedded in early, canonical documents from the National Park Service, such as the original *Preservation Briefs 3* in 1978.[7] It also shaped the evolution of building energy codes. Since the early energy conservation standards were written chiefly with new construction in mind, the initial recommendation was to develop separate standards for existing and historic buildings.[8] Instead, successive versions of these standards became less prescriptive and began to include explicit exemptions for designated historic spaces and buildings. By ASHRAE Standard 90.1-1999, a wholesale exemption for historic buildings had been written into the standard, which remains in place today.

The Late 1970s through the Present: CBECS and RECS Surveys
From the late 1970s through the present, the primary source of data on building energy performance has been federal surveys collected by the US Energy Information Administration (EIA). While the 1977 study cited above was limited in scope to office buildings in New York City,

1
Data from 2003 CBECS Table C3, Consumption and Gross Energy Intensity for Sum of Major Fuels for Non-Mall Buildings.

2
Relative standard error (RSE)

3
Author's estimates based on analysis of the 2003 CBECS microdata

| Year built | Gross energy intensity[1] | | Building-level energy intensity[3] | | | | |
| | kBtu/sq.ft. | RSE[2] | Mean | 95% CI | Percentiles | | |
					25th	Median	75th
Before 1920	80.2	13.5	92.6	(74.8, 110.4)	30.6	57.4	109.1
1920 – 1945	90.3	13.7	101.1	(88.0, 114.1)	27.5	59.6	114.6
1946 – 1959	80.3	10.6	81.7	(71.9, 91.5)	27.5	58.2	106.4
1960 – 1969	90.9	8.5	92.2	(76.6, 107.8)	28.2	59.2	105.7
1970 – 1979	95.0	7.8	97.8	(84.5, 111.0)	32.1	63.5	116.4
1980 – 1989	100.1	10.4	102.7	(88.6, 116.7)	28.5	57.5	109.6
1990 – 1999	88.8	8.6	111.0	(92.1, 129.9)	25.9	55.6	120.0
2000 – 2003	79.7	11.5	85.1	(66.4, 103.7)	11.9	44.2	94.9

FIG. 2: Energy intensity by year of construction, 2003 CBECS.

4
Data from 2009 RECS Table CE1.1, Summary Totals and Intensities, U.S. homes.

5
Author's estimates based on analysis of the 2009 RECS microdata.

| Year built | Gross energy intensity[4] | | Building-level energy intensity[5] | | | | |
| | kBtu/sq.ft. | RSE | Mean | 95% CI | Percentiles | | |
					25th	Median	75th
Before 1940	51.6	2.4	71.3	(66.3, 76.3)	36.1	53.1	80.6
1940 – 1949	52.0	3.2	62.9	(61.1, 64.6)	37.0	53.2	78.9
1950 – 1959	52.5	1.8	61.4	(59.6, 63.2)	37.1	52.7	75.6
1960 – 1969	50.2	2.1	58.8	(57.6, 60.1)	35.2	50.1	73.1
1970 – 1979	46.9	1.7	55.6	(54.5, 56.6)	33.3	46.6	68.8
1980 – 1989	43.5	1.8	49.8	(49.0, 50.6)	30.9	44.0	62.5
1990 – 1999	39.9	1.7	46.7	(45.9, 47.5)	29.7	42.3	58.0
2000 – 2009	37.1	1.9	42.8	(42.0, 43.5)	27.7	38.2	51.9

FIG. 3: Energy intensity by year of construction, 2009 RECS.

these federal surveys provide information on the building stock of the entire United States.

The Commercial Building Energy Consumption Survey (CBECS) and the Residential Energy Consumption Survey (RECS) are national sample surveys that collect data on the energy performance and energy-related characteristics of commercial and residential buildings, respectively, in the United States. They have been conducted by the EIA roughly every four years since the late 1970s. Energy performance data is collected via utility bills for the survey year, and information about other energy-related characteristics (also termed "asset data") is collected through interviews. Asset data collected in the CBECS and RECS includes information about the physical characteristics of the building (such as wall type, window type, and HVAC system type), as well as operational characteristics (such as number of occupants and hours of operation). CBECS and RECS data is widely used, most often for benchmarking energy performance. This benchmarking is typically performed using summary tables from the CBECS or RECS, or through CBECS-based benchmarking tools, such as the US Environmental Protection Agency's ENERGY STAR score.

The CBECS and RECS data has also been used by the historic preservation community, chiefly to reinforce the narrative about energy efficiency in historic buildings. The National Park Service's web page on energy efficiency and preservation provides a plot of data from the

9
"Energy Efficiency,"
Technical Preservation
Services, National
Park Service, US
Department of the
Interior, https://
www.nps.gov/tps/
sustainability/
energy-efficiency.htm.

10
Jo Ellen Hensley and
Antonio Aguilar,
*Improving Energy
Efficiency in
Historic Buildings,
Preservation Briefs* 3
(Washington, DC:
National Park Service,
US Department of the
Interior, 2011), https://
www.nps.gov/tps/
how-to-preserve/
preservedocs/
preservation-briefs/
03Preserve-Brief-
Energy.pdf.

11
Karen Palmer and
Margaret Walls, "Using
Information to Close
the Energy Efficiency
Gap: A Review of
Benchmarking
and Disclosure
Ordinances," *Energy
Efficiency* 10, no. 3
(June 2017): 673–691.

2003 CBECS showing EUI by year of construction, which concludes that "per square foot, historic commercial properties rank among the best in terms of energy consumption." 9 The 2011 revision to *Preservation Briefs* 3 mentions this same CBECS data and also provides a table of data from the 2005 RECS showing EUI by year of construction. 10 The 2005 RECS, in contrast to the CBECS, appears to show an improvement in EUI in more recent construction, and *Preservation Briefs* 3 treats this data as an indicator of potential energy savings, suggesting that 30–40 percent energy savings in a historic residential building is a realistic goal. *FIG. 2, 3*

A New Era: Municipal Benchmarking Data

Over the past decade, an increasing number of US cities have enacted mandatory energy benchmarking and disclosure ordinances, requiring buildings to report energy consumption on an annual basis. These policies represent a shift in the way we collect data about the built environment and in our understanding of the building stock, effectively leading us into a new era of energy performance data. Whereas the CBECS and RECS provide a nationally representative picture of energy performance, municipal benchmarking data offers a fine-grained perspective that is locally focused.

The structure of these policies is fairly similar across the cities that have adopted them. Most have the following features in common:

- *Scope*: There is a building type and size threshold above which buildings must comply, typically commercial buildings (and sometimes multifamily residential buildings) larger than 50,000 square feet.
- *Data collected*: Building owners are required to report annual energy consumption each year, along with a small number of other details such as property address, square footage, building type, and year of construction.
- *Additional requirements*: There may be additional requirements beyond energy reporting, such as water consumption reporting or an energy audit.
- *Reporting and benchmarking mechanism*: The US Environmental Protection Agency's ENERGY STAR Portfolio Manager tool collects the required data and determines building performance relative to the rest of the building stock.
- *Disclosure*: There is typically a provision for making the reported data publicly available.

The first city to adopt such a policy was Washington, DC, in 2008, followed by Austin and New York City. 11 Since then more than two dozen US cities and counties have followed suit, including many of the largest metropolitan areas in the country, such as Chicago, Philadelphia, and San Francisco.

The resultant data differs from the CBECS and RECS in several ways that are notable for preservationists. First, the benchmarking data is a census rather than a sample, which has implications for how the data is analyzed (namely, survey weights do not need to be used). Second, the benchmarking data has greater spatial and temporal frequency than the CBECS and RECS. This creates longitudinal data through repeated annual disclosure by the same set of buildings and allows for record linkage with other datasets (e.g., registers of listed historic buildings) as building addresses are provided in the data. Third, the benchmarking data contains minimal asset data compared to the CBECS; little is disclosed about the physical and operational characteristics of the benchmarked buildings beyond square footage, building type, and year of construction.

To date, this emerging data has been only minimally explored for how it might change or add to our understanding of the energy performance of older and historic buildings. Because the year of construction is collected for benchmarked buildings, most cities provide charts of EUI (typically mean or median values) by year of construction in their annual benchmarking reports. For example, the annual benchmarking report for the City of Chicago plots median EUI by decade of construction, as well as ENERGY STAR score by decade of construction. 12 In addition to graphing the data, a few cities, such as Philadelphia and Seattle, overlay information about building EUI and year of construction onto publicly available maps of the city, enabling the potential identification of geographic trends.

12
City of Chicago, *2015 Chicago Energy Benchmarking Report*, 2015, 31, http://www.cityofchicago.org/content/dam/city/progs/env/EnergyBenchmark/2015_Chicago_Benchmarking_Report_Web_16DEC2015.pdf.

13
Syska & Hennessy and Tishman Research Corporation, *Energy Conservation in Existing Office Buildings*, III–20; Constantine E. Kontokosta, *Local Law 84 Energy Benchmarking Data: Report to the New York City Mayor's Office of Long-Term Planning and Sustainability*, 2012, 17–19, http://www.nyc.gov/html/gbee/downloads/pdf/ll84_kontoska_report.pdf.

● PROBLEMS WITH THE PRESERVATION
   PERSPECTIVE ON ENERGY DATA

The preservation community has long made use of energy data, as both a tool to understand the performance of older buildings relative to newer ones, and as a mechanism for reinforcing the narrative about preservation and energy efficiency. A more detailed view of this data, however, points to several problems and suggests that the prevailing perspective of energy data in preservation has been a limited one.

The Problem with Age and EUI
The preservation community's perspective on energy data is typically encapsulated in charts or two-way tables (such as Figures 1–3) exploring the bivariate relationship between EUI and year of construction (sometimes this variable is given as building age). There are a number of limitations to framing the data in this way that are not always explicitly addressed:

- *Categorization*: Year of construction, while in reality a continuous variable, is typically grouped into periods in order to summarize the data in charts and tables. Categorizing a continuous variable can result in loss of detail about the variation in values, and there is little consistency in categorization from study to study. Some analyses divide year of construction according to developments in building code, while others have simply organized data into five- or ten-year increments, or on another basis. 13
- *Misleading tables*: Presenting EUI in two-way tables can be misleading, as it is not always clear what the EUI value in the table represents—the mean EUI, the median EUI, or some other metric. For most populations of buildings, EUI is a positively skewed variable (the mean falls to the right of the median), and the

median may therefore be a more useful metric than the mean, depending on how the data will be used. In fact, the CBECS and RECS EUI values shown in *Preservation Brief 3* are not per building means or medians but gross energy intensities—that is, intensities computed by taking the total energy consumption for an age category and dividing it by the total square footage for that category. *FIG. 2, 3* For comparison, the mean building-level EUI is also provided in Figures 2 and 3, along with the 95 percent confidence interval for the mean estimate. Estimates are provided as well for the 25th, 50th (median), and 75th percentiles for each year of construction category. Note that for some age categories, these three estimates—gross intensity, building-level mean EUI, and building-level median EUI—differ by a large amount. Critically, the building-level median EUIs for the 2003 CBECS data shown in Figure 2 (which are the most appropriate metric to use from a building performance standpoint) show a different trend than the gross intensities used in *Preservation Brief 3* and do not support the same narrative of better energy performance in older buildings. The interquartile range (spread between the 25th and 75th percentiles) across all age categories is also relatively even, indicating that there are high- and low-performing buildings within each grouping.

- *Limitations of EUI*: EUI itself may not be the best (or at least should not be the sole) metric for understanding the energy performance of buildings. EUI is a coarse measure, eliding seasonal and hourly differences in building energy and thermal performance; these differences may be important in understanding the energy-saving features in older buildings.

- *Lack of statistical analysis*: Conclusions about the relationship between age and EUI are typically drawn only from measures of central tendency; measures of spread (for example, standard deviation or standard error) are seldom considered, and more detailed statistical analysis is rarely performed. While these conclusions can be a useful first step, statistical measures and tests of association such as correlation coefficients, chi-square tests, and linear regression provide a more robust understanding of the relationship between two variables.

In cases where statistical analysis has been performed to examine the relationship between year of construction and EUI, the results have shown that the relationship, while sometimes statistically significant, is generally weak.

Simple (bivariate) regression analysis of the relationship between age and EUI using nationally representative data (the 2003 CBECS and 2009 RECS) shows that, for commercial buildings, year of construction is a statistically significant predictor of EUI, but that the model R^2 (a measure of goodness of fit) is very low, with year of construction explaining less than 1 percent of the variation in EUI ($R^2 = 0.002$) and the best-fitting model being a cubic relationship between the two variables. For residential buildings, year of construction was also found to be a significant predictor of EUI, but with a low R^2 ($R^2 = 0.044$) and a negative linear relationship,

implying that EUI decreases with a more recent year of construction. [14]
In both datasets, many of the survey variables were found to be significant
bivariate predictors of EUI, partially because of the large sample size of
the survey. But these low R^2 values indicate that year of construction is
not an especially strong predictor of EUI in commercial or residential
buildings and that the relationship between the two variables is weak.

While not explicitly focused on the relationship between building
age and EUI, the US Environmental Protection Agency's ENERGY STAR
models have also used the CBECS data to consider the relationship between
building characteristics (including age) and EUI. Early work developing
these models from the 1992 CBECS data found year of construction to be
a significant predictor of EUI for K-12 school buildings in several census
divisions, but it was not a significant predictor of electric EUI in office
buildings. [15] The current ENERGY STAR models, most of which are based
on the 2003 CBECS data, only include year of construction as a possible
predictor for one of the building types (K-12 schools); it is not a predictor
in the final regression model. [16]

Studies looking at the relationship between age and EUI using
municipal benchmarking data, while limited to date, show fairly similar
trends. Analysis of early benchmarking data in New York City found—
using a multiple regression model—that building age was a significant
predictor of source EUI for office and multifamily buildings. In contrast
to site EUI, source EUI includes the energy consumed on site, in addition to the energy consumed during the generation and transmission
of that energy. Still, the overall model R^2 values were still fairly low for
engineering models ($R^2 = 0.20$ and $R^2 = 0.16$ for office and multifamily
buildings, respectively). [17] A comparative study of benchmarking data in
six US cities found the relationship between age and site EUI to be weak
in each case; correlation coefficients ranged from nearly 0 to a maximum
of around 0.3 for K-12 schools in Boston and Chicago. In two cities, the
correlation coefficients were negative across all building types, indicating
that newer buildings in these cities have lower EUIs. Overall, there were
few clear trends in the direction of this relationship. [18]

The Problem with Age

Beyond the problems of bivariate analysis of EUI and year of construction, year of construction is itself a highly problematic variable.
From a practical standpoint, this data is typically collected through a
questionnaire or form—this is true of the CBECS, the RECS, and municipal
benchmarking data—but this leads to two problems.

First, the person answering the questionnaire often does not actually know a building's exact year of construction. The CBECS and RECS
address this by asking respondents two questions about the year of construction: an open-ended question prompting respondents to give the
exact year of construction and, next, a closed question with ranges. The
second question is asked only if respondents don't know the answer to
the first, with the expectation that they will be more likely to answer at
all if they can choose from ordered categories. [19]

The success of this strategy is shown in the data. In the CBECS and
the RECS, an imputation procedure fills in the missing data (imputation

[14] Amanda L. Webb, "Evaluating the Energy Performance of Historic and Traditionally Constructed Buildings" (PhD diss., Pennsylvania State University, 2017).

[15] Terry Sharp, "Benchmarking Energy Use in Schools," in Proceedings from the 1998 ACEEE Summer Study on Energy Efficiency in Buildings, vol. 3 (American Council for an Energy-Efficient Economy, 1998): 305–316; Terry Sharp, "Energy Benchmarking in Commercial Office Buildings," in Proceedings from the 1996 & 1994 ACEEE Summer Study on Energy Efficiency in Buildings, vol. 4 (American Council for an Energy-Efficient Economy, 1996): 321–329.

[16] Portfolio Manager Technical Reference: ENERGY STAR Score for K-12 Schools (Washington, DC: US Environmental Protection Agency, 2014), https://www.energystar.gov/sites/default/files/tools/K12%20Schools.pdf.

[17] Kontokosta, Local Law 84 Energy Benchmarking Data, 24–25.

[18] Amanda L. Webb, L. Beckett, and M. D. Burton, "Examining the Energy Performance of Older and Historic Buildings Using Municipal Benchmarking Data," in Proceedings of the 3rd International Conference on Energy Efficiency in Historic Buildings (Visby, Sweden, forthcoming).

[19] US Energy Information Administration, Commercial Buildings Energy Consumption Survey (CBECS) for 2003: Building Questionnaire—Form EIA-871A, US Department of Energy, http://www.eia.doe.gov/survey/form/eia_871/2003/cbecs2003-871A-building-ques.pdf.

20
Robert M. Groves et al.,
Survey Methodology,
2nd ed. (Hoboken, NJ:
Wiley, 2009), 238.

is standard procedure in large surveys, and many different imputation methods are available). The public-use microdata for these surveys contains the imputed values, as well as a set of "imputation flag" variables to indicate whether a given value was reported or imputed. *FIG. 4* The data shows that in both the 2003 CBECS and the 2009 RECS, year of construction has one of the higher imputation rates—10.5 percent and 14.9 percent, respectively—although the rate drops to 1.0 percent for the CBECS and 2.5 percent for the RECS for the categorical (closed) form of the question. The implication is that, relative to other variables in the surveys, respondents are less likely to know the exact year of construction for their building.

Second, while open-ended survey questions have the potential to elicit more exact information, respondents tend to provide inexact answers, often rounding to multiples of five and ten.[20] This tendency can be seen in both the CBECS and the RECS data. *FIG. 5*

Year of construction is also problematic from a conceptual standpoint. While a building may have a single original date of construction, buildings are not static. Collecting data on the year of original construction

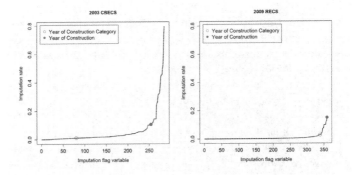

FIG. 4: Imputation rate for variables in the 2003 CBECS and 2009 RECS. The imputation rate is the total number of items imputed for each variable over the total sample size, arranged in increasing order. The imputation rates for year of construction and year of construction category are highlighted.

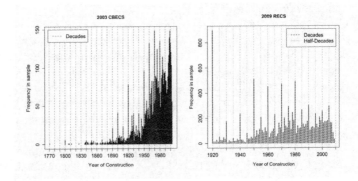

FIG. 5: Frequency of survey responses for the year of construction question in the 2003 CBECS and 2009 RECS. Grid lines are plotted at each decade for the CBECS and for each decade and half-decade for the RECS. Both plots show that the survey responses tend to cluster around the decade and half-decade years.

may capture something about the building's form and style, but it will not adequately account for additions or alterations, many of which would likely impact the building's energy performance. Consider a building originally constructed in the 1920s, with a substantial addition in the 1950s, a window replacement in the 1970s, and a boiler replacement in the 2000s: How old is this building? How old should we consider it to be for the purposes of energy-related data collection and analysis? Even when these distinctions are made explicit in the way data is collected—the 2003 CBECS, for example, specifically states that if the building has had major additions, the respondent should give the year of construction of the largest portion of the building—the data is still able to represent only a single point in the building's lifetime.

Building age may be a principal criterion for defining a building as historic and worthy of preservation, but a deeper look at how this variable is collected and paired with energy data suggests limits to its usefulness and questions its value in discussions about energy efficiency.

● PRESERVATIONISTS AS STAKEHOLDERS IN ENERGY DATA

To date, the preservation community's use of energy data has been largely reactive. But now that energy performance data is being collected at greater spatial and temporal frequencies and through locally controlled mechanisms, preservationists have the opportunity to move from a reactive stance to a proactive one: to become not just passive consumers of energy data, but active stakeholders.

The Mutual Benefits of Preservation and Energy Efficiency

Over the past four decades, preservationists' relationship to energy data has worn into a pattern. As new datasets materialize over time, they are examined for what they say about the relationship between age and EUI, and the findings are then incorporated into existing narratives. Only when these findings suggest that older buildings perform well compared to newer buildings are they highlighted, with the tacit (and in some cases explicit) implication that these buildings should not be targeted for energy retrofits.

But the use of energy data in this way—to support a specific narrative—largely misses the point. There are genuine, tangible benefits to older and historic buildings that can come from improving their energy efficiency. When the discussion about energy efficiency is based in narrative (even narrative reinforced by data), these benefits take a back seat to preservation philosophy; the focus is placed on how to minimize change to these buildings, rather than how to maximize the potential benefits of energy efficiency.

The primary benefit of energy efficiency is energy savings for older buildings—in terms of annual consumption and peak demand savings—both for their cost savings and as an environmental strategy to mitigate climate change. FIG. 6 But energy savings can also have ancillary positive effects. If the retrofit involves the building envelope, improving energy efficiency can also improve thermal comfort of inhabitants, especially

21
Giovanni Carbonara,
"Energy Efficiency
as a Protection Tool,"
Energy Build 95
(May 2015): 9–12.

22
Mark Huppert et al.,
*Realizing the Energy
Efficiency Potential
of Small Buildings*
(Washington, DC:
National Trust for
Historic Preservation,
Preservation Green
Lab, 2013).

23
Constantine E.
Kontokosta, "Energy
Disclosure, Market
Behavior, and
the Building Data
Ecosystem," *Annals of
the New York Academy
of Sciences* 1295
(August 2013): 34–43.

24
Palmer and Walls,
"Using Information
to Close the Energy
Efficiency Gap."

Benefits of energy efficiency to preservation:	Benefits of preservation to energy efficiency:
• Energy savings (peak and annual) • Energy cost savings • Improved thermal comfort • Improved delivered services • Keeping the building in use	• Improved cooling season thermal comfort • Reduced peak cooling demand • Increased resilience • Neighborhood scale efficiencies

FIG. 6: *Mutual benefits of preservation and energy efficiency.*

near previously cold windows and walls. Energy retrofits may also improve delivered services; an upgraded HVAC system, for example, may provide improved thermal comfort and indoor air quality using the same (or less) energy. Ultimately, if the goal of preservation is to keep a building in use, a comfortable, efficient building is more likely to stay in use, and improving energy efficiency can therefore be viewed as a tool for protecting and preserving the building, rather than as a threat.[21]

Conversely, there are real benefits of preserving older buildings for achieving energy efficiency goals. The inherent energy-saving features in some older buildings are effectively passive design strategies that can aid in thermal comfort and reduce peak cooling loads. These features also help increase resilience to climate change and extreme weather events. Consider the presence of operable windows, which provide a building with ventilation even through a power outage. There are also potential neighborhood scale benefits, as historic districts are often composed of buildings with similar physical characteristics and thus can take advantage of district-scale energy efficiency solutions.[22]

The Potential Uses of Energy Data in a Preservation Context

Focusing on these benefits can provide a new framework for preservationists' relationship to energy data. Currently, six major end users—owners, tenants, lenders, service providers, community groups, and utilities—make specific use of the data.[23] If we introduce preservationists into this ecosystem as a set of stakeholders in energy data (particularly municipal benchmarking data), what could we do?

To start with, there are at least four potential uses:

• *Retrofit targeting:* Our current approach to energy efficiency, with its blanket energy code exemption, treats historic buildings as a uniform segment of the building stock. In truth, energy performance is highly variable, even within the same building type (for example, source EUI for the 95th percentile of office-type buildings in New York City is seven times higher than for the 5th percentile).[24] Similarly, some older and historic buildings perform well and others perform poorly. Instead of looking at trends, looking at variability in the performance of older and historic buildings could allow us to target the worst performers for retrofits and tout the best performers as exemplars. This would represent an important shift away from making retrofit decisions based on age or listing status and toward data-driven decision-making.

- *Outcome-based code support:* In recent years, outcome-based energy codes have been explored by the preservation community as a solution to the shortcomings of prescriptive requirements and performance modeling methods in current energy codes and as an alternative to blanket exemptions for historic buildings.[25] However, several challenges have been identified, including setting credible targets and finding consistent reporting mechanisms. Municipal benchmarking data has the potential to address these challenges and support the implementation of outcome-based codes.

- *Policy evaluation:* Energy data could be used to evaluate the effectiveness of sustainable development policy in historic districts. As one example, the City of Cincinnati currently provides a property tax abatement for buildings with LEED certification. Local developers are coupling this with historic tax credits to finance large-scale rehabilitation projects in some of Cincinnati's historic districts. Since LEED certification is typically based on modeled rather than measured energy performance, energy data could be used to examine how well these retrofits actually perform.

- *Urban-scale energy modeling:* There has been a recent shift from modeling individual buildings to modeling at the district scale. Municipal benchmarking data may have some potential to help build and calibrate those models. This possibility is particularly interesting in the context of historic buildings and districts, as it enables better energy planning at the neighborhood scale. Boundaries for net-zero energy could be drawn around neighborhoods, rather than buildings—for example, historic buildings that restrict the installation of on-site renewables because of visual impact could become net-zero energy by locating renewable energy elsewhere within the expanded boundary.[26]

25 Liz Dunn, Sean Denniston, Jayson Antonoff, and Ralph DiNola, "Toward a Future Model Energy Code for Existing and Historic Buildings," in *Proceedings from the 2010 ACEEE Summer Study on Energy Efficiency in Buildings,* vol. 8 (American Council for an Energy-Efficient Economy, 2010): 88–99.

26 Ben Polly et al., "From Zero Energy Buildings to Zero Energy Districts," in *Proceedings from the 2016 ACEEE Summer Study on Energy Efficiency in Buildings,* vol. 10 (American Council for an Energy-Efficient Economy, 2016): 1–16.

● THE FUTURE OF PRESERVATION AND ENERGY DATA

As newly constructed buildings are increasingly able to achieve net-zero energy consumption and deep energy retrofits of existing buildings result in substantial energy savings, the historic building stock will fall behind in terms of energy performance. Recognizing this, several projects based in the European Union—for example, 3ENCULT, RIBuild, and IEA Task 59—have been dedicated to developing retrofit options compatible with preservation, but a similarly aggressive approach has yet to gain widespread traction in the United States.

The future is data-driven. This is true for energy efficiency as much as it is for any other industry, and the preservation community would do well to follow along. Adopting a more aggressive approach to energy efficiency in historic buildings here in the United States requires that preservationists become active stakeholders, helping to shape the policies and processes by which we collect energy data, and using the data in transparent ways to inform (not simply reinforce) preservation policy and practice.

27
David Hsu, "How
Much Information
Disclosure of Building
Energy Performance
Is Necessary?," *Energy
Policy* 64 (January
2014): 263–272.

Municipal benchmarking ordinances, in particular, present a ripe context for preservationists to engage as active stakeholders with energy data. This is due partly to the relative newness of these ordinances, and partly because their urban scale and local jurisdiction matches well with the goals of municipal preservation agencies and grassroots urban preservation advocacy groups. Engaging with energy data at this scale raises several considerations for the preservation community writ large.

First, how can we look beyond EUI to total kBtu or total carbon emissions? Benchmarking policies are typically designed to measure and track a large proportion of a city's energy consumption using a small number of buildings. Because bigger buildings use more energy, benchmarking policies focus on the largest buildings. Preservationists could similarly look away from intensity measures like EUI and toward measures of magnitude like total kBtu to develop an approach to energy efficiency that has the greatest impact while retrofitting the fewest buildings. Only a subset of older and historic buildings—those over 50,000 square feet—fall under the scope of typical benchmarking ordinances, and it is these that warrant the most immediate consideration.

Second, we must also ask what data it is important to collect. Some cities, such as New York and Austin, require periodic energy audits in addition to benchmarking and disclosure of utility data. The audit collects information far more detailed than utility bills, including building characteristics such as HVAC system type and occupancy. While recent research suggests that audit data may not provide additional information for predicting building energy performance, it may be useful from the standpoint of preservation. 27 Given that year of construction is a problematic variable, there may be other variables that could easily be collected that could help improve approaches to energy efficiency in older and historic buildings.

Finally, how might strategies for preservationists' use of and advocacy for energy data differ from city to city? Some cities, such as New York, represent mature energy data markets. New York was among the early adopters of benchmarking ordinances and has comparatively robust and transparent data publicly available about both its historic and nonhistoric building stock, through efforts like the NYC Planning Labs and Discover NYC Landmarks. Other cities, such as Cincinnati, could be considered a less mature but developing energy data market. Cincinnati has recommended a benchmarking ordinance as part of its latest Green Cincinnati Plan but has not yet adopted one. While it has made some municipal data easily available through its CincyInsights portal, little of this data is about the building stock. These two types of markets may benefit from different engagement strategies and expectations.

Developments in the collection and use of energy performance data have opened up a new set of possibilities for historic preservation and energy efficiency. We have the opportunity to take a more expansive position toward energy data than the one we have held for the past forty years and to reflect on what we might be able to gain from this new era of data. Just as energy efficiency can be seen as a tool to protect historic buildings and keep them in use, energy data can similarly be seen as a guide toward better, more well-informed stewardship of the historic built environment.

Using New Data to Demonstrate
Why Old Buildings Matter

Michael Powe

Building Evidence-Based Narratives

The National Trust for Historic Preservation's Research & Policy Lab was developed to serve as a national resource for data and analysis about older and historic buildings. The field of historic preservation has long sought to demonstrate how old buildings contribute to quality of life in cities (beyond their aesthetic and historic value), and the availability of new forms of data presents an increasing number of possibilities for doing so. The lab now establishes and shares baseline information about the existing built fabric of cities in order to demonstrate how older buildings play a unique, underappreciated role in supporting equitable, healthy, and resilient cities. Founded in Seattle in 2009 and now with staff across the country, the Research & Policy Lab advocates for reuse and preservation as tools for building better cities and explores opportunities to support the reuse of all existing buildings, not simply those with clear historical or architectural significance. 1 Even further, it has also worked to estimate the reuse and infill development potential in areas with underutilized buildings and land.

1
The Research & Policy Lab operated as the Preservation Green Lab until it was renamed in June 2018. The new moniker better describes the lab's work, which now includes research on issues outside of environmental sustainability as well as a stronger focus on policy innovation in cities.

● ESTABLISHING BASELINE INFORMATION ABOUT
THE BUILT ENVIRONMENT OF US CITIES

In 2016 a colleague and I presented some city-specific research findings to a room full of planners and elected officials. As we shared basic information about the number of buildings in this particular city, the percentage of those buildings built before 1945, and the proportion listed on the local and national historic registers, I noted curious faces and many audience members hurriedly scratching down the numbers on the screen. It seemed that this information was new, even to an expert audience.

Management of the built environment is the focus of cities' planning and preservation departments. It makes sense, then, that planners, preservationists, and policy makers should have a good general grasp of the characteristics of their city's buildings. Shouldn't the number and the relative age and size of a city's buildings be readily available? Shouldn't

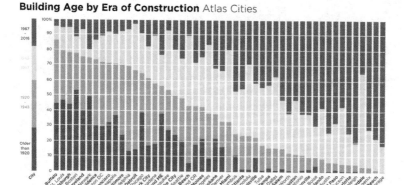

Building Age by Era of Construction Atlas Cities

FIG. 1: *Chart of building age by era of construction, from* The Atlas of ReUrbanism. *Image courtesy of Research & Policy Lab.*

2
Preservation Green
Lab, *The Atlas of
ReUrbanism: Summary
Report*, National
Trust for Historic
Preservation, 2016,
http://forum.saving
places.org/view
document/report-
atlas-of-reurbanism-
buildi.

3
Preservation
Green Lab, *Atlas of
ReUrbanism*, 6.

4
Note that we count all
parcels or buildings
that fall within historic
districts and not simply
those that are listed as
"contributing" to the
district's character,
so our analysis likely
represents an overes-
timate of the structures
that are actually desig-
nated or protected.

5
Preservation
Green Lab, *Atlas of
ReUrbanism*, 5.

that information inform decisions about how our cities develop and manage change? As it turns out, blame for ignorance shouldn't fall on the shoulders of city officials alone. Data about the built environment is often siloed in different parts of city and county governments. County assessor offices, not city staff, often own and manage property information. Furthermore, while the data may be accessible upon the request of city staff, it isn't frequently referenced, let alone visualized in a digestible way.

Gathering, processing, and visualizing this information is now a core component of the Research & Policy Lab's work. Our 2016 *Atlas of ReUrbanism* report—named for the National Trust's organization-wide focus on reinforcing the highly functional older buildings, blocks, and neighborhoods of cities—serves as a compendium of this basic information on building characteristics of fifty US cities, from Portland, Maine, to Portland, Oregon. 2

By capturing building characteristics from county assessor data, we can compare the relative age of cities' buildings. *FIG. 1* Though the accuracy of this data may vary from city to city, the broad patterns likely hold up. Cities with industrial legacies like Buffalo, St. Louis, Pittsburgh, Cleveland, Newark, and Providence have among the highest percentages of prewar buildings, while Boston stands above the rest in its fabric of buildings built before 1920. In Houston, Phoenix, and other cities that experienced considerable population growth in the second half of the twentieth century, most buildings were built after 1967. 3

Furthermore, combining building and parcel data with historic preservation data allows us to begin to understand the reach of one of preservation's core tools: historic designation. By using GIS shapefiles for historic districts and landmarks, and by counting all parcels that either fall within the bounds of a historic district or have landmark status or individual listing, we can estimate the total percentage of a city's build-ings that are designated or protected. 4 In nearly 40 percent of the cities for which we have data, fewer than 2 percent of the city's structures are locally designated. St. Louis, Pasadena, and Washington, DC have the highest local designation rates among our sample set of cities. Across the thirty-six cities for which we have local designation data, we find an average local designation rate of 4.2 percent. 5

Proportions of buildings listed on the National Register of Historic Places tend to be somewhat higher in these cities. We find an average of 6.6 percent of properties listed on the National Register, though a few outlier cities raise the average. For instance, in Baltimore, nearly 35 per-cent of properties are either individually listed or fall within National Register districts. In Salt Lake City, Atlanta, and St. Louis, between 15 and 30 percent of buildings are either individually listed or in National Register districts.

This sort of information represents more than mere trivia. Our goals with *The Atlas of ReUrbanism* are to inform better conversations about land use policy, preservation practice, and development decisions and, ultimately, to bring about a better future for US cities. As an example, in Seattle, as well as in other cities with strong real estate markets and clear geographical constraints on development, vocal advocates of development argue that historic preservation limits possibilities for much-needed additional housing, driving up housing prices and making the city less affordable and more exclusive.[6] This argument echoes the views of Edward L. Glaeser and others.[7] While *The Atlas of ReUrbanism* does not directly address questions relating to housing supply, demand, and affordability, it does illuminate the fact that local historic designation—perhaps the most powerful preservation tool—actually impacts very few properties.[8] In Seattle fewer than a thousand buildings are locally designated and protected—less than 0.5% of the city's built environment.[9] There are forces that directly limit new development, but historic preservation is not the pervasive barrier it is sometimes portrayed as.

● MERGING DATASETS TO SHOW OUTSIZE PERFORMANCE

Much of our work is focused on leveraging newly assembled data to demonstrate why old buildings matter. At the Research & Policy Lab, we draw inspiration especially from the writings of Jane Jacobs, who suggests that "cities need old buildings so badly it is probably impossible for vigorous streets and districts to grow without them."[10] By bringing together data on the built environment with data on social, economic, and cultural vitality, we're able to show how the characteristics of buildings influence the performance of city blocks and neighborhoods, backing up Jacobs's observational insights from a select few cities with numbers from more than fifty cities throughout the United States.

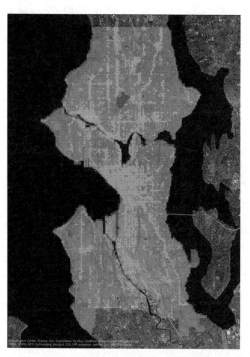

FIG. 2: *A 200-meter-by-200-meter grid lattice over the city of Seattle. Orange squares indicate commercial or mixed-use areas; blue squares represent all other areas. Image courtesy of Research & Policy Lab.*

6
Dan Bertolet, "When Historic Preservation Clashes with Housing Affordability: And What Seattle Can Do to Better Balance the Two and Create More Homes for Everyone," Sightline Institute, December 19, 2017, http://www.sightline.org/2017/12/19/when-historic-preservation-clashes-with-housing-affordability.

7
Edward L. Glaeser, *The Triumph of the City: How Our Greatest Invention Makes Us Richer, Smarter, Greener, Healthier, and Happier* (New York: Penguin, 2011), 148–152.

8
Preservation Green Lab, *Atlas of ReUrbanism*, 5.

9
Preservation Green Lab, *The Atlas of ReUrbanism: Seattle Factsheet*, National Trust for Historic Preservation, 2016, http://forum.savingplaces.org/HigherLogic/System/DownloadDocumentFile.ashx?DocumentFileKey=ae67753a-f52b-034d-13ef-9432b10c94bf&forceDialog=0, 2.

10
Jane Jacobs, *The Death and Life of Great American Cities* (New York: Vintage, 1961), 187.

11
Preservation Green Lab, *Older, Smaller, Better: Measuring How the Character of Buildings and Blocks Influences Urban Vitality*, National Trust for Historic Preservation, 2014, http://forum.saving places.org/connect/ community-home/ librarydocuments/ viewdocument? DocumentKey=83 ebde9b-8a23-458c-a70f-c66b46b6f714.

12
Jacobs, *Death and Life of Great American Cities*, 187–199.

13
Preservation Green Lab, *Older, Smaller, Better.*

14
Z transformation involves adjusting individual values in relation to the overall distribution of data. In our use, we subtract the average citywide value from the individual grid square's value and divide by the standard deviation. So, for instance, if a particular grid square has a median building age of 100 years, the citywide average median building age is 40 years, and the standard deviation of median building age is 30, that grid square would have a *z* value of 2 for median building age, indicating that its value is two standard deviations greater than the citywide average. Computing and combining *z* values for median building age, diversity of building age, and granularity thus gives us a clear, simple metric for representing the character of a grid square relative to the rest of the city.

Our approach to merging different datasets to relate building characteristics to performance was first established in the Research & Policy Lab's 2014 study, *Older, Smaller, Better*. 11 Seeking to statistically test Jacobs's seminal hypothesis that a diverse mix of old and new buildings supports various forms of urban vitality, we used GIS to overlay a 200-meter-by-200-meter lattice grid over the geographies of Seattle, San Francisco, and Washington, DC. 12 *FIG. 2* In these cities, each square on the grid captures approximately one and a half square city blocks. We then apportioned data from parcels, building permits, census blocks and tracts, and other sources so that each square represented only the data that was geographically coincident, regardless of its original form and format. These sources ranged from decennial census data and county assessor parcel data to data from web services like Flickr, Walk Score, Craigslist, and Yelp. We were even able to utilize data on the intensity of cell phone activity.

We also developed a new composite metric for representing the aggregation of multiple aspects of the built environment in a single data point: the Character Score. 13 Using parcel data, we computed the median building age, the diversity of building age, and the density of buildings or parcels within each grid square. We then adjusted this data using a z transformation so that all values were placed in relation to the city's total building stock and summed the z-transformed data points for these three composite metrics. 14 The results show that areas with older, smaller, mixed-age buildings have relatively high Character Scores and areas with mostly large, new buildings have relatively low scores.

FIG. 3: *Infographic depicting the link between Character Score and women- and minority-owned businesses in Seattle. Image courtesy of Research & Policy Lab; original photography (edited) by Caffe Vita, Flickr/Creative Commons 2.0 license (https://creativecommons.org/licenses/by/2.0).*

New York, NY
301.5 mi² | Pop: 8,550,405 | Most Populous U.S. City | Est. 1624

Blocks of older, smaller, mixed-age buildings play a critical role in fostering robust local economies, inclusive neighborhoods, and sustainable cities. The Preservation Green Lab report, *Older, Smaller, Better*, leveraged the ideas of **Jane Jacobs** to show why preservation and building reuse matter for successful communities. The *Atlas of ReUrbanism* expands this research to 50 U.S. cities, demonstrating that **Character Counts.**

In **New York**, compared to areas with large, new structures, character-rich **blocks of older, smaller, mixed-age buildings** contain...

Nearly twice as many women and minority-owned businesses

Twice the number of jobs in small and new business

More diverse residents in terms of race, country of origin, and sexual orientation

The building blocks for an inclusive, diverse, economically vibrant city, New York's older, smaller buildings are irreplaceable assets. For more information about New York's high-character areas, **please see reverse.**

■ **The Atlas of ReUrbanism** | *A Tool for Discovery*
Developed by the Preservation Green Lab, the Atlas of ReUrbanism is part of the National Trust for Preservation's ReUrbanism initiative. Explore the buildings and blocks of New York and other American cities further by visiting:
www.atlasofreurbanism.com

Preservation Green Lab

FIG. 4: *Front of New York factsheet from* The Atlas of ReUrbanism. *Image courtesy of Research & Policy Lab.*

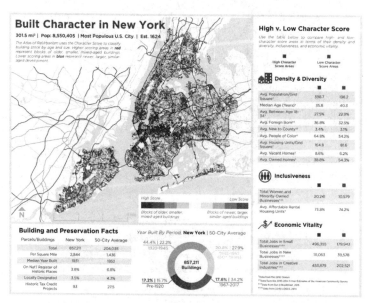

FIG. 5: *Back of New York factsheet from* The Atlas of ReUrbanism. *Image courtesy of Research & Policy Lab.*

15
Preservation Green Lab, *Older, Smaller, Better*, 28–36.

16
Preservation Green Lab, *Older, Smaller, Better*, 32–33.

17
Preservation Green Lab, *Older, Smaller, Better*, 28–36.

18
Jacobs, *Death and Life of Great American Cities*, 187–199.

19
Preservation Green Lab, *Older, Smaller, Better in Tucson: Measuring How the Character of Buildings and Blocks Influences Urban Vitality in a Southwestern City*, National Trust for Historic Preservation, 2016, http://forum. savingplaces.org/view-document/older-small-er-better-in-tucson; Preservation Green Lab, *Reuse and Revitalization in Jacksonville: Discovering the Value of Older Buildings and Blocks*, National Trust for Historic Preservation, 2017, http://forum.saving places.org/view document/reuse-and-revitalization-in-jackson. We also published a peer-reviewed study that expanded upon our analysis of San Francisco, Seattle, Tucson, and Washington, DC: Michael Powe, Jonathan Mabry, Emily Talen, and Dillon Mahmoudi, "Jane Jacobs and the Value of Older, Smaller Buildings," *Journal of the American Planning Association* 82, no. 2 (Spring 2016): 167–180.

20
Preservation Green
Lab, *Older, Smaller,
Better in Tucson*, 13–30.

21
Michael Peel,
"Transform Tucson's
Vintage Buildings
to Create Greater
Economic Impact,"
*Inside Tucson
Business*, August 18,
2017, https://www.
insidetucson
business.com/news/
transform-tucson-s-
vintage-buildings-to-
create-greater-
economic-impact/
article_01422128-
837a-11e7-98ef-
6bad45ee8bf8.html.

22
Preservation Green
Lab, *Reuse and
Revitalization in
Jacksonville*, 23–24.

23
Preservation
Green Lab, *Atlas of
ReUrbanism*, 8–14.

24
Preservation
Green Lab, *Atlas of
ReUrbanism*, 15–18.

25
Preservation
Green Lab, *Atlas
of ReUrbanism:
Factsheets*, National
Trust for Historic
Preservation, 2016,
http://forum.saving
places.org/act/pgl/
atlas/atlas-factsheet.

26
Preservation
Green Lab, *Atlas
of ReUrbanism:
Factsheets*.

27
Preservation
Green Lab, *Atlas of
ReUrbanism*, 8–14.

Leveraging spatial regression analysis, *Older, Smaller, Better* showed that high–Character Score areas significantly outperform areas with mostly large, new buildings in terms of walkability, economic vitality, residential density, and cultural activity, even when differences in recent development, income, and transit accessibility are taken into account. [15] We found significant, positive links between the Character Score and jobs in small businesses, jobs in new businesses, proportion of women- and minority-owned businesses and nonchain businesses, and density of jobs and businesses per commercial square foot. [16] *FIG. 3* True to Jacobs's observations, we found that older, smaller buildings punch above their weight class in supporting neighborhood vitality. [17] Jacobs may have known that places with a mix of old and new buildings would attract more bustling human activity, but she could not have foreseen that data from cell phone activity would be used to demonstrate the veracity of her ideas. [18]

Since the publication of *Older, Smaller, Better*, we have used the grid overlay and Character Score metric in a variety of studies. We leveraged new sources of data to illuminate the value of older, smaller buildings in relation to local concerns in Tucson and Jacksonville. [19] Our 2016 *Older, Smaller, Better* in Tucson study revealed a significant link between high Character Score areas and greater tree canopy and cooler surface temperatures, in addition to many of the same findings related to economic, social, and cultural vitality found in the original *Older, Smaller, Better* study. [20] The publication of the Tucson study was instrumental in the creation of a pilot Adaptive Reuse Program in late 2016. [21] We also leveraged spatial regression analysis to explore statistical links between built character and the presence of civic commons spaces—churches, nonprofit organizations, libraries, and the like—in Jacksonville, as reported in our *Reuse and Revitalization in Jacksonville* report, published in 2017. [22]

As previously mentioned, the Research & Policy Lab leveraged the grid overlay and Character Score metric to demonstrate findings in *The Atlas of ReUrbanism*. [23] Though the research is focused on simple correlations between Character Score and various neighborhood performance metrics, that information can be incredibly useful for policy makers and urban advocates. [24] To make this information more accessible, we developed a dashboard of the resultant information for each of the fifty cities in the atlas. [25] *FIG. 4, 5* Each city-specific dashboard is captured in a factsheet that includes an array of statistics that relate character and performance. In keeping with our goal to make for a better conversation about cities' futures, we include the same metrics for each city—we do not cherry-pick this data to drive a particular argument. [26]

By bringing together property characteristics with data on residents, jobs, and businesses, the Research & Policy Lab has been able to demonstrate strong links between older buildings and positive urban planning and policy outcomes. [27] We've also recently explored places where the performance of older buildings is more muted, and we highlight areas of cities that could benefit from infill development or targeted attention and investment in older buildings.

28
Preservation Green Lab,
*Partnership for Building
Reuse*, National Trust for
Historic Preservation,
2017, http://forum.
savingplaces.org/act/
pgl/pbr.

Old buildings do not always provide benefits that are immediately clear. In many older neighborhoods, decades of disinvestment, inattention from city officials, and racial bias have led to high levels of vacancy, poverty, and poor service provision. In areas that have middling levels of performance, strategic investment could tip neighborhoods and commercial corridors toward healthier outcomes. And in areas with promising levels of vitality as well as a wealth of vacant lots, smart infill development should be part of a revitalization strategy.

Between 2012 and 2016, we partnered with local Urban Land Institute District Councils to produce reports focused on improving opportunities for building reuse in Baltimore, Chicago, Detroit, Los Angeles, and Philadelphia. 28 As part of this work, we developed a process to expand our grid overlay, Character Score metric, and range of datasets to explore changes over time and identify areas that could benefit from targeted attention and investment. The Reuse Opportunity Model highlighted areas that were near transit stops, good schools, and healthy economic areas

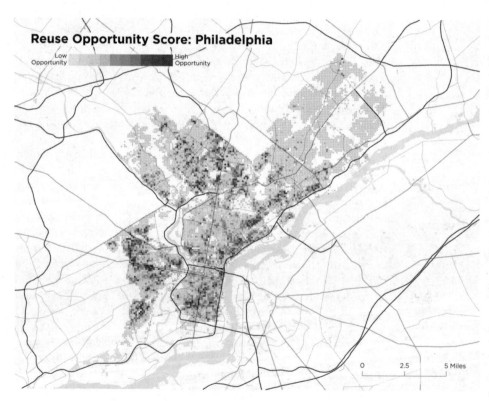

FIG. 6: *Map of reuse opportunity modeling for Philadelphia. Red areas show greatest opportunity for building reuse, as indicated by economic vitality, demographic characteristics, neighborhood amenities, and real estate activity. Reuse opportunity modeling focuses on areas with middling levels of job and population growth, proximity to good schools and transit, and concentrations of older, smaller buildings and mixed-age blocks. Image courtesy of Research & Policy Lab.*

29
Preservation Green
Lab, *Untapped
Potential: Strategies
for Revitalization and
Reuse*, National Trust for
Historic Preservation,
2017, http://forum.
savingplaces.org/
viewdocument/
untapped-potential-
strategies-for.

30
National Trust for
Historic Preservation,
"National Treasures:
Little Havana," 2016,
https://savingplaces.
org/places/little-
havana.

31
Research & Policy
Lab, *From Vacancy to
Vitality: Quantifying
Infill Opportunity in
Little Havana, Miami*,
National Trust for
Historic Preservation,
forthcoming.

32
Research & Policy Lab,
From Vacancy to Vitality.

33
Research & Policy Lab,
From Vacancy to Vitality.

but had vacant buildings and little or no population or job growth. 29 *FIG. 6* We projected that these areas could benefit from a closer look from real estate developers, community development organizations, and city policy makers and planners.

This evolving understanding of how to leverage and combine various datasets to visualize the built environment allowed the Research & Policy Lab to play a role in a larger National Trust effort in Miami's Little Havana neighborhood. 30 Little Havana's low-rise housing and commercial strips are located adjacent to the gleaming condominium and office towers of Miami's downtown and Brickell neighborhoods, and developers are now actively pursuing opportunities to build mid- and high-rise structures within the historic heart of Miami's Cuban American community.

Given this development pressure, we tried to understand what growth potential exists in Little Havana without demolishing existing buildings. Using parcel data, vacant lot and building data, and satellite and Google Street View imagery, we identified a total of 451 vacant lots, 99 lots used exclusively for surface parking, and 28 vacant buildings totaling approximately 4.6 million square feet of idle land. 31 *FIG. 7* Using census data to calculate neighborhood-wide average population, job, and business densities, we estimated that about 10,000 new residents, 2,500 new jobs, and 550 new businesses could be housed in the previously identified vacant areas, even without maximizing allowable building heights as spelled out in the city's zoning code. 32 This represents potential for a 16 percent increase in population, a 32 percent increase in the number of jobs, and a 22 percent increase in the number of businesses in this already bustling neighborhood, all while retaining its current cultural heritage and built character. 33

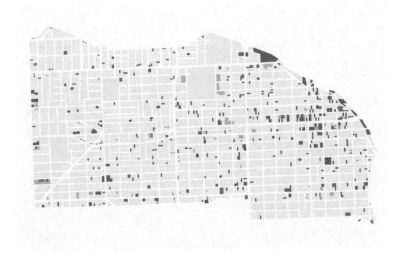

FIG. 7: *Map of vacant space in Little Havana, Miami. Using parcel data from the Florida Department of Revenue, vacant property data from the City of Miami Neighborhood Enhancement Team, and imagery from Google, we identified 451 vacant lots (red), 99 surface parking lots (orange), and 28 vacant buildings (blue), representing a total of about 4.6 million square feet of vacant space in an already bustling neighborhood. Image courtesy of Research & Policy Lab.*

By building upon the strengths of old buildings with targeted rein- 34
Jacobs, *Death and Life of Great American Cities*, 187–199.
vestment and new infill development, cities can accommodate growing
populations gracefully, welcome new industry and enterprise, and pursue
resilient and sustainable futures. Just as Jacobs argues in *The Death and Life of Great American Cities,* new infill construction offers a path to vigorous blocks and neighborhoods when it is paired with conservation and reuse of older, smaller, complementary structures. [34]

● EXPANDING THE USE OF DATA

As the research and policy development arm of the nation's leading historic preservation advocacy organization, the Research & Policy Lab has aimed to equip preservationists with data, analysis, and research that demonstrate why old buildings matter. We also aspire to move preservation and reuse into the broader conversation among urbanists, real estate developers, community development professionals, policy makers, and planners. As our research has shown, old buildings undergird the efforts of economic development officials, developers of affordable housing, and public health professionals. Our data can illuminate the path to new partnerships and better outcomes for the public at large.

And the number of ways that we can leverage data and analysis to meet these goals is constantly increasing. We plan to explore mapping sea-level rise and chronic inundation against data on older and historic structures. We will work toward developing dashboards and scenario planning tools for city officials to understand how decisions related to land use policy and real estate development influence cities' carbon impacts, jobs in small businesses, residential and commercial affordability, and risk of displacement. We will also work to translate our data and research into policy, in collaboration with local partners in communities across the country. Finally, we hope to refine our abilities in visualizing baseline data, to provide more data for download and exploration, and to offer training for preservationists, urbanists, and other individuals interested in using data to support work in their own communities.

Historic Buildings, Chain Stores, and Mom-and-Pop Retail

Emily Talen

Building Evidence-Based Narratives

Retail in the United States has been going through profound change in recent decades. This is especially true of small-scale retail along urban main streets, where changes are unfolding in a sector long thought of as a major contributor to quality urbanism.[1] Along the traditional main street composed of mom-and-pop stores, shopping was always equated with daily life and a neighborhood-based community. But retail in the age of chain stores and e-commerce challenges those foundations. How changes in the retail sector impact urban neighborhoods is a special concern. The classic urban main street—composed of these mom-and-pop stores, pedestrian oriented, mixed in use, and serviceable to the surrounding neighborhood—has been in decline for decades. There seems to be a wide distance between the main street ideal and urban commercial corridors composed of chain stores and strip malls or boutiques and restaurants.

Historic buildings have played a central role in these retail changes—a connection famously laid out by Jane Jacobs, who argued that healthy neighborhoods require a mix of old and new buildings.[2] This is because old buildings and new buildings require differing levels of economic yield, and new businesses often emerge naturally in buildings with low economic overhead. But there has been limited empirical testing of this hypothesis, and criticism by Edward Glaeser and others has discounted the value of older buildings in keeping space affordable.[3]

As a first step in understanding these linkages, some basic correlations must be quantified between historic buildings, chain stores, and mom-and-pop retail. Mom-and-pop retail—termed "main street retail"—is important, and we can see that by better understanding the connection between main street retail and historic buildings in Chicago. To what degree is main street retail connected to historic buildings? Are small-scale retailers more likely to be located in areas with newer buildings or older buildings? How are these locations different from chain stores?

● FRAMING THE ARGUMENTS

Main street decline is tied to the broad urban transformation that, by the early twentieth century, had weakened localized economic interdependence and diminished the need for neighborhood-based servicing.[4] Technological innovations decreased the importance of a local urban existence, such that in many places daily life was no longer tied to walking and the corner store was no longer the place where local identity and social contact flourished.[5] Companies that started small and reached behemoth size were implicated in the process of "creative destruction," in which the growth of one retailer translated to the death of smaller mom-and-pop stores.[6] Large corporate chain stores took their toll: one study found that Walmart accounted for half of small retail closures;[7] another estimated that within five years of a Walmart's opening, four smaller competitors, on average, will close.[8]

Against this backdrop of long-term structural transformation, sustaining independent retail along an urban main street has been a constant struggle. Small-scale, independently owned retail on urban main streets is increasingly threatened by online shopping, commercial

1
Emily Talen and Hyesun Jeong, "Does the Classic American Main Street Still Exist? An Exploratory Look," Journal of Urban Design (2018): 1–21, https://doi.org/10.1080/1357 4809.2018.1436962.

2
Jane Jacobs, The Death and Life of Great American Cities (New York: Random House, 1961).

3
Edward Glaeser, The Triumph of the City: How Our Greatest Invention Makes Us Richer, Smarter, Greener, Healthier, and Happier (New York: Penguin Books, 2011).

4
James Howard Kunstler, The Geography of Nowhere: The Rise and Decline of America's Man-Made Landscape (New York: Free Press, 1994); Robert M. Fogelson, Downtown: Its Rise and Fall, 1880–1950 (New Haven: Yale University Press, 2003); Douglas W. Rae, City: Urbanism and Its End (New Haven: Yale University Press, 2005).

5
Sam Griffiths et al., "The Sustainable Suburban High Street: A Review of Themes and Approaches," Geography Compass 2, no. 4 (July 2008): 1155–1188; John Dawson, "Futures for the High Street," Geographical Journal 154, no. 1 (March 1998): 1–22.

6
Marc Levinson, The Great A&P and the Struggle for Small Business in America (New York: Hill and Wang, 2012).

7
Panle Jia, "What Happens When Walmart Comes to Town: An Empirical Analysis of the Discount Retailing Industry," Econometrica 76, no. 6 (November 2008): 1263–1316.

8
Emek Basker, "Job Creation or Destruction? Labor Market Effects of Wal-Mart Expansion," Review of Economics and Statistics 87, no. 1 (February 2005): 174–183.

9
Michael Corkery, "Is American Retail at a Historic Tipping Point?," *New York Times*, April 15, 2017; Hayley Peterson, "The Retail Apocalypse Has Officially Descended on America," *Business Insider*, March 21, 2017.

10
Greg Hinz, "Why Are So Many Stores Closing in Chicago?," *Crain's Chicago Business*, August 12, 2017, http://www.chicagobusiness.com/article/20170812/ISSUE05/170819949/chicago-is-losing-neighborhood-retailers.

11
Manhattan Borough President's Office, *Small Business Big Impact: Expanding Opportunity for Manhattan's Storefronters* (New York, 2015).

12
Dana Berliner, "Land Use Regulation: What's It Worth Anyway?," Policy Debates Forum, Urban Institute, July 19, 2017, https://www.urban.org/debates/land-use-regulation-whats-it-worth-anyway.

13
Sharon Zukin, Philip Kasinitz, and Xiangming Chen, *Global Cities, Local Streets: Everyday Diversity from New York to Shanghai* (London: Taylor & Francis, 2015).

14
Jacobs, *Death and Life of Great American Cities*.

15
William L. Yancey and Eugene P. Ericksen, "The Antecedents of Community: The Economic and Institutional Structure of Urban Neighborhoods," *American Sociological Review* 44, no. 2 (April 1979): 253–262.

16
Rocco Pendola and Sheldon Gen, "Does 'Main Street' Promote Sense of Community? A Comparison of San Francisco Neighborhoods," *Environment and Behavior* 40, no. 4 (July 2008): 545–574.

gentrification, and other forces making its retention more urgent. With one in ten American workers employed in retail, the store and mall closures, bankruptcies, and job losses of the "retail apocalypse" are being compared to the job losses that occurred in manufacturing in the latter half of the twentieth century—hinting at the associated social, political, and economic changes that could come with it. While some economists view this scenario as simply "the way the market is supposed to work," with changes signaling a form of "creative destruction," others lament the loss of job opportunity. [9]

Surveys have documented how many small retailers are burdened with high rents and high taxes, and in some cities, minimum-wage laws, shopping-bag fees, and mandatory paid sick leave add costs that small retailers say they are unable to bear. [10] A survey of New York City's "shopfronters" cited factors affecting businesses like commercial rent, more affluent clientele, burdensome zoning rules that block innovation, commercial spaces that are too large, code inspectors with a "guilty until proven innocent" attitude, and Business Improvement Districts (BIDs) that cater to property owners rather than business owners. [11] The parking that zoning requires adds additional costs, and through the use of variances, well-connected larger businesses manage to escape certain requirements. [12]

Commercial corridors composed of historic buildings may provide the look of traditional retailing without the social and servicing functionality. Such places do not provide for the needs of daily life and instead may harbor what has been called the "ABCs" of gentrification—art galleries, boutiques, and cafes. [13] Such areas have the physical lineage of a traditional main street but are dominated by boutiques and bars that cater to tourists rather than neighborhood residents. As retail shifts and as products and services change—perhaps in a way that is more attractive to a "creative class" clientele—tensions emerge. But against larger structural forces, changes in urban form, and shifting behaviors and preferences, main street as the walkable locale of small, independent retailers should still be valued.

Main street retail is focused on servicing local residents, and these businesses are responsive to local need, supporting Jacobs's argument that a quality main street is activated by exchange and that exchange, in turn, is enabled through the provision of services that range from daily needs to optional amenities. [14] This fosters economic interdependence, social interaction, and neighborhood stability. [15] For example, a study of San Francisco neighborhoods found that neighborhoods that coalesce around commercial main streets have a "significantly higher sense of community" than those without a main street. [16] Relatedly, research in the Netherlands concluded that the strongest predictors of "community" are the sharing of resources and common activities, which foster mutual interdependence. [17] A study of retail turnover in New York City found that chain stores were more footloose, moving across neighborhoods more frequently than stores that service daily life. [18]

Secondly, there are social and cultural benefits associated with neighborhood-based businesses. Small businesses rooted in a neighborhood are the embodiment of what it means to be "local," with a "geographic immediacy [of] inputs and outputs" defined by business owners who tend to live locally, customers who live within walking distance, and their joint influence on the social, cultural, and economic life of the neighborhood.[19] Retail has been described as playing a major role in the "foundations of the social and economic structure" of cities, where shopping is a cultural experience and retail resiliency a matter of tapping cultural needs.[20]

Social contact is maintained when interaction is routine rather than specialized. This makes main street shopping distinct from e-commerce, which not only is incapable of attending to a local customer base and "personalized shopping experiences" but also fails to provide "surprise encounters."[21] Neighborhood-based retail promotes quotidian social exchange: people coming together to buy or sell, teach or learn, greet or glance.[22] The ability of commercial streets to operate as successful social spaces is a driving force behind their economic value.[23]

Corporate retailing lacks the ability to foster these neighborhood-based social connections. Researchers have argued that personalized customer service—actually knowing the person behind the product or service—is both gratifying and difficult to reproduce.[24] As Stacey Sutton puts it, the problem is that "corporate decision makers respond to national or regional strategy and capricious markets rather than local needs."[25] Large retailers, like Sears and Walmart, are focused on "financial engineering" and hedge fund strategies that appeal to shareholders and private-equity investors. Their concern is not really about the "operations side" and neighborhood servicing.

Thirdly, small retail is "a stepping stone" for other small business owners and entrepreneurs to launch businesses; a certain degree of clustering can "establish the multiplier effects that no one business can achieve on its own."[26] The employment generated by small, independently operated main street businesses is valued because it is neighborhood-based and because it may provide a role for those left out of the "urbanized knowledge economy."[27] At the most fundamental level, small, local, and independent retailing creates jobs.[28] The multiplier effect— including direct, indirect, and induced impacts—is substantially higher compared to corporate-owned chain stores. The calculation of a local economic premium by groups like the American Independent Business Alliance and the firm Civic Economics generates multiple supporting statistics— for example, that $68 out of $100 spent at a local business remains in the community, while just $43 spent at a chain store remains. Retail studies conducted in ten American cities showed that the local economic benefit of independent stores, taken together, was 3.7 times higher than the economic benefit of shopping at chains.[29]

Finally, main street retail as an ideal has what is known as active frontages—frontages that do not have blank walls or fences but instead have verticality, façade articulation, and transparency revealing active uses within. In this sense, they are capable of stimulating social exchange—i.e., daily social encounters that happen in public space, on the sidewalk. Jacobs chronicles these benefits, writing that "sidewalk contacts are the small change from which a city's wealth of public life may grow."[30] Street-based exchange promotes liveliness, sociability, and a sense of safety.[31]

17
Beate Völker, Henk Flap, and Siegwart Lindenberg, "When Are Neighbourhoods Communities? Community in Dutch Neighbourhoods," *European Sociological Review* 23, no. 1 (February 2007): 99–114.

18
Rachel Meltzer and Sean Capperis, "Neighbourhood Differences in Retail Turnover: Evidence from New York City," *Urban Studies* 54, no. 13 (October 2017): 3049.

19
Rachel Meltzer, "Gentrification and Small Business: Threat or Opportunity?," *Cityscape* 18, no. 13 (2016): 59; Derek S. Hyra, *The New Urban Renewal: The Economic Transformation of Harlem and Bronzeville* (Chicago: University of Chicago Press, 2008).

20
Herculano Cachinho, "Consumerscapes and the Resilience Assessment of Urban Retail Systems," *Cities* 36 (February 2014): 131–144.

21
Brenda Parker and Rachel Weber, "Second-Hand Spaces: Restructuring Retail Geographies in an Era of E-Commerce," *Urban Geography* 34, no. 8 (2013): 1096.

22
Mike Greenberg, *The Poetics of Cities: Designing Neighborhoods That Work* (Columbus: Ohio State University Press, 1995).

23
Matthew Carmona, "London's Local High Streets: The Problems, Potential and Complexities of Mixed Street Corridors," *Progress in Planning* 100 (August 2015): 1–84; Colin Jones, Qutaiba Al-Shaheen, and Neil Dunse, "Anatomy of a Successful High Street Shopping Centre," *Journal of Urban Design* 21, no. 4 (2016): 495–511.

24
John Rampton, "6 Benefits for You and Your Community from Supporting Local Entrepreneurs," Entrepreneur, April 17, 2015.

25
Stacey A. Sutton, "Are BIDs Good for Business? The Impact of BIDs on Neighborhood Retailers in New York City," Journal of Planning Education and Research 34, no. 3 (September 2014): 309–324.

26
Department for Communities and Local Government, Parades of Shops—Towards an Understanding of Performance and Prospects (London, 2015), 7.

27
Richard Florida, The New Urban Crisis: How Our Cities Are Increasing Inequality, Deepening Segregation, and Failing the Middle Class—and What We Can Do About It (New York: Basic Books, 2017).

28
Elizabeth A. Mack, review of Small Business and the City: The Transformative Potential of Small Scale Entrepreneurship by Rafael Gomez, Andre Isakov, and Matt Semanskey in Journal of Regional Science 55, no. 5 (November 2015): 874; Rafael Gomez et al., Small Business and the City: The Transformative Potential of Small Scale Entrepreneurship (Toronto: University of Toronto Press, 2015).

29
American Independent Business Alliance, "Ten New Studies of the 'Local Economic Premium,'" October 2012, https://www.amiba.net/resources/studies-recommended-reading/local-premium.

30
Jacobs, Death and Life of Great American Cities, 72.

Researchers argue that these social experiences cannot be replicated in other retailing contexts, such as shopping malls.[32] Even where positioned along a street, corporate retailing undermines the principles of active frontage because of their formulaic retailing requirements. For example, corporate retailers often insist on main entrances being on the parking lot at the rear of a commercial building and on not allowing a second entrance on the street side ("because format retailers don't want to deal with that"). Corporate retailers also miss the way window transparency is a way to show life inside, obscuring their windows with advertisements.[33]

● CONNECTING MAIN STREET RETAIL AND HISTORIC BUILDINGS

How should the link between historic buildings and main street retail be conceptualized? One framework to start with is the one posed by Jacobs, who argues that healthy neighborhoods require old buildings interspersed with new ones. While Edward Glaeser has argued otherwise,[34] the Preservation Green Lab at the National Trust for Historic Preservation has produced empirical evidence of the value of older buildings in sustaining economic diversity.[35] Nevertheless, the lab's work distinguishes preserved historic districts from Jacobs's focus on "plain, ordinary, low-value old buildings."[36] Others have pointed out that older buildings are more adaptable to multiple uses and more capable of responding to business expansion and contraction.[37] Ewing and Clemente found that older buildings are statistically related to greater pedestrian activity and provide an essential aspect of place design.[38] Researchers have also connected older buildings with the arts and the creative economy.[39]

Quantifying Mom-and-Pop and Main Street Retail

To differentiate between independent and chain stores, my primary data sources are geocoded business license data from Chicago's Department of Business Affairs and Consumer Protection, parcel data from the county assessor, and GIS data identifying street environment characteristics. To differentiate main street versus chain store blocks, I measure the kind and mix of uses the block provides, the degree to which independently operated businesses are present, and the ability of the street to satisfy a minimum threshold of pedestrian quality.

Only those blocks that had services (including public services like schools, community centers, and public facilities) are scored. This constitutes about 15 percent of Chicago's blocks (7,005 out of 46,311 blocks). I exclude blocks that are residential only or do not include services (such as blocks with only manufacturing). Main street and chain store blocks are differentiated by use and ownership rather than by pedestrian quality. Both sets of blocks meet a minimum threshold of pedestrian quality if they are free of certain degrading factors: automotive uses (gas stations, convenience stores attached to gas stations, automobile repair shops, car washes, and car dealers), parking facilities (surface parking lots and parking garages), city-owned vacant lots, and abandoned buildings as reported in 311 service requests. With rare exceptions, all blocks have sidewalks.

Block defined as	Criteria
Main street block	1. At least one basic service: grocery store, day care center, library, school, senior center, community center, or neighborhood health clinic
	2. At least one optional amenity: restaurant, café, coffee shop, bookstore, bar, fitness and health use, clothing or other shop, arts and entertainment
	3. Residential use (1 or more units)
	4. Less than 50% of services are chain stores
	5. No parking facilities, vacant lots, abandoned buildings, or automotive uses
Chain store block	1. No basic services (as defined above)
	2. At least one optional amenity: restaurant, café, coffee shop, bookstore, bar, fitness and health use, clothing or other shop, arts and entertainment
	3. No Residential use
	4. 90% or more of services are chain stores
	5. No parking facilities, vacant lots, abandoned buildings, or automotive uses

FIG. 1: Characteristics of main street and chain store blocks. Chain stores were identified using the following sources: Technomic's "Top 250 Chain Restaurant Report" (2016), Balance's report "Top 100 Largest U.S. Based Retail Companies" (2016), and Wikipedia's list of chains (https://en.wikipedia.org/wiki/List_of_restaurant_chains_in_ the_United_States). For Chicago blocks, more than a half of the chain stores are bars and restaurant (57%), followed by convenience stores (31%). Data sources: City of Chicago Business License data; City of Chicago parcel data (2016/2017); Cook County Illinois parcel data(2016/2017); City-Owned Land Inventory; 311 Service Requests (vacant and abandoned buildings); and Overpass Turbo, a web based data mining tool from Open Street Map.

The ideal main street block has services that relate to daily needs, such as grocery stores, libraries, and community centers; these uses are supplemented with amenities such as bars and restaurants, cafés and coffee shops, fitness centers, and entertainment venues. In addition, an ideal main street has residential uses, so that the street is mixed in use—perhaps with residences above stores—rather than exclusively commercial. Finally, main street blocks have a significant level of local ownership: less than 50 percent of their businesses are owned by chain stores. Chain store blocks, in contrast, consist only of optional amenities, lack residential use, and have more than 90 percent chain stores. In other words, they are main street blocks in appearance only: they are dominated by corporate retail, lack housing, and lack services geared to daily life. Thus, of the 7,005 scored blocks, I classified about 241 blocks, or 3.4 percent, as "main street" blocks. In addition, 70 blocks, or 1 percent of the scored blocks, are identified as chain store blocks.

Quantifying Historic Buildings

For building age, I used data provided by the National Trust for Historic Preservation's Preservation Green Lab (now called the Research & Policy Lab). [40] Using data from the Cook County assessor's office (Cook County is where the city of Chicago is located), the Preservation Green Lab estimates the number of buildings built prior to 1945 within each 1/8-mile (or 200-by-200-meter) square of the city. FIG. 2 The statistical results show how historic building age is correlated with small businesses in

31
Emma Heffernan, Troy Heffernan, and Wei Pan, "The Relationship between the Quality of Active Frontages and Public Perceptions of Public Spaces," Urban Design International 19, no.1 (Spring 2014): 92–102.

32
Eric Muhlebach and Richard Muhlebach, "The 'Malling' of American Retail and How to Re-Discover Street Retailing," Journal of Property Management 78, no. 3 (May 2013): 22–25.

33
Scott Doyon, "The Sidewalk to Hell Is Paved with Good Intentions," Placemakers blog, December 13, 2017, http://www.placemakers.com/2017/12/13/the-sidewalk-to-hell-is-paved-with-good-intentions.

34
Glaeser, Triumph of the City.

35
Michael Powe, Jonathan Mabry, Emily Talen, and Dillon Mahmoudi, "Jane Jacobs and the Value of Older, Smaller Buildings," Journal of the American Planning Association 82, no. 2 (Spring 2016): 167–180.

36
Jacobs, Death and Life of Great American Cities, 187.

37
Stewart Brand, How Buildings Learn: What Happens After They're Built (New York: Penguin Books, 1995).

38
Reid Ewing and Otto Clemente, Measuring Urban Design: Metrics for Livable Places (Washington, DC: Island Press, 2013).

39
Carl Grodach et al., "The Location Patterns of Artistic Clusters: A Metro- and Neighborhood-Level Analysis," Urban Studies 51, no. 13 (October 2014): 2822–2843.

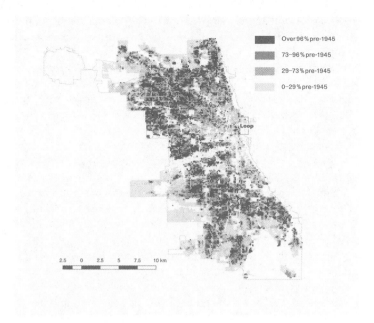

Fig. 2: *Quartiles of building age in Chicago . Each category has an equal number of cells. Data from Preservation Green Lab.*

two ways—by main street versus chain store block, and by chain store versus small business as point locations.

Main street blocks overlap the most with grid cells that have 73 to 96 percent historic buildings. *FIG. 3* They overlap the least with the newest building stock (i.e., grid cells with only 0 to 29 percent historic buildings). Chain store blocks have a somewhat reversed association—that is, chain store blocks overlap the most with the newest grid cells.

These associations vary by type of business. *FIG. 4, 5* The trends are fairly consistent across all small business types: businesses are more likely to be located in areas in the midrange of building age distribution than in areas with predominantly new or all old building stock. The distribution of chain stores indicates that, compared to small businesses that are not chains, these stores are more distributed in the newer grid cells than in the midrange. Also, there is more variation with chain stores than with small businesses: fitness and health-related businesses, and to some degree general merchandise businesses, are located in grid cells with more new buildings. *FIG. 6*

● PRESERVATION AND MAIN STREET

As a general trend, there is empirical support for the notion that mom-and-pop retailers are more likely to be located in older building fabric—measured both by their location within "main street" blocks and by their point locations. Overall, when compared to chain stores, small businesses are associated with areas with older buildings. But there is

141

also a significant amount of variation within these categories: there are still chain stores in historic buildings and mom-and-pop stores in new buildings. *FIG. 7*

What are the implications of this kind of analysis? Preservationists should develop a clear, empirical understanding of how their goals intersect with support for small, independent retailing, especially in quantifying the link between these two goals: preservation of main street fabric and the continued health of small, independent retailing. This is only one approach to looking at the connection; more investigations are needed. This kind of quantified analysis is now possible thanks to the expansion of public access to geospatial data at the city level. Preservationists can use this data to assess the connections between preservation goals and other goals, changing thresholds in ways that make sense for alternative understandings of what a quality main street might mean and which preservation goals are realistic.

Ultimately, understanding the connection between alternative (but not incompatible) goals could help clarify not only what main streets and historic buildings are up against but how their shared values can be leveraged. Perhaps some blocks could be stabilized and maintained because of how they have been able to attain both main street retail and preservation goals. Other areas could be targeted as representative of main street and preservation quality—an essential part of a multistrategy approach to neighborhood revitalization. In other words, blocks that retain preservation and main street qualities despite everything stacked

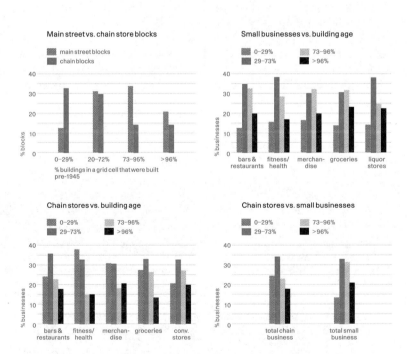

FIG. 3: Comparing pre-1945 buildings in relation to main street and chain store blocks.
FIG. 4: Comparing pre-1945 buildings in relation to small business type.
FIG. 5: Comparing pre-1945 buildings in relation to chain store type.
FIG. 6: Comparing pre-1945 buildings in relation to chain store and small business totals.

against them—car-dependence, formula retail, online shopping—should be paid attention to.

But it is also important that zoning codes be attended to. Once blocks that have both main street and preservation qualities are identified, it is essential to ensure that codes work in a supportive rather than a destructive manner. Do zoning codes reflect the needs of small businesses and historic buildings, rather than solely the needs of developers? Are they supportive of neighborhood-servicing and pedestrian quality, or are there rules (like parking requirements) that impose unnecessary burdens? Relatedly, are there design guidelines supportive of small-scale retail in historic buildings? Are the unique qualities of streets supported such that cultural expressions of identity are enhanced and boilerplate streetscape design is avoided?

Zoning for main street faces the broader problem that small-scale, independently owned retail on a walkable, mixed-use urban street is increasingly threatened by forces outside government control, especially e-commerce. While major shifts in retail and consumer behavior may be both inevitable and immutable, it is difficult to envision a form of urbanism in which localized retailing in walkable, historic neighborhoods is no longer a part of the landscape. Planners, residents, and political leaders need to decide what the response to these changes should be. As long as the concept of walkable, mixed-use main streets is still something to be valued, policy makers need to understand how the tools they impart—from regulation to investment—impact the long-term health and viability of these streets.

FIG. 7: Map showing the varying contexts of small business and building age in Chicago. Numbered areas point to four different combinations of building age and small business frequency.

Big and Deep Heritage Data:
The Social HEritage Machine (SHEM)

Jeremy C. Wells
Vanilson Burégio
Rinaldo Lima

Building Evidence-Based Narratives

A problem long discussed in critical heritage studies, with little resolution or consensus, is the fact that laypeople value and perceive the historic environment in multifarious ways. To be sure, this is a problem grounded in broad, qualitative meanings, so to assume that there is a singular resolution is misguided. But what is broadly acknowledged is that the conservation of built heritage is intractably grounded in expert rule— so, at least from the perspective of conservation/historic preservation practice, there tends to be little interest in resolving this problem. [1] Urban planners, however, still have an interest in understanding the relationship between people and place, as do researchers and practitioners guided by evidence-based design principles. Even as built heritage conservation practice succeeds in preserving (or ossifying) its own methods, others would like to understand the meanings and values of built heritage in the unadulterated, natural language used by most stakeholders—meanings and values that would then complement the language traditionally used by conventional experts. [2]

In the United States, three-quarters of historic preservation practice is driven by regulatory requirements that are intended to sideline the values of most stakeholders. [3] Or, in another sense, rules, laws, and regulations require practitioners to be ignorant of public values in the name of efficiency and avoiding politics. [4] Curiously, most laws and policies around the world that mandate the protection of the historic environment (e.g., historic buildings, structures, places, landscapes) justify such protection as a public good but do not make good on this laudable goal. The United Nations Educational, Scientific, and Cultural Organization (UNESCO) identifies and protects monuments, groups of buildings, and sites for the "benefit of all humanity"; [5] the National Historic Preservation Act of the United States proclaims that "the preservation of... heritage is in the public interest"; [6] and the Brazilian Constitution states that the promotion and protection of all forms of cultural heritage (material and immaterial) is to be conducted "with the cooperation of the community." [7] Yet the ways that heritage laws and policies are implemented and the way that heritage conservation is conducted privilege expert rule and marginalize the values of laypeople by design.

In practice, conventionally trained experts, such as historians, control the meanings associated with the identification and protection of the historic environment; these values are based on "objective" art/historical facts and leave little, if any, room for the more subjective meanings that everyday people have for places that are important to them. Laurajane Smith refers to this disconnect between conventional experts and everyday people as the "Authorized Heritage Discourse," which demands that "the proper care of heritage, and its associated values, lies with the experts, as it is only they who have the abilities, knowledge, and understanding to identify the innate value and knowledge contained at and within historically important sites and places." Smith describes how preservation/ conservation doctrine provides the basis of a "self-referential authority of conservation and management philosophy of practice" used by heritage experts to "sideline" the "values and meanings that are situated outside the dominant [expert-driven] discourse." [8] A significant body of empirical research has confirmed the influence of this "authorized" discourse; it is

1
Lucas Lixinski, "Between Orthodoxy and Heterodoxy: The Troubled Relationships between Heritage Studies and Heritage Law," *International Journal of Heritage Studies* 21, no. 3 (2015): 203–214; John Schofield, ed. *Who Needs Experts? Counter-mapping Cultural Heritage* (Farnham, UK: Ashgate, 2014); Laurajane Smith, *Uses of Heritage* (New York: Routledge, 2006); Frits Pannekoek, "The Rise of the Heritage Priesthood or the Decline of Community Based Heritage," *Historic Preservation Forum* 12, no. 3 (Spring 1998): 4–10; Rich Hutchings and Marina La Salle, "Archaeology As Disaster Capitalism," *International Journal of Historical Archaeology* 19, no. 4 (December 2015): 699–720; and Rodney Harrison, *Heritage: Critical Approaches* (New York: Routledge, 2013).

2
Jeremy C. Wells and Lucas Lixinski, "Heritage Values and Legal Rules: Identification and Treatment of the Historic Environment via an Adaptive Regulatory Framework (part 2)," *Journal of Cultural Heritage Management and Sustainable Development* 7, no. 3 (July 2017): 345–363; Jeremy C. Wells, "In Stakeholders We Trust: Changing the Ontological and Epistemological Orientation of Built Heritage Assessment through Participatory Action Research," in *How to Assess Built Heritage? Assumptions, Methodologies, Examples of Heritage Assessment Systems,* ed. Bogusaw Szmygin (Florence and Lublin: Romualdo Del Bianco Foundation and Lublin University of Technology, 2015).

3
Jeremy C. Wells,
"Challenging the
Assumption of a
Direct Relationship
Between the Fields of
Historic Preservation
and Architecture
in the United
States," *Frontiers of
Architectural Research*
(forthcoming); Smith,
Uses of Heritage.

4
Jeremy C. Wells, "Are
We 'Ensnared in the
System of Heritage'
Because We Do Not
Want to Escape?,"
*Archaeologies:
Journal of the World
Archaeological
Congress* 13, no. 1
(2017): 26–47.

5
UNESCO, *Operational
Guidelines for the
Implementation of
the World Heritage
Convention*, July 2015,
http://whc.unesco.org/
document/137843.

6
US National Historic
Preservation Act,
amended December
16, 2016, https://www.
achp.gov/sites/default/
files/2018-06/nhpa.pdf.

7
Brazilian Constitution of
1988 (Constituição da
República Federativa
do Brasil de 1988),
http://www.planalto.
gov.br/ccivil_03/
Constituicao/
Constituicao.htm.

8
Smith, *Uses of Heritage*,
94, 106.

9
John Schofield,
"Being Autocentric:
Towards Symmetry in
Heritage Management
Practices," in *Valuing
Historic Environments*,
ed. Lisanne Gibson
and John Pendlebury
(Farnham, UK: Ashgate,
2009); Schofield, *Who
Needs Experts?*; Emma
Waterton and Laurajane
Smith, "The Recognition
and Misrecognition of
Community Heritage,"
*International Journal of
Heritage Studies* 16, no.
1–2 (2010): 4–15; Sharon
Milholland, "In the
Eyes of the Beholder:
Understanding and
Resolving Incompatible
Ideologies and
Languages in US
Environmental and

experts who control the official meanings of heritage and, in the process, discount local or community values.[9]

Today, there is an increasing interest in trying to understand the values of people other than experts in order to make the planning and management process for built heritage more relevant to an increasing number of stakeholders.[10] This desire is also linked to making heritage-planning processes reflect the values of participatory democracy. In our digital world, social media is increasingly relevant and offers the tantalizing possibility of efficiently tapping into these community values. In the scientific community, social media applications have been used to understand how people perceive and value physical places and the ways in which meanings are communicated. For instance, services such as Twitter provide a wealth of information on how individuals communicate within their social network; a quick search on the phrases "historic buildings" and "charming places" results in many thousands of posts in which people share their feelings about such places. Similar examples exist on Facebook, Pinterest, Google+, Tumblr, and Instagram, as well as on travel sites, such as TripAdvisor.

In comparison with more formal modes of communication, tweets frequently reflect the author's opinions and emotional states rather than objective facts. The collection of tweets has therefore become a new data source for understanding people's experiences of the world—the study of which is called sentiment analysis or opinion mining.[11] The rise of social media has attracted significant academic interest in the potential of sentiment analysis.[12] Opinion mining has, for example, been applied to novels, news headlines, and art perception.[13] Other research has focused on developing a larger-scale understanding of consumer sentiments toward certain products or the stock market.[14] However, opinion mining of this nature has not yet been applied to built cultural heritage and cultural landscapes.

There are a range of obstacles to using computational tools to support built cultural heritage and cultural landscape planning and management. Given that heritage conservation is supposed to benefit citizens, the first problem is the lack of effective computational tools for representing the perspectives of nonexperts in the conservation management process. But it is not just that computational tools are missing: in the social sciences, methods of understanding people's values, meanings, and perceptions are resource intensive, in terms of both time and money. In general, the only work that combines built heritage conservation and information systems simply documents the objective characteristics of buildings (e.g., location integrity, size, height, architectural style), usually in combination with geographic information systems (GIS); these systems do not consider or incorporate stakeholders' values. While heritage management often involves stakeholders, laws and policies ensure that only the significations that coincide with the values of experts are considered; other meanings are discarded. In effect, we know very little about how people value, describe, and perceive the historic built environment because these impressions are not important to orthodox planning and management processes.

In this light, there is a need to facilitate a greater comprehension of the relationship between laypeople and the historic environment, especially by using information from social media networks, including Twitter, Facebook, TripAdvisor, and blogs. In order to substantially increase our understanding of how people describe and value built heritage and cultural landscapes, we propose the development of a specialized web-based platform called the Social HEritage Machine (SHEM). The SHEM platform is envisioned as a tool that will help cultural heritage researchers and managers to better understand how lay people relate to tangible cultural heritage, from both local and global perspectives. Furthermore, the proposed platform will combine social engagement with planning processes to allow stakeholders to participate directly in making decisions about the recognition, treatment, and management of built heritage.

● COMPUTATIONAL BACKGROUND

In a simplistic sense, SHEM will understand and geocode (map) the meanings associated with built heritage. It will make use of social media and other data sources to understand the relationship between people and heritage or historic environments. SHEM will access a broad range of stakeholder values by mining data on how people describe and value cultural landscapes. Beyond that, it will also provide some participatory-democracy services to support the recognition and treatment of built heritage. This cloud-based tool will be built using computational methods such as the semantic web, ontologies, linked open data, natural language processing, opinion mining, data mining, and social machines.

Semantic Web. The semantic web started with the idea that computers should be able to understand and handle information from the web. 15 Specifically, the initial vision was to transform the web into a resource that humans can read and that machines can also interpret. The basic parts of the semantic web include ontologies and annotations on web resources. Ontologies use logical expressions or axioms to create a knowledge base for a specific domain. Annotations then ensure that the data is interpretable by both humans and machines.

The key idea is that syntactic metadata structures, based on shared semantic specifications founded on formal logic, make web content understandable to machines. This makes it possible to create more interoperable and intelligent web services. A computer that cannot interpret the data it is dealing with is like a telephone that relays information: while it provides a valuable service, it cannot be very helpful in more complicated information-processing tasks. The advantage of the semantic web is that it uses common formats for data derived from heterogeneous sources and languages to describe the relations of data to real-world objects. Several existing standards, such as resource description framework (RDF) and ontology web language (OWL), are already able—to a certain extent—to bridge contents with related meanings.

Ontologies. An ontology is a shared and common understanding of some domain that can be communicated across people and computers and therefore can be shared and reused across different applications. 16

Cultural Laws in Relationship to Navajo Sacred Lands," *American Indian Culture and Research Journal* 34, no. 2 (2010): 103–124; Lisanne Gibson, "Cultural Landscapes and Identity," in *Valuing Historic Environments*; Peter Howard, "Historic Landscapes and the Recent Past: Whose History?," in *Valuing Historic Environments*; Laurajane Smith, "Deference and Humility: The Social Values of the Country House," in *Valuing Historic Environments*; Emma Waterton, Laurajane Smith, and Gary Campbell, "The Utility of Discourse Analysis to Heritage Studies: The Burra Charter and Social Inclusion," *International Journal of Heritage Studies* 12, no. 4 (July 2006): 339–355; Jeremy C. Wells, "Our History Is Not False: Perspectives from the Revitalization Culture," *International Journal of Heritage Studies* 16, no. 6 (November 2010): 464–485; James Maitland Gardner, "Heritage Protection and Social Inclusion: A Case Study from the Bangladeshi Community of East London," *International Journal of Heritage Studies* 10, no. 1 (March 2004): 75–92.

10
Wells, *In Stakeholders We Trust*.

11
Bing Liu, *Sentiment Analysis: Mining Opinions, Sentiments, and Emotions* (Cambridge, UK: Cambridge University Press, 2015).

12
Bo Pang and Lillian Lee, "Opinion Mining and Sentiment Analysis," *Foundations and Trends in Information Retrieval* 2, no. 1–2 (2008): 1–135.

13
Saif M. Mohammad, "From Once Upon a Time to Happily Ever After: Tracking Emotions in Novels and Fairy Tales," in *Proceedings of the 5th ACL-HLT Workshop on Language Technology for Cultural Heritage* (2011), 105–114; Carlo Strapparava and Rada

Mihalcea, "Learning to Identify Emotions in Text," in *Proceedings of the ACM Conference on Applied Computing* (2008); Matteo Baldoni et al., "Sentiment Analysis in the Planet Art: A Case Study in the Social Semantic Web," in *New Challenges in Distributed Information Filtering and Retrieval*, Studies in Computational Intelligence, vol. 439 (Berlin: Springer, 2013), 131–149.

14
Johan Bollen, Huina Mao, and Xiaojun Zeng, "Twitter Mood Predicts the Stock Market," *Journal of Computational Science* 2, no. 1 (2011): 1–8.

15
Tim Berners-Lee, James Hendler, and Ora Lassila, "The Semantic Web," *Scientific American*, May 2001, 29–37.

16
Berners-Lee, Hendler, and Lassila, "Semantic Web."

17
Martin Doerr, "The CIDOC CRM, an Ontological Approach to Schema Heterogeneity," *Semantic Interoperability and Integration* (2005).

18
Christian Bizer, Tom Heath, and Tim Berners-Lee, "Linked Data—The Story So Far," *International Journal on Semantic Web and Information Systems* 5, no. 3 (2009): 1–22.

19
Zhiqiang Zeng, Hua Shi, Yun Wu, and Zhiling Hong, "Survey of Natural Language Processing Techniques in Bioinformatics," *Computational and Mathematical Methods in Medicine* 2015, no. 6 (2015): 1–10.

20
Zeng et al., "Survey of Natural Language Processing Techniques."

21
Liu, *Sentiment Analysis*.

In order to describe subject matter, ontologies use concepts, instances, and relations, which are organized in taxonomies through which inheritance mechanisms can be applied.

In the field of cultural heritage, CIDOC-CRM is a formal ontology intended to facilitate the integration, mediation, and interchange of heterogeneous cultural heritage information. [17] It was developed by experts from fields such as computer science, archaeology, museum documentation, history of the arts, natural history, library science, physics, and philosophy, under the aegis of the International Committee for Documentation (CIDOC). CIDOC-CRM was created to capture the richness typical of cultural heritage information: its classes and properties work to capture the concepts underlying database structures, providing a high level of data integration.

Linked Open Data. [18] Recently, a need to connect datasets across the web has created a movement toward linked data—a method of publishing structured data so that it can be interlinked with other data. Linked open data builds upon standard web technologies such as hypertext transfer protocol (HTTP) and RDF and extends them to share information in a way that can be automatically read by computers, enabling data from different sources to be connected and queried. The linked open data paradigm extends data commons on the web by publishing various open datasets as RDF triples and establishing RDF links among entities. A key idea of linked open data is that different parts of a database can come from different data sources. For example, metadata about a person, such as Pablo Picasso, may come from an authority database, whereas information about a place, such as Málaga (the Spanish city where Pablo Picasso was born), may be provided by a land survey organization.

Natural Language Processing. [19] Natural language processing is a field of computer science, artificial intelligence, and computational linguistics concerned with the interactions between computers and human (natural) languages, and as such, it is related to the field of human-computer interaction. One of the biggest challenges is natural language understanding (that is, the ability of computers to derive meaning from human or natural language input); other challenges involve natural language generation.

One of the most important subtasks for natural language processing in SHEM is named entity recognition, a form of information extraction. Its main goal is to locate elements and classify them in categories defined in advance, such as people, location, and so on. [20] One basic feature in the majority of named entity recognition systems is the ability to take a text block as input and to output the same block of text with the names of entities highlighted.

Opinion Mining. [21] Opinion mining, also known as sentiment analysis, refers to the use of natural language processing, text analysis, and computational linguistics to identify and extract subjective information from textual sources. Sentiment analysis is widely applied to reviews and social media for a variety of applications, ranging from targeted marketing to customer service. More broadly, the main goal of opinion mining is to determine the attitude of a writer with respect to some topic or to the overall contextual polarity of a document. The writer's attitude may include judgment, evaluation, the writer's own emotional state, or the emotional effect the writer wishes to have on the reader. With SHEM, we are mainly interested in the writer's judgment or evaluation, specifically of some aspect of built heritage.

Data Mining. In addition to opinion mining, data mining can also be of great help. Data mining is an interdisciplinary subfield of computer science that looks for patterns in datasets by using methods at the intersection of artificial intelligence, machine learning, statistics, and database systems. [22] The overall goal of data mining is to extract information and transform it into an understandable structure for further use. Data mining is the analysis step of the "knowledge discovery in databases" process.

Social Machines. Broadly speaking, social machines combine both computational and social processes into a sociotechnical system that exploits the large scale of interaction between humans and machines. [23] Social machines represent a natural evolution of web-enabled systems, and companies such as Google, IBM, Microsoft, and others have recently expressed interest in the topic. [24] In practice, social machines are a generic way to describe social web applications (like Twitter, Facebook, and Ushahidi) as a combination of building blocks that have a behavior, communicate, and obey certain rules or constraints. [25] At the same time, these social machines "wrap"—or facilitate exchange between—internal and external data sources. [26] Such building blocks can also be used to wrap information-processing systems (like social media) to provide a dynamic set of specialized application programming interfaces (APIs). These are the *socially connected computing units* we have used to derive social machines from individuals, businesses, and governments. [27] With SHEM, we intend to develop an online platform that combines the social machine paradigm and the aforementioned technologies (such as linked open data, natural language processing, and data mining) as a way to include more people's opinions in place-based conservation initiatives.

● RELATED WORK

Previous studies on local sensitivities and public opinions on cultural heritage have been conducted, although—with a few exceptions—the focus is usually not on built heritage. In a study on transforming relational database content, Kate Byrne outlines a method that integrates RDF data with annotations from free text; she suggests that in order to connect cultural data in different formats, the RDF schema should be quite simple. She uses a named entity recognition technique to detect and categorize objects in text, and then makes use of classification methods to find binary relations between them. Finally, these relations are converted to RDF triples and integrated in the basic schema—a system that opens the way to a true integration of the hybrid data so common in heritage management. The

22
Pang-Ning Tan, Michael Steinbach, and Vipin Kumar, *Introduction to Data Mining* (Boston: Pearson Addison Wesley, 2005).

23
Nigel R. Shadbolt et al., "Towards a Classification Framework for Social Machines," in *Proceedings of the 22nd International Conference on World Wide Web* (New York: ACM, 2013), 905–912.

24
SOCIAM: The Theory and Practice of Social Machines, "Partners," https://www.sociam.org/about.

25
Ushahidi is a crowd-sourcing application designed to gather, manage, and analyze data submitted by users; see https://www.ushahidi.com.

26
Vanilson Burégio, Silvio Meira, and Nelson Rosa, "Social Machines: A Unified Paradigm to Describe Social Web-Oriented Systems," in *Proceedings of the 22nd International Conference on World Wide Web*, 885–890.

27
Vanilson Burégio et al., "Personal APIs as an Enabler for Designing and Implementing People as Social Machines," in *Proceedings of the 23rd International Conference on World Wide Web* (New York: ACM, 2014), 867–872; Vanilson Burégio, Zakaria Maamar, and Silvio Meira, "An Architecture and Guiding Framework for the Social Enterprise," *IEEE Internet Computing* 19, no. 1 (January 2015): 64–68; and Vanilson Burégio et al., "Towards Government as a Social Machine," in *Proceedings of the 24th International Conference on World Wide Web* (New York: ACM, 2015), 1131–1136.

28
Kate Byrne, "Putting Hybrid Cultural Data on the Semantic Web," *Journal of Digital Information* 10, no. 6 (2009), https://journals.tdl.org/jodi/index.php/jodi/article/view/700.

29
Baldoni et al., "Sentiment Analysis"; Federico Bertola and Viviana Patti, "Emotional Responses to Artworks in Online Collections," in *Proceedings of the 21st Conference on User Modeling, Adaptation, and Personalization* (Rome, June 10–14, 2013).

30
Vasco Monteiro et al., "Sensing World Heritage: An Exploratory Study of Twitter as a Tool for Assessing Reputation," *Computational Science and Its Applications, ICCSA 2014* (Berlin: Springer, 2014), 404–419.

31
Monteiro et al., "Sensing World Heritage."

dataset that was used was a small sample, but the results are encouraging. [28]

Another example is ArsEmotica, an ontology-driven framework that creates a semantic social space where artworks can be dynamically organized according to an ontology of emotions. This system analyzes tagged artworks and outputs, for each artwork, a set of related emotions that might be felt by the viewer. By exploiting and combining semantic web tools and lexical resources, the program can identify the emotions that capture the affective meaning that visitors collectively give to the artworks. [29]

More recently, Vasco Monteiro, Roberto Henriques, Marco Painho, and Eric Vaz conducted an exploratory study of Twitter as a tool for assessing the reputation of World Heritage. Their work collected two months' worth of information (from December 2013 to January 2014, for a total of 11,839 tweets) from Twitter about local and global sensitivities regarding World Heritage and submitted this data to temporal, spatial, and some simple text mining analysis. Their objective was to explore the potential of using Twitter feeds in order to understand both local and global sensitivities regarding heritage sites—specifically, those that are UNESCO World Heritage sites. [30]

While these projects have produced interesting results, their capacities for both data management and analysis are limited compared to the SHEM platform. Indeed, SHEM differs from the aforementioned projects in a number of ways. For example, none of the other projects integrate data from several data sources; more interesting insights will be possible when one correlates different sources of information. Similarly, in contrast to the project led by Monteiro, which reports on a two-month period, the SHEM platform intends to continually update its knowledge base on historic places of interest. [31] SHEM will not be limited to an exploratory analysis, which means that useful online analysis will be possible at any time.

SHEM will perform several kinds of temporal, spatial, and (mainly) natural language analysis for opinion mining. The opinion mining done by ArsEmotica is limited to curated collections of artworks, whereas SHEM intends to provide sentiment analysis for cultural heritage buildings, sites, and landscapes. Although all of these other programs can be applied to cultural heritage data management, they do not take into account the one aspect more specific to heritage in the built environment: participatory democracy. In SHEM, we aim to consider everyone's opinions as input to the process of planning, management, and treatment of built heritage and cultural landscapes.

● THE PROPOSED APPROACH:
   OBJECTIVES AND COMPONENTS OF SHEM

SHEM is a cloud-based platform to help cultural heritage researchers and managers better understand how laypeople relate to tangible cultural heritage, from both local and global perspectives. Considering SHEM through the lens of social machines suggests that urban planning is capable of mediating the interaction and participation of citizens by listening, engaging, and learning from different groups of people.

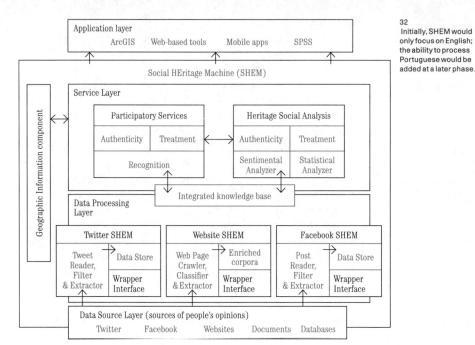

FIG. 1: Proposed architecture overview for SHEM platform.

32
Initially, SHEM would only focus on English; the ability to process Portuguese would be added at a later phase.

As stated earlier, one of the issues with tangible (built) heritage conservation is that practitioners do not have a good understanding of how ordinary people describe and value built heritage and cultural land-scapes, as law and policy require the meanings of heritage to be conveyed in the language of experts, such as architects and historians. That creates the need for research into the following questions, which we hope that SHEM will be able to answer: What is the language that laypeople use to describe and value historic places? How can a computational tool effec-tively gather metadata about this language from social media networks in order to inform heritage planning processes? What does it mean for places to be authentic, and how can places retain this authenticity?

In order to answer these questions, we want to test our working hypothesis that data from social media services and linked open data can be exploited to improve our understanding of how laypeople people relate to cultural heritage. Such an analysis could be a valuable tool for cultural heritage research, planning, and management. SHEM aspires to provide meaningful insights on specific historic places, but it has other objectives as well. It offers a platform for natural language analysis of strong asso-ciations among words and phrases related to particular aspects of built heritage and historic places; it can also investigate cultural differences by comparing English and Portuguese descriptions of built heritage. 32 Developing a web-based and user-friendly interface will help make descriptive statistics about buildings, structures, or landscapes more accessible and help identify historic places that conventional experts may be missing. SHEM will provide geolocation layers on a map for the names of all known objects within a boundary area, so that it will be clear if the place as a whole contains data on recognition, authenticity, and treatment. And importantly, SHEM strengthens advocacy for heritage conservation by making arguments in the language and values of most stakeholders.

In order to accomplish these objectives, SHEM adopts a four-layered software architecture. *FIG. 1* The layers, from bottom to top, are the following:

Data Source Layer. In the bottom layer, there is a set of people's opinions on heritage environments from different sources. Such data sources include online social media (e.g., Twitter, Facebook), specific heritage-related databases, and possibly other websites/services (e.g., TripAdvisor).

Data Processing Layer. Above the data layer, a set of *wrappers* (e.g., Twitter-SHEM, Facebook-SHEM) is responsible for integrating specific data sources. Each wrapper has a set of specialized data-processing components in charge of reading, filtering, and extracting information of interest prior to storing it in a *data store/enriched corpora* for future analysis and integration. The *integrated knowledge base* provides a unified access point for managing the data gathered by the different wrappers. Further, it provides additional metadata to leverage, among other things, linked open data and spatial/geographical information.

Service Layer. This layer uses the integrated knowledge base to provide several services, such as keyword, sentiment, and statistical analyzers. These services are disseminated as APIs and are grouped into two categories—namely, *participatory services* and *heritage social analysis*.

The term *participatory services* refers to the key features of critical heritage studies: recognition, authenticity, and treatment. *Recognition* refers to the names/phrases/concepts and the process by which laypeople distinguish, understand, and conceptualize the historic environment as different from other kinds of environments. *Authenticity* refers to the way in which a historic environment and/or elements of a historic environment feel "real" or "genuine" to laypeople. *Treatment* refers to how changes can be made to the historic environment and/or elements of a historic environment to conserve its feeling of authenticity for laypeople.

Heritage Social Analysis is based on a set of knowledge-intensive tasks that derive higher-level insights from social data in order to support the recognition, treatment, and management of built heritage. Such services include opinion mining, sentiment analysis, word frequency, and statistical analysis.

It is worth noting that both the data-processing layer and the service layer are supported by a *geographic information component*. This component enables, among other things, the integration of SHEM with geographic information systems, like ArcGIS and Google Maps. Such integration will facilitate the implementation of services that allow users to visualize heritage-related data on a map; for example, a user could draw a boundary on a map, and SHEM would show any relevant data on recognition, authenticity, and treatment.

Application Layer. The top layer supports the applications that can be built on top of the SHEM platform, which can combine different SHEM

153

services to make web-based tools, mobile apps, and mapping solutions, to mention just a few possibilities.

Ideally, SHEM's services will provide online open APIs, which means that the SHEM platform can naturally facilitate a plethora of cultural heritage-related applications and services, built by developers with an interest in a more effective place-based conservation process. In this way, SHEM can facilitate a heritage conservation planning process that is based on participatory democracy, allowing for a far greater number of stakeholders to become engaged in these processes and for heritage experts to be better informed of the nature of the public good.

● MORE POSSIBILITIES FOR SHEM

While the goal of SHEM is to focus on heritage values in the built environment, there is no reason that, once the platform is built, it could not be expanded to focus on mapping other meanings associated with the built environment. As such, it could provide a broad-based tool of potentially great value to urban planners as well as cultural heritage planners. It also can provide a foundation for further research into the everyday language people use to describe the built environment. Imagine, for instance, sustainability arguments developed and delivered using the language of laypeople rather than the more academic language of experts. For policy advocates, SHEM could effectively gather heritage meanings and values from the public, not only to better inform planning processes but also to formulate policies that have the potential to change people's behavior as it relates to the built environment.

To be sure, given the issues around online privacy and the use of people's data without permission—Facebook's abuse of people's trust is a ready example—SHEM could be perceived as a threat when characterized superficially. But the essential difference is that SHEM makes no attempt to personally identify individuals. From the moment data is mined, it is immediately aggregated and dissociated from any personal identifiers. There is no opportunity to utilize the raw data, the lexicon data, or data presented through the user interface to associate certain meanings with specific individuals. We view the ability to associate meanings with specific individuals as unnecessary to our endeavor; by not allowing this possibility, our work is ethically positioned to protect people from possible intrusion. In addition, data mining processes in SHEM will access only publicly available data and will not take advantage of loopholes to gain access to data nefariously. In the spirit of planning for the public good, SHEM is a tool based on the ethical collection and use of information publicly shared by millions of people.

The principles embodied in SHEM have the potential to revolutionize how we plan for the conservation of the built environment. By making it very easy to access the "unauthorized" meanings associated with heritage, SHEM may prove to be a significant force for destabilizing the expert-driven, top-down regulatory process of most built heritage conservation in the United States, as well as in many other countries around the world.

○ Institutionalizing Data
○ Co-Producing Knowledge
○ Building Evidence-Based Narratives
● Informing Policy Agendas

Perspectives on Data in
Urban Historic Preservation Policy

Douglas S. Noonan
Tetsuharu Oba

Informing Policy Agendas

Early in 2003, a colleague passed along a copy of the *Chicago Tribune* with an imposing headline: "Research and Destroy." [1] In a series on historic landmark preservation in the city, the *Tribune* referenced a comprehensive survey of historic resources that the city's planning department had undertaken years before. The journalists used that data in order to reach a startling and controversial conclusion—namely, that the city was doing a poor job of preserving its historic buildings. Yet the appeal of the article extended beyond a catchy title and exciting journalism; it raised issues of both theory and data that grabbed the attention of at least one graduate student.

The story relied on the Chicago Historic Resources Survey, a rare and detailed set of data that would later inform some of our own scholarship. [2] It provided an early example of how data informs the practice of urban heritage preservation as well as how it empowers analysis and advocacy. The "Research and Destroy" story told a tale of a preservation policy based on listing special resources and using "command and control" regulation to preserve them. Even environmental policies, which had yielded ample research on such an approach for endangered species, produced the same unfortunate, unintended consequences of the landmark preservation experience described in "Research and Destroy." [3]

The course was set, and our interest in historic preservation policies followed. Yet a data fix for a graduate student does not necessarily mean data can fix the problems of historic preservation and its policies. A world with more and better data will not necessarily advance a preservation agenda, or any agenda, for that matter. Carrying the conversation forward and including a variety of perspectives is vital to ultimately shaping how data can and will be used.

1
Blair Kamin and Patrick T. Reardon, "A Squandered Heritage: Research and Destroy," *Chicago Tribune*, January 13, 2003.

2
Douglas S. Noonan, "Finding an Impact of Preservation Policies: Price Effects of Historic Landmarks on Attached Homes in Chicago, 1990–1999," *Economic Development Quarterly* 21, no. 1 (February 2007): 17–33; Douglas S. Noonan and Douglas J. Krupka, "Determinants of Historic and Cultural Landmark Designation: Why We Preserve What We Preserve," *Journal of Cultural Economics* 34, no. 1 (February 2010): 1–26.

3
Paul J. Ferraro, Craig McIntosh, and Monica Ospina, "The Effectiveness of the US Endangered Species Act: An Econometric Analysis Using Matching Methods," *Journal of Environmental Economics and Management* 54, no. 3 (November 2007): 245–261.

● KYOTO CITY CASE STUDY

Kyoto offers a valuable case study as the city faces preservation challenges common to other global cities while its specificity points to new ideas and approaches. Kyoto, surrounded by mountains on three sides, connects a natural landscape with a 1,200-year history and abundant cultural heritage. It served as Japan's capital city from 794 to 1868 and contains the various historical structures that position implies. Its historical structures range from shrines and temples to *Kyo-machiya* (a type of townhouse distinctive to Kyoto) and modern architecture. Kyoto's building inventory includes many locally important cultural sites, including monuments designated as a UNESCO World Heritage site. Perhaps most important and most challenging for Kyoto, however, are its historical landscapes, which have grown from the harmonization of these historic structures with the surrounding natural landscapes.

Preserving the built environment in Kyoto thus involves more than just preserving particular buildings or even districts: it also involves preserving the broader landscape around these important cultural sites. The approach to historic preservation taken in Kyoto recognizes these "perspective landscapes" and "borrowed landscapes" (*shakkei*) as central to the conservation of its built heritage. The ancient city of Kyoto contains significant landscapes that have appeared in traditional Japanese *waka* and

4
Dennis E. Gale, "The Impacts of Historic District Designation Planning and Policy Implications," *Journal of the American Planning Association* 57, no. 3 (Summer 1991): 325–340.

5
Peter V. Schaeffer and Cecily Ahern Millerick, "The Impact of Historic District Designation on Property Values: An Empirical Study," *Economic Development Quarterly* 5, no. 4 (November 1991): 301–312.

6
David E. Clark and William E. Herrin, "Historical Preservation Districts and Home Sale Prices: Evidence from the Sacramento Housing Market," *Review of Regional Studies* 27, no. 1 (1997): 29–48.

7
Mark van Duijn, Jan Rouwendal, and Richard Boersema, "Redevelopment of Industrial Heritage: Insights into External Effects on House Prices," *Regional Science and Urban Economics* 57 (March 2016): 91–107.

8
Vicki Been, Ingrid Gould Ellen, Michael Gedal, Edward Glaeser, and Brian J. McCabe, "Preserving History or Restricting Development? The Heterogeneous Effects of Historic Districts on Local Housing Markets in New York City," *Journal of Urban Economics* 92 (March 2016): 16–30.

9
Gabriel M. Ahlfeldt, Kristoffer Moeller, Sevrin Waights, and Nicolai Wendland, "Game of Zones: The Political Economy of Conservation Areas," *Economic Journal* 127, no. 605 (October 2017): F421–F445.

10
Hans Koster and Jan Rouwendal, "Historic Amenities and Housing Externalities: Evidence from the Netherlands," *Economic Journal* 127, no. 605 (October 2017): F396–F420.

haiku poems. The landscapes include everything visible between a viewer and a particular landmark, with borrowed landscapes emphasizing the mountain scenery visible from within gardens and perspective landscapes emphasizing views of historic buildings and other natural scenery. Thus, conserving historic resources in Kyoto involves preserving views *from* historic sites as well as preserving views *of* those sites.

● YESTERDAY TO TODAY

Tracing the evolution of data's role in informing our understanding of historic preservation shows how dramatically the use of data has changed. Looking back, there has been a remarkable growth in the size, depth, and variety of data employed in empirical analysis of historic preservation. The earliest articles on the topic used rather limited data, such as averages of assessed property values in a handful of neighborhoods, [4] or research based on just 250 total observations in two historic districts in a single community. [5] Those studies from the early 1990s were followed a few years later by David Clark and William Herrin's study of the impact of historic preservation on housing prices in Sacramento. [6] Their data sample employed 683 observations, showing an improvement over their predecessors, although they were still using manually constructed maps rather than the digital tools that would dominate shortly thereafter.

Looking at later studies on this topic—price differentials associated with historic landmark designations—we see a very different picture. For example, a recent study of twenty-six years of residential property transactions in the Netherlands included 200,000 observations. [7] Another excellent project analyzed 500,000 observations—thirty-five years of residential transactions in New York City—from several massive, complex datasets related to properties and policies. [8] Other studies have used mortgage data for over 1,000,000 properties in England, [9] and 2,000,000 housing transactions over thirty-six years in the Netherlands were used to examine four decades of subsidies for cultural heritage investments. [10] Seen in this light, it is little wonder that people refer to our era as an age of "big data." Yet we are only twenty years removed from the first generation of studies that employed just a few hundred observations.

This development continues as research frontiers expand. A sample of 7,000 participants was used to train computer algorithms (using machine learning) to predict safety ratings for streetscapes across several cities. [11] Advanced tools like this algorithm point to new ways that we will be able to systematically and objectively evaluate our built environment. Another recent study coupled neighborhood-level data on energy consumption and adoption of energy-efficient technologies with information on historic preservation policies across England. [12] Moving beyond price differentials, we can look at energy and environmental impacts of historic buildings by connecting previously disconnected datasets.

Kyoto Then and Now: More Data in Practice
Kyoto has a strong tradition of policy to preserve such historical resources. In 1930, prior to World War II, the city designated areas totaling

3,400 hectares as scenic areas. In 1966 the Ancient Capitals Preservation Law was promulgated to prevent loss or degradation of historical resources due to rapid urbanization. Kyoto accordingly designated some special preservation areas for historic landscapes. Kyoto has also passed ordinances regarding the formation and preservation of urban landscapes and established preservation districts for groups of historic buildings under the national Law for the Protection of Cultural Properties (1950).

Under Japan's 2004 Landscape Act, Kyoto thoroughly redesigned its previous policy and implemented a new landscape policy in 2007. This new policy employs five regulatory and incentive measures:

- revised building height regulations
- revised building design standards and designated districts
- strengthened preservation measures for perspective and borrowed landscapes
- more stringent regulations on outdoor advertisements
- advocacy for conservation and revitalization of historical buildings, including *Kyo-machiya*

11
Nikhil Naik, Jade Philipoom, Ramesh Raskar, and César Hidalgo, "Streetscore—Predicting the Perceived Safety of One Million Streetscapes," in *2014 IEEE Conference on Computer Vision and Pattern Recognition Workshops* (Piscataway: IEEE, 2014), 793–799.

12
Christian A. L. Hilber, Charles Palmer, and Edward W. Pinchbeck, "The Energy Costs of Historic Preservation" (SERC Discussion Paper 217, July 2017), http://eprints.lse.ac.uk/86563/1/sercdp0217.pdf.

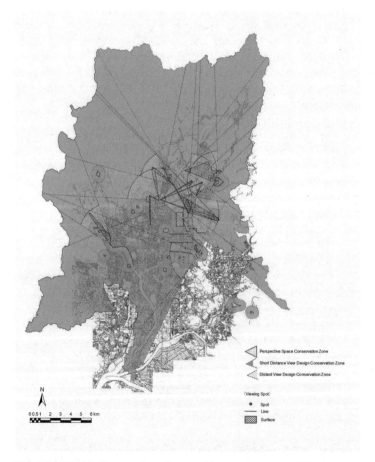

FIG. 1: *Designation of perspective and borrowed landscape areas. Partial processing of the digital data provided by and used by permission of Kyoto City.*

FIG. 2: *Panoramic view of Mount Daimonji seen from the bank of the Kamo River.*

13
A viewpoint site is a high-profile public location that provides excellent perspective landscapes, such as shrines, temples, castles, the Imperial Palace, historical structures, parks, rivers, bridges, and roads.

14
These are landmarks that can be seen from a viewpoint site and that contain some elements of excellent landscapes, such as mountains, rivers, historical structures, aesthetic townscapes, and traditional cultural objects that are infused into nature. Mount Daimonji is one of five locations where giant bonfires are lit during the annual Gozan Okuribi festival held annually on August 16.

Kyoto City had previously imposed uniform height limitations within designated areas to prevent the degradation of its historical landscapes, but as they were based on height from the ground surface, they proved insufficient to preserve perspective landscapes. In order to protect the area between the viewpoint and the subject to which the view is directed, Kyoto became the first city in Japan to enact a City Ordinance on the Preservation of View in September 2007. These sightlines are now regulated based on elevation above sea level. Regulating to preserve views has long been practiced in other cities, such as London (London View Management Framework), Paris (Fuseaux de Protection Generale de Site), and Vancouver (View Cones). *FIG. 1*

Kyoto's ordinance designates perspective landscape and borrowed landscape areas where building heights included in a three-dimensional space are regulated by standards for form, design, and color. Perspective and borrowed landscape areas are grouped into three types of zones: the perspective space conservation zone, the short-distance view design conservation zone, and the distant view design conservation zone. The perspective space conservation zone is the most important: these zones are generally fan-shaped, originating from the viewpoint site. 13 Buildings located in these zones are regulated so that they do not obstruct specific views, such as of Mount Daimonji. 14 *FIG. 2* The short-distance view design conservation zones regulate the design and appearance of visible structures nearer to the viewpoint site. Farther out, the distant view design conservation zones set standards for exterior and roof colors to preserve the view. *FIG. 3* Today, thirty-eight sites are designated as perspective and borrowed landscape areas to preserve and create excellent perspective and borrowed landscapes.

Since initiating the new landscape policy, Kyoto has also begun developing a system to assess its policy. It has developed a new database to track implementation of the landscape view policy and the impact of

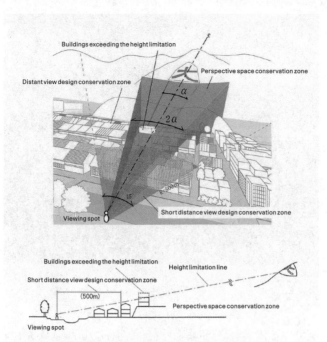

15
Kyoto City, "White
Paper on Landscape
in Kyoto City 2015"
(in Japanese), 2016,
http://www.city.
kyoto.lg.jp/tokei/
page/0000146590.
html.

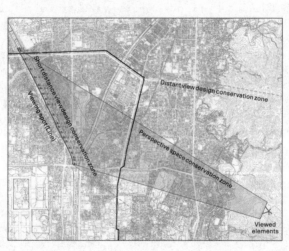

FIG. 3: *Conceptual scheme of perspective and borrowed landscape areas.*
Conservation zones regulate height restrictions in the perspective space
(orange area), appearance and design in the short-distance view (green area),
and colors in the distant view. As seen in the bottom map, the viewing site
could be a line along a river as well as a single point. Partial processing of the
digital data provided by and used by permission of Kyoto City.

related policies on construction and civic awareness. The results have
been published as the "White Paper on Landscape in Kyoto City."[15] As
we enter an era of large-scale data utilization, this new database—which
includes quantitative, textual, and image-based data—is expected to
greatly contribute to developing and improving evidence-based historic

preservation policies in Kyoto. It is also intended to support the planning of brand-new policy measures. As preservation policies become more sophisticated, the database is developing as well. Kyoto is exploring better ways to use the database for policy-making (e.g., planning, development, validation), granting approvals for applications under relevant regulations, disseminating information about landscape policies, and increasing public awareness.

Creating and conserving perspective and borrowed landscapes entails combining data on buildings and topographical information in geographic analyses. Kyoto has complemented field surveys of actual views with validation of those views using image data as well as three-dimensional GIS analyses. For example, creating topographical cross-sections along sight lines between viewpoints and visual targets allows detection of possible obstacles in perspective landscapes. This improves enforcement of elevation-based building-height regulations. These additional examinations and confirmations are made possible by the development of three-dimensional GIS data and tools in the new database.

Kyoto's preservation efforts also include conservation of *Kyo-machiya*, traditional wooden houses in Japan that are typically quite deep and have a small frontage. *Kyo-machiya* have standard layouts and features, and characteristically stand in a row facing out onto small alleys. Yet development pressures and maintenance costs have led to a decline in the number of *Kyo-machiya*. The city has conducted major field surveys on a regular basis to prevent the loss and alteration of *Kyo-machiya*. Data collection has included appearance surveys as well as questionnaires for inhabitants. The 2008–2009 survey employed digital devices, instead of conventional paper maps and questionnaires, to limit data-entry errors and the cost of digitizing survey results. Ongoing and improving data-collection efforts around the preservation of these distinctive buildings can support preservation policies going forward. *FIG. 4*

FIG. 4: *View of* Kyo-machiya, *traditional townhouses, in a preservation district for groups of historic buildings* (Gion-shinbashi).

The striking improvement in quality and availability of data happens only within the context of broader institutions and processes. Back in graduate school, one instructor said that institutions are best characterized by the incentives and information that they provide. It is a useful shorthand. Even burgeoning data resources should be appreciated in light of their institutional contexts, especially the incentives offered in those systems.

In terms of policy related to historic preservation, both those that are directly related (e.g., landmark designations, regulation of historic conservation zones) and those more indirectly related (e.g., zoning rules, spatially targeted economic development strategies, infrastructure plans) must be considered. Development dynamics throughout a city have a large impact on the options for and constraints on preservation well before the overt preservation policy instruments are involved. In the broader policy framework, our institutions help determine the types of historic resources that we preserve: what they are, where they are, etc. The built environment in any given city can be characterized as a multidimensional distribution of different types of structures, of different ages, at different locations, and so on. Of course, different urban areas have different distributions that evolve over time. This portfolio or distribution is sort of a dynamic equilibrium, as the various forces at play (development pressures and preservation pressures, among many others) establish and alter that portfolio over time.

Direct and indirect policies emerge from a variety of processes that take place in legislative bodies, agencies, commissions, and other organizations, which in turn determine the instruments through which we undertake—implicitly or explicitly—historic preservation: regulation, subsidies, information (e.g., labeling schemes, data clearinghouses), and direct provision (e.g., of government-owned sites). The menu of policy tools (such as property rights and taxes) is even more extensive. Thus, crucially, the matter of how data affects historic preservation largely depends on how additional data affects these processes.

The processes to select both the portfolio of built environment to conserve and the instruments by which we effect that conservation are influenced by competing interests, budget constraints, and other incentives. Although there are examples of timely studies and salient data that have substantially influenced policy, there may be even more instances where policy has been driven with complete or near complete disregard of relevant studies, data, and available evidence. Politics, charisma, ideology, and other forces have mattered in the past and will remain pertinent, for better or worse, regardless of how much we call for evidence-based policy. Still, incentives alone do not explain everything: data and information can play a role.

How More and Better Data Enter Historic Preservation Processes
Whether or not the choices made in historic preservation are optimal, desired, or even intentional, decisions about what should be preserved are made and do change, and so do the policy instruments that affect them.

But the consequences of adding more data into these complex systems is still unclear, due to the mediated and negotiated nature of these processes. More and better data is not exclusive to a particular political or ideological agenda or preference. Rather, it should be available to many relevant parties and interests. An era of bigger data may be more empowering to interests aligned against or orthogonal to historic preservation than it is to those in favor of it.

There are many ways that new data can enter into these processes. First, more and better data might trigger more or new procedural attention or regulatory processes, either automatically or through greater demand for new action. It was this sort of story—where enhanced data led to greater oversight—that the *Chicago Tribune* published: a story that unintentionally helped avoid the destruction of historic landmarks. 16 A world with better data might include better identification of the historic inventory, more awareness of its value, and more awareness of the threats it faces, which in turn can result in reconsideration of plans that undermine preservation. Of course, more and better data, in principle, could also be used to undermine or restrict historic preservation—for instance, in the case of other priorities (e.g., environmental or social equity) that might trump a preservation agenda.

Kyoto's historic preservation policy illustrates some ways that more data matters. In October 2018, an amendment to Kyoto's ordinance will designate eleven new viewpoint sites for perspective and borrowed landscape zones. There will also be a new scheme for landscape design review to prevent construction projects at viewpoint sites and in short-distance view design conservation zones from disturbing designated landscapes. The city's new urban database, combined with these new procedures, will ensure more thoughtful reviews for development projects as the city expands its inventory of regulated areas.

A second hope is that data may actually inform these processes. This simple (and possibly naive) idea is that if regulators, developers, residents, or any other group are better informed about these historic resources, they can make better preservation choices. Kyoto offers an excellent example of this simple story. To understand the current state of the 47,735 *Kyo-machiya* confirmed in the 2008–2009 survey, the city updated the surveys in 2016–2017. Only 40,146 *Kyo-machiya* remained. An average of 800 of these traditional townhouses (or 1.7 percent) disappeared annually over seven years. The preservation of *Kyo-machiya* then became an urgent priority. The city quickly passed the Ordinance on the Preservation and Succession of *Kyo-machiya*, which will be in full force beginning in May 2018. This ordinance requires residents of *Kyo-machiya* to notify the city government if they are considering changes to their houses. The city can then provide the residents with a range of ways to preserve and utilize their houses in hopes of preservation or restoration.

Still, it is an open question whether better data will produce more knowledgeable stakeholders and whether that knowledge will actually affect any outcomes. It is not clear that agents in these processes are systematically underappreciating a preservation agenda due to a lack of data. More awareness of the inventory of built environment might instead undermine what was seen as "special" about a particular property or resource. While more and better data may improve our awareness, it also does not mean that it will benefit any one particular historic resource (especially at those sites for which excellent data already exists).

It should also be noted that this world of more and better data also involves learning about policy priorities that compete with or oppose a preservation agenda. Even if better data helps policy makers, regulators, or residents better appreciate preservation values, it can also help them realize the importance of affordable housing, jobs, energy efficiency, or some other policy priority. While better data can translate into stronger evidence to justify particular policy choices or help coordinate and connect people engaged in these processes, that can also be true for those with competing agendas. There is nothing special about this "data age" that privileges historic preservation over other interests.

Kyoto has actively considered ways to use data to promote the dissemination of information and mutual communication in ways that help preserve historical landscapes. Specifically, the city government is planning to compile and publish profiles of twenty-seven historical resources, identifying each resource's appearance, value, importance, history, and the culture of surrounding areas. The intent is to foster public discussion of the design review associated with these twenty-seven resources, each of which are under the perspective landscape design review scheme. In addition, the city plans to develop and publish a web-based landscape sharing system in 2018. This GIS system will integrate the profiles of historical resources and the surrounding areas as well as information about the city's policy measures into digital maps available online. This will not only allow the city to transmit information, but will also enable citizens, businesses, shrines, and temples to post and exchange ideas regarding Kyoto's landscapes. These data-sharing efforts are expected to proactively enhance coordination and collaboration between an owner of historical resources and the community.

Similarly, to preserve the *Kyo-machiya*, the city of Kyoto provides financial support for the repair and beautification of these houses. The city has launched the *Kyo-machiya Machi-Dukuri* (town-creating) Crowdfunding Support Scheme, which is the first of its kind in Japan. People who want to repair or utilize a *Kyo-machiya* for their business can collect funds for necessary repairs via the city's crowdfunding program. Eligible projects must meet certain requirements for the *Kyo-machiya*, its repairs, future use, and certain other aspects. The city pays the initial cost, up to ¥1 million. Then, after half of the project's target amount is collected via crowdfunding, the city funds the remainder (up to ¥3 million). In addition, investors receive dividends according to profitability during the crowdfunding term (one to five years, depending on the project). Business operators who repair the *Kyo-machiya* also offer traditional Japanese cultural experiences (like tea ceremonies or flower arrangements), lunch, or hotel rooms as a reward to backers. This *Machi-Dukuri* support scheme is enabled by better data: without it, the government would not have had clear information on the population of *Kyo-machiya*, let alone the threats to their preservation. Establishing this kind of platform may yet catalyze additional preservation and lead to more programs tailored to the needs of historic preservation.

We anticipate that the data age will see its most revolutionary impacts by offering the possibility of designing superior policy instruments that make use of that data. What those instruments might look like is a pressing matter for future research and experimentation, but the crowdfunding scheme provides some hints. At present, discussions and research tend strongly to concentrate on conventional (mostly regulatory) policy tools, leaving "out of the box" thinking an important but underexplored frontier. Better data can unlock policy tools (such as preservation easements) previously underutilized or overlooked.

Frontiers in Data

Given the transformation in available data over the past few decades, there are many opportunities for data to inform future historic preservation policy. Many new datasets and analytic tools are already available and are awaiting integration with historic resources data. This includes data on neighborhood context (e.g., views, aesthetics, traffic), time-series and longitudinal datasets that continue to expand, data on building attributes (e.g., permits, investments, performance), and data on residents' tastes and local histories. Datasets that directly measure our heritage resources, quantitatively and qualitatively, are also growing. These databases can include field surveys, couple together other "big data" sources, and accommodate volunteer data. Data provided by individual volunteers, sometimes inadvertently (for example, in social media posts), can be particularly useful.

In addition, we can still improve how we use data. How we can use data to make better decisions is a question not asked often enough, but it presents important practical challenges that should be faced. Perhaps most interesting is the prospect of improved access to and sharing of data to improve monitoring, coordination, and mobilization. More data transparency and sharing can mobilize support for historic preservation as well as improve our ability to monitor what is happening to the resources we have today.

● MORE DATA AND BETTER DECISIONS

We must be careful to avoid the assumption that more and better data will inevitably lead to better decisions. We have been able to make decisions with imperfect information before, and imperfect information will persist even with better data access. There are still significant gaps in our knowledge, and too little is known about the different effects of our policy efforts on built heritage. Too little is known about how individuals have voluntarily created and maintained historic resources, and we have little sense of how we can promote more of that voluntarism, even as we fixate on policy interventions after assets have already been identified and maintained. We should also be mindful that data is typically very unevenly distributed, and there will be regions, organizations, and resources that more readily benefit from more and better data, while others may be left behind.

Whether data tilts policies more toward preservation or toward other priorities remains an open question. But an ambiguous outcome does not mean that the outcome cannot be influenced by effective action (or inaction). There will be competitions to leverage data in favor of various policy agendas, and urban preservationists would do well to compete vigorously on this front. That includes making sure that municipal data warehouses and portals fully incorporate heritage-related data.

Lastly, we should reiterate that the area in which we see the biggest potential for more and better data to positively impact historic preservation policy is policy that goes beyond the conventional designation and command-and-control regulatory approaches. Better data can make more property rights-oriented and more rewarding approaches (carrots rather than sticks) more viable than ever before. Kyoto's recent experience with coupling crowdfunding with historic building renovations illustrates the promise of this approach. Additional attention to these sorts of alternative policy instruments and how they can leverage new and bigger data is particularly welcome.

Acknowledgments

The authors would like to thank the members of the Scenic Beauty Policy Section, City Planning Bureau of Kyoto City for the useful discussions and provisions of materials and data. This work was supported by the JSPS KAKENHI Grant Number 17K06704 and the Obayashi Foundation.

Social Actors in Urban Heritage Conservation: Do We Know Enough?

Eduardo Rojas

Informing Policy Agendas

Urban heritage conservation is facing challenges that go beyond those foreseen by the 1964 Charter of Venice and the subsequent international agreements and technical documents issued by the United Nations Educational, Scientific, and Cultural Organization (UNESCO) and the International Council on Monuments and Sites (ICOMOS).[1] These documents advocate for the conservation of the sociocultural values—historic, aesthetic, and social—of monuments, historic centers, and neighborhoods. In contrast, current approaches to conservation recognize a wider variety of values associated with intangible and tangible urban heritage—values that include an expanded appreciation of the role that urban heritage plays in the social and economic development of communities, such as the economic value of protecting urban heritage itself.[2]

The UN Sustainable Development Goals emphasize the role of intangible heritage in social cohesion and the role of material heritage in providing communities with a sense of place.[3] Furthermore, UN HABITAT's New Urban Agenda acknowledges the multiple contributions made by inherited buildings, public spaces, and infrastructures to the social and economic development of communities—such as the provision of space to accommodate contemporary activities (economic use value); a physical platform for social events and festivities (social value) and religious practices (spiritual value); or an intergenerational transmission of traditions and cultural uses (educational value).[4]

The recognition of this larger role has occurred in parallel with UNESCO's advocacy for a more integrated approach to the valuation and management of urban heritage, as stated in the "Recommendation on Historic Urban Landscapes" issued in 2011.[5] This approach was further developed in UNESCO's contribution to the 2016 UN HABITAT III Conference.[6]

Under this enlarged conceptualization of the role of heritage in development, urban communities are given the task of deciding what to conserve and with what means. Decision makers seeking to benefit from this expanded approach to the role of urban heritage in communities need to move away from narrowly focused decision-making processes driven by the interests of a limited set of social actors and instead involve all individuals and organizations (community, public, and private) with an interest in urban heritage. Furthermore, achieving a balance between conservation and development—objectives that are neither entirely public nor fully private—requires close public-private cooperation that in turn requires effective institutions and political support lacking in many communities.

To effectively confront these challenges, the conservation of urban heritage must be more closely integrated into the management of cities and not just be an ancillary activity controlled by cultural institutions.[7] This way, a wider variety of social actors could participate in critical decisions like heritage site designations, the adoption of conservation regulations, and the allocation of public resources to conservation. Currently, these activities take place mostly within the confines of cultural institutions and participation is restricted to a small set of interested individuals and institutions. Assimilating conservation into city management will also allow for better coordination of heritage preservation with urban

1
For more information, see UNESCO, "Publications," World Heritage Convention, http://whc.unesco.org/en/publications, and ICOMOS, "Charters and Other Doctrinal Texts," Documentation Centre, https://www.icomos.org/en/charters-and-other-doctrinal-texts.

2
David Throsby, "Heritage Economics: A Conceptual Approach," in The Economics of Uniqueness: Investing in Historic Cores and Cultural Heritage Assets for Sustainable Development, ed. Guido Licciardi and Rana Amirtahmasebi (Washington, DC: World Bank, 2012), 45–73.

3
UN General Assembly, Resolution 70/1, "Transforming Our World: The 2030 Agenda for Sustainable Development," A/RES/70/1 (September 25, 2015), http://www.un.org/ga/search/view_doc.asp?symbol=A/RES/70/1.

4
UN Conference on Housing and Sustainable Development, Resolution 71/256, "New Urban Agenda," A/RES/71/256 (October 20, 2016), Quito, Ecuador, https://habitat3.org/the-new-urban-agenda.

5
UNESCO General Conference, "Recommendation on the Historic Urban Landscape," 36 C/23 Annex (May 27, 2011), Paris, France, http://unesdoc.unesco.org/images/0021/002110/211094e.pdf.

6
UNESCO, Culture Urban Future: Global Report on Culture for Sustainable Urban Development (Paris: UNESCO, 2016), http://unesdoc.unesco.org/images/0024/002462/246291E.pdf.

7
Dennis Rodwell,
"Celebrating
Continuity," *Context*
136, no. 54 (2014).

8
Philippe C. Schmitter,
"Governance"
(paper presented
at the Democratic
and Participatory
Governance: From
Citizens to "Holders"
conference, European
University Institute,
Florence, September
2000), quoted in
Erik Swyngedouw,
"Governance Innovation
and the Citizen:
The Janus Face of
Governance-beyond-
the-State," *Urban
Studies* 42, no. 11
(October 2005): 1995.

9
Stephen Bell, *Economic
Governance and
Institutional Dynamics:
The Market, the
State, and Networks*
(Melbourne: Oxford
University Press, 2002).

rehabilitation programs and for more transparent management of issues that are hotly contested by conservators, like the adaptive reuse of heritage properties and the introduction of new buildings, modern infrastructure, and public spaces in heritage areas. Yet it will be difficult to integrate heritage conservation and city management without more knowledge of the preferences, goals, and commitments of the social actors interested in the conservation and development of urban heritage. In most studies and urban heritage preservation plans these actors are broadly called "stakeholders," but this denomination—and the underlying conceptualization—does not take into account their diversity or the variety of their interests in urban heritage conservation.

The first step in bridging this knowledge gap is to gain more clarity about the diversity of the interested social actors. Today, those interested in historic preservation are no longer limited to the cultural elite, scholars, and philanthropists who supported conservation in the mid-twentieth century. Now, the list has expanded to include long-time residents of historic districts for whom the urban heritage is a symbol of their identity, local property owners seeking profits from their heritage properties, entrepreneurs who trade in heritage areas, and households interested in living in them. Still, there are marked differences in the motivations and roles played by these various social actors. Some are actively engaged in activities to promote the conservation of urban heritage, whereas others directly benefit (or lose) from the process, and yet others are only marginally interested. There are also social actors who finance conservation efforts directly (like government institutions or philanthropists) or indirectly (for instance, property owners in heritage areas who cannot develop their properties to the market's "full and best use" as a result of conservation regulations) and others who are not invested but nevertheless benefit from conservation efforts (like tourists).

Designing and implementing sustainable urban conservation programs requires a strong understanding of the motivations, expectations, and commitments of the social actors involved. It is no longer sufficient to talk generically of "stakeholders." One possible approach—suggested by Philippe Schmitter—is to organize social actors according to the "significance" they assign to their involvement in the conservation process and to analyze their concerns and motivations.[8] Social actors who own property in protected heritage areas are often concerned with economic returns; thus, their priorities and preferences would be quite different from, for instance, those of nonresident scholars concerned with historic value. Different social actors will also be affected differently by the conservation effort. Restrictive regulations commonly promoted by nonresident scholars and conservation practitioners, for example, have a significant impact on the daily life of residents and on the financial standing of property owners.

A better understanding of the types of interested actors has important consequences for the design and implementation of structures of authority and institutions that coordinate and allocate resources for the conservation of urban heritage.[9] Nonresidents or nonowners of property are more inclined to promote regulations and design guidelines aimed at full conservation than residents and property owners who often prefer a more flexible approach. Among residents differences may exist between owners and renters, with the former benefiting from higher property prices after gentrification and the latter group often at risk of losing low cost accommodation. Differences also exist among nonresidents: scholars advocate for the integrated preservation of heritage areas, whereas philanthropists prefer to finance the conservation of high-impact monuments. The correct identification and mapping of these interests is necessary to provide an accurate depiction of their variety, their coincidences, and their differences.

10
Schmitter,
"Governance."

The set of social actors that promote conservation of urban heritage generally include those with knowledge about an area's cultural or social importance: the "knowledge holders." This group is made up of a wide variety of individuals and institutions ranging from academic entities studying the aesthetic value of buildings to individuals holding the collective memory of a community. There are also the individuals residing in the heritage area or community organizations concerned with the loss of the physical structures that support their ways of life. As their daily life is affected by the loss of these assets, they can properly be called "stakeholders," and their interests may range from the conservation of corner stores (where daily encounters among neighbors may take place) to the conservation of public spaces used for community celebrations (religious feasts, carnivals, or charity events). Private philanthropists have been known to promote (and finance) conservation for positive publicity or to fulfill their social responsibility commitments; they represent a form of "special interest holders." Elected officials in national, state, and local governments that promote conservation for their constituencies are what Schmitter calls "status holders" since they represent others—the voters—who, in turn, are "right holders" because they influence the allocation of public resources and the application of conservation regulations with their votes. [10]

Social actors may benefit (or lose out) from heritage conservation. Property owners stand to gain in cases where government conservation programs increase the attractiveness of an urban heritage area; they may also experience economic losses as a result of the restrictions imposed by conservation regulations. They are "shareholders" as their wealth is affected by social conservation preferences. Residents—particularly renters—are affected when heritage conservation results in gentrification and they are displaced by the disappearance of affordable rentals, losing not only their homes but also access to jobs and services. They are one class of "space holders" as their fortunes depend on what happens in their area. Other classes of "space holders" are those who use heritage areas regularly—for example, to access government services, cultural activities, or shopping. Tourists are a particular class of "space holders" who, because of the transient nature of their activity, usually have only a passing interest in the heritage area. Each class has a specific set of concerns that significantly impact that class's attitudes toward conservation efforts.

The involvement of different social actors in financing heritage conservation varies widely. Typically, the most significant source of funds is the government—frequently the central government and, less commonly, a city government—caring for the bequest value of the heritage. However, the many demands on the public budget limit the amounts and reliability of the funds allocated. Philanthropists are another potential source of financing, but their contributions are sporadic, in amounts not always commensurate with the needs of complex urban heritage areas, and are usually focused on projects that respond to their preferences rather than the priorities of the community. In most countries, the involvement of other social actors in financing urban heritage preservation is still limited. Some of the shareholders—for instance, property owners—are known to invest in their own properties, but generally only after government-sponsored rehabilitation programs are implemented and gentrification begins. In the most advanced conservation programs, there is a greater variety of shareholders actively involved, including real estate investors and entrepreneurs interested in the economic use value of the heritage areas.

Monetary contributions are but one of the means by which social actors manifest their support for the conservation of urban heritage. Other ways include involvement in the design of conservation regulations and support for their enforcement. The extent of this support is closely connected with the social actors' objectives, their preferences, and the benefits they get from the process. In turn, this leads social actors to a range of levels of commitment: from full commitment to only sporadic relations to the conservation effort. Social actors can be "core participants" in conservation—fully engaged with a long-term and deep concern for the many dimensions of the task— or "committed participants" who only fully engage when matters of interest to them are at stake. Some are "peripheral participants" holding occasional and narrow interests, and only intermittently contributing a limited amount of resources. In an urban heritage conservation process with wide support, it would be reasonable to expect that stakeholders, shareholders, and right holders would make up the bulk of the core actors and that knowledge holders, special interests, status holders, and space holders may play a committed or a peripheral role.

Another dimension of analysis is the way in which social actors engage others in furthering conservation objectives. Some actors will be willing to cooperate with others by contributing knowledge, financing, and political support while also preparing to work in tandem with other actors, either formally (through institutions) or informally (through voluntary agreements). For instance, shareholders who are strongly invested in a heritage area are more likely to enter into public-private partnership with government entities than are peripheral space holders, like tourists. However, sharing an interest in preservation is not enough to guarantee cooperation; the international experience indicates that private and public social actors are more willing to cooperate when there is a clear and shared vision for the future of an urban heritage area and when government institutions demonstrate a clear commitment to the conservation process.

On the other hand, social actors sometimes enter into conflict. This is the case when shareholders feel that conservation regulations are imposed from above and reduce the development options (or value) of their properties without clear compensation. In these situations, shareholders often oppose the regulations and in certain circumstances prevent their implementation altogether. Some nonresident right holders are also indifferent to conservation either because they are unaware of the sociocultural values of the heritage area or they are unwilling to support the allocation of funds.

These arguments point to the need to develop better methodologies to reliably identify, evaluate, and consult with social actors about what they value and to find ways to harmonize their often-conflicting goals. Current approaches do not clearly distinguish between the different social actors, treating them mostly as a single entity: stakeholders. Further, the available methodologies for stakeholder analysis are frequently limited to capturing citizens' perceptions of urban heritage and documenting their preferences concerning the conservation of different components of that heritage—they do not allow a more in-depth understanding of the motivations, commitments, and potential contributions of each social actor. Valuable as they are, these tools also do not help to identify the drivers that would move social actors to work together—which is a basic necessity for the enforcement of urban heritage conservation and development regulations. A study of urban heritage conservation programs in four Latin American World Heritage sites suggests that sustainability of the conservation effort increases with the involvement of a wider variety and a larger number of social actors interested in a multiplicity of sociocultural and economic values of the heritage. [11]

In short, social actors' interests, enthusiasms, and willingness to cooperate are crucial in urban heritage conservation. The identification of their diversity, concerns, commitment to the task, and capacity to cooperate allows for the adoption of socially supported conservation regulations and guidelines, effective institutional arrangements to foster cooperation among interested actors, and the ability to attract more resources—public and private—and to better allocate resources. This knowledge about social actors will enhance the sustainability of the conservation process and the contribution of urban heritage to the social and economic development of urban communities.

[11] Eduardo Rojas, "Governance in Historic City Core Regeneration Projects," in The Economics of Uniqueness: Investing in Historic Cores and Cultural Heritage Assets for Sustainable Development, ed. Guido Licciardi and Rana Amirtahmasebi (Washington, DC: World Bank, 2012), 143–181.

Connecting Preservation to Urban Policy in a Data-Rich Future

Randall Mason

Informing Policy Agendas

175

We are living in extraordinarily data-rich times, but the implications of this circumstance for historic preservation planning are unclear. Established preservation policies were formed in a quite different era—one of painstakingly researched data, crafted and interpreted by historians and other preservation experts. Now, however, data seems ubiquitous, harvested and analyzed by ever more novel means and by new cadres of (nonpreservation) experts. The gap between preservation designation reports and, for instance, Sidewalk Labs' recent proposals to adapt part of the historic Toronto waterfront into a smart city seems vast. These advances in data science and technology create new opportunities for both decision-making and reform in the governance cultures of historic preservation. Understanding and playing off the history, governance, and professional culture around data can enable preservation policy actors (in *all* sectors) to shape decisions more purposefully, integrate preservation into broader policy frameworks more deeply, measure outcomes more convincingly, and advocate more effectively.

Data richness brings both opportunities and threats to preservation policy. There is promise in asking new questions and answering old questions with greater insight, relentlessly seeking new data and data-analysis tools that shed light on how preservation works in society or that simply allow us to be better informed. There is also the risk that more data will devalue or substitute for the traditional politics, design, and craft of preservation expertise—automating what we don't want to automate. The threat this presents to self-identified preservationists shouldn't be underestimated: proposals that substitute algorithms for human decisions are already out there (namely, the Sidewalk Toronto proposal).

So, while data *quantity* is way up, it's not the answer to every question of policy research and decision-making. The *quality* of data and access to it are never guaranteed, and we have to be vigilant in choosing the right kinds of data to inform the very different sorts of analyses and decisions relevant to historic preservation. At least three distinct and overlapping types of data (produced variously by humanities, social science, and geographic/spatial analysis professionals) are discernible and relevant in relation to different modes of preservation analysis and decision-making:

- More and better visual, graphic, and narrative data for valuing and interpreting historic places and buildings: the increasing availability of photographs, museum collections, full-text historical documents, and genealogical collections is nothing less than a data revolution already happening, and flourishing, in the digital humanities.
- More cogent data and analysis of social behaviors and conditions associated with historic preservation and historic buildings and places: this remains a research frontier of great potential, as market, social media, psychological, and other behavioral data can offer insight on how and why individuals and institutions make decisions affecting historic preservation.
- Drawing from both of the streams just noted, geographic data on historic built environments and their uses/values in GIS-based inventories and analytical pathways can better connect

preservation to planning, development, and other broader policy-making processes at the municipal level (a revolution already in the works).

Issues with data are rooted in issues with research (what we *do* with data) and the varied uses of research for decision-making and governance (the emphases here), as well as for knowledge creation and evaluation. The greatest promises and difficulties of data-richness revolve around *integrating* data-driven analyses into larger preservation policies and decision-making processes. The big question, in other words, is: How will political and professional processes of governance *use* new supplies of data and new modes of analysis?

● CULTURES OF POLICY

With new technologies for creating and capturing data, for analyzing and representing it, and for extending the breadth and depth of phenomena on which we can harvest data, the potential effects on decision-making are dizzying. In historic preservation, where many decisions are based on idiosyncratic, expert appraisal of humanistic or visual data, the introduction of quantified, mapped data documenting historic fabric—or mapped data illuminating the effects of preservation decisions (on social behavior, public health, economic factors, environmental performance, and so on)—is potentially revelatory. Could this newly available data, for instance, enable a shift from rules-based preservation regulation to regulation based on outcomes that are monitored by data from new sources?

To illuminate the opportunities (and risks) of investing in more data creation, analysis, and management, one needs to acknowledge three broad framing issues, common to all arenas of urban and environmental policy but particularly vexing for historic preservation policy:

- Policy is underpinned by *governance*, defined here as a collection of institutions, actors, laws, policies, political traditions/habits, and resource stocks and flows (money, people, power, visibility), as well as how these elements interact as a system of realizing public goods. Governance spans the public and private sectors, in addition to NGOs. In the United States, systems of governance have changed significantly over the past generation as a result of pressures like privatization and grassroots empowerment.
- Governance, in turn, relies on *decision-making* and the behavior of decision makers. Whereas these processes and people have traditionally been treated as black boxes, we need to know more about how different kinds of data (quantitative, qualitative, visual, crowd sourced, expert created, etc.) result in different decisions in empirical situations.
- The effectiveness of urban and environmental policies is strongly shaped by how well policies are *integrated* across departments and disciplines (economic and community development, public

177

health, education, and more). In other words, isolating preservation (like isolating any other issue) weakens our ability to understand effects across whole urban systems (social and environmental) and even hampers the effectiveness of preservation in the first place.

So, in order to take advantage of the data revolutions still to come, preservation policy institutions and actors need to acknowledge the structures and habits underpinning governance, to examine more closely and empirically the factors shaping corporate and individual decisions, and to better integrate with other types of policy (especially "urban" policy). The *barriers* to policy integration within governance structures also have to be addressed.

At the risk of overgeneralizing, urban and land use policy in the United States tends to be bottom heavy (that is, locally oriented) and weakly guided from the top (at the federal level). This is particularly true with regard to land use regulation; federal resources are usually aimed at creating incentives for local governments through competitive funding schemes or establishing best-practice standards and guidance. There is a mixed legacy of federal intervention involvement in municipal-level decisions—mostly as a result of the federal government's lack of intervention. There are few instances of the federal government incentivizing or integrating resource programs; for example, rehabilitation and low-income tax credits remain separate, though numerous individual projects try to combine them. Regulation of land, buildings, and development in the United States tends toward the minimal; the market is presumed to be the best means of allocating goods and opportunities, putting environmental and public goods always on the defensive. Urban policies usually are changed only incrementally. Given the dominance of interest-group politics, competition between different policy outcomes is maximized, and there is little incentive to work across policy areas, which would involve potential trade-offs.

More specific to historic preservation: at the municipal level, preservation can be a quite powerful but inconsistently applied land use policy, though only with regard to the very limited areas mapped as locally "significant" and isolated from its effects vis-à-vis other arenas of urban policy. The isolation of preservation means that interest groups often take advantage of preservation to advance their own goals, like discouraging in-migration, new construction, and increased density.

The local-federal dynamics outlined here—as well as the absence of meaningful regional governance in the United States—have evolved over many decades. The pattern of strong local power and weak federal power over land and buildings satisfies the private-property-rights, "home rule" culture of American politics, and competitive interest-group politics, but it hampers governance or policy-making aimed at citywide, regional, or national resources (such as ecosystems, watersheds, etc.). Cities, for example, are too often treated as nothing more than a collection of neighborhoods or economic outputs.

This geography of American governance has been further entrenched by vitriolic debates over the reach of federal governance and pressures

1
Bruce Katz and Jeremy Nowak, *The New Localism: How Cities Can Thrive in the Age of Populism* (Washington, DC: Brookings Institution Press, 2017).

2
Stephen Goldsmith and Neil Kleiman, *A New City O/S: The Power of Open Collaboration and Distributed Governance* (Washington, DC: Brookings Institution Press, 2017).

3
Municipal preservation policies are not federally mandated, though financial incentives and reference documents (particularly the Secretary of the Interior's Standards and Guidelines and the National Register of Historic Places criteria for listing) have created some consistency. The detailed character and implementation of municipal preservation policies, though, can vary significantly from place to place.

around the privatization of public functions and assets. In the current political/policy climate, the federal government promises only further retreat, extending neoliberal tendencies and incidentally making way for new assertions of municipal power. Realizing the opportunity this leaves for asserting city-scale governance, some recent research highlights the need to integrate across policy silos within municipalities [1] and embrace "distributed" (decentralized and automated) governance fueled by digital technology and data richness in whichever sectors data becomes available. [2]

● CULTURE OF PRESERVATION

Against these general outlines of urban policy (defined broadly to encompass preservation policy), several factors specifically shape historic preservation as an arena of policy. Acknowledging the specific structure, culture, and evolution of the historic preservation field in the United States is crucial for understanding whether and how innovations in data and data analysis are embraced.

Historic preservation is a field, not a discipline; it applies the methods, analytics, insights, and the like of various disciplines to the core set of issues that define the field. Those issues, deeply embedded in modern culture, revolve around the construction of usable pasts through acts of collecting, curating, protecting, storytelling, and so on that have buildings, landscapes, and sites as their object. Aspects of preservation centering around management of land and property bring the field squarely into the realm of policy. Preservation is also deeply aligned with the modern state, though governance arrangements specific to preservation needs take many forms, and the philanthropic/NGO sector has long played a (if not *the*) leading role. Indeed, the leaders and agents driving preservation governance are drawn equally from NGOs and the public sector; the relationships between advocates and public officials, characterized by both collaboration and tension, dominate the governance of preservation. In an increasingly neoliberal environment, this creates opportunities for private owners and firms to "capture" governance functions related to heritage sites.

As a function of the state, historic preservation has been inscribed in law as a public good and has thus been embraced as one among many rationales for creating regulations, incentives, and other policies to shape land use, development, urban form, and environmental quality in the broadest sense. Preservation law and policy's most vital achievement in the United States has been creating a space for culture as a public good. The National Historic Preservation Act of 1966 reinforced a hierarchical "ecosystem" of national and state policy to support and encourage local governments. The hard-won legal standing of historic preservation has made preservation a stand-alone policy issue in most urban jurisdictions. [3]

Preservation tends to be isolated from other forms of urban policy by the progrowth, prodevelopment cultures of governance in US cities. Partly this status was fought for by preservationists: the self-righteous, proselytizing strain of preservationist discourse, concerned with high culture, has successfully narrowed the audience for preservation as well as isolated it from other valid urban policy concerns/constituencies. One result has been creation of separate preservation agencies within many city governments.

4
"UNESCO Recommendation on the Historic Urban Landscape," 2011, https://whc.unesco.org/en/hul.

Integrating policy means not merely breaching the metaphoric preservation silo vis-à-vis other planning, environmental, and cultural fields. I see it as consisting of "vertical" integration (across scales of governance, from grassroots organizing to municipalities to state, regional, and national governments) as well as "horizontal" integration (across departments/functions within and between scales of governance). Practically, one might regard the big issue of integrating preservation with other policies as a question of balancing regulations and incentives in a regional real-estate/development market. While this discussion is critical, it too often devolves to zero-sum decisions about preservation or development of discrete sites.

Historic preservation is not only an end in itself (protecting the cultural significance reflected in buildings and sites) but also a means to other ends (like affordable housing, local retail and job creation, walkable neighborhoods, greater participation in arts and culture, public health, and more). This is where data innovation has played a role in revealing opportunities and new research agendas; the effectiveness of rehabilitation tax credits, affordable housing investments, and the like can be analyzed only by relating data on preservation to data on *other* social conditions and outcomes. The Preservation Green Lab's mapping work, for example, has been a signal contribution to realizing the data requirements and analytic pathways necessary to create policy-focused research spanning both preservation and urban planning.

The need for integrating preservation policy with other urban policy is recognized not only in preservation circles but in the international-development and development-banking communities as well. The adoption of UNESCO's Historic Urban Landscape Recommendation in 2011, for instance, was an endorsement of integrating historic preservation into existing urban planning and development decision processes worldwide.[4] It was published as a best-practice model after a lengthy international process of consultation and is now being piloted informally in various cities.

Why is data innovation so important in fighting historic preservation's isolation as a social project of elites? If historic preservation is recognized to be a means to several policy ends (and not just an end in itself), it stands to gain much greater support and feed an ideal of engaged preservation.

● ADDRESSING FRAGMENTED GOVERNANCE
WITH NEW DATA ANALYSIS TECHNIQUES

Novel uses of data and new data analysis techniques will have important ramifications for preservation policy and its integration with urban policy. GIS-enabled spatial analysis, for example, promises to ease collaboration by acting as a kind of analytical lingua franca across disciplines and agencies. But in tandem with that promise, we must ask the interesting question, what kinds of data (quantitative or qualitative)

5
Preservation Green
Lab, *Older, Smaller,*
Better: Measuring
How the Character of
Buildings and Blocks
Influences Urban
Vitality (Washington,
DC: National Trust for
Historic Preservation,
2016).

influence the individual preferences of decision makers in preservation policy and governance?

Spatial Data as Commons

Fragmentation of ownership, governance, and responsibility for the public built environment means that no one agency actually manages "the historic built environment." The scope of the fragmentation problem is revealed by a quick thought experiment: in a five-minute walk through your neighborhood, how many policy jurisdictions of how many municipal agencies do you enter? Half a dozen? In my imaginary neighborhood walk, the list includes streets, parks, planning and zoning, building codes, parking, business licenses, and historic buildings—not to mention police, fire, water, and sewer. Data to support the management of each fraction was generated and kept separately until quite recent advances in GIS and spatial databases.

Mapping diverse data in GIS environments has been established as the preeminent tool for linking big data and urban policy (including historic preservation policy). It quickly enables analysis and visualization of preservation and other data about the built environment, analyses to explore how different data interact, and even scenarios to explore how policy change in one aspect of the system might affect others (for instance, how older and mixed building stock tends to support more diverse social life by several measures).[5]

If partnerships can be formed around a "public realm of data" (as opposed to realms owned by different owners and managed by different city agencies), there might be an opportunity for preservation to find a stronger purchase on its public-good arguments. Could "smart city"-generated data create a new commons for data? Perhaps. Conceptually, big data has the capacity to address this fragmentation by drawing more holistic connections between the fragmented parts of the built environment, as managed and as experienced. Smart-city initiatives that generate much more data about more social and environmental phenomena should be regarded both as potential solutions and as potential threats to the notion of the public realm as a commons: solutions in the sense that rich, real-time data about the built environment and our uses of it could enable integrated, seamless, efficient management; threats in light of the reality that whoever generates, owns, and controls this data wields undue power over the commons.

Governing Spatial Data

The bureaucratic architecture of municipal historic preservation agencies is one factor in preservation's integration/isolation, though it is not necessarily decisive. Preservation is sometimes the sole function of an independent agency (in New York City, for instance) and other times is organized as a more or less discrete function within a planning agency (for instance, in San Francisco). In Philadelphia, the Historical Commission was for a long time independent but was recently folded into a new Department of Planning and Development. The question of which structure is more effective depends on the local political culture and on qualities of governance beyond the formal arrangement of government offices.

Practically, bureaucratic structure affects how data is shared. The legibility and openness of GIS-enabled data across departments within a municipal government and with external/NGO partners and the public is a potentially powerful agent for integrating political decisions and enabling analysis across silos. The ease of sharing and analyzing data in a common GIS environment is also a powerful boon to collaborating across the usual silos. An open data policy, inventory standards, and a shared GIS environment should be regarded as necessities, not just conveniences.

At the University of Pennsylvania, we've worked with several City of Philadelphia agencies to improve the quality and shareability of data important to preservation policy and likewise helpful for other policy applications (including tax assessment and urban design/zoning). Our character-study projects estimate building age (data that exists but is notoriously poor in quality) by using historical mapping and oblique aerial photography to quickly gauge building type and age for wide swaths of the city. Commissioned by the Office of Property Assessment, the analysis was shared with the Historical Commission and the Planning Commission. The availability of a digitized, geocoded historical map series, high-resolution aerial photography for the entire city, and a robust, publicly shared GIS framework made the character-study surveys a useful interim alternative to a painstaking parcel-by-parcel survey of the entire city. Looking forward, we and others are experimenting with machine-learning tools to automate the analysis of oblique aerial photos, which would yield results useful for several policy applications even more quickly.

Behavioral Data: Stories or Numbers

A second kind of fragmentation is also at play in preservation decision-making: not in the realm of spatial analysis and technical innovation but rather in the realm of individual preferences and decision-making when it comes to weighing the economic and cultural values of heritage places.

The availability of data about decisions, performance, use, and meaning of the historic built environment is vexed by the divide between cultural and economic modes of valuation, producing incommensurable tranches of qualitative data that is difficult to analyze at scale and quantitative data that poorly captures the range of valued qualities in heritage environments. Market data is too poor a proxy on which to base decisions about heritage values, and qualitative data is too resistant to quantification to plug in to standard policy-evaluation frameworks.[6]

There is a general assumption that decision makers (leaders in government and firms) base their decisions on quantitative data. If it can be quantified, it counts. However, some anecdotal evidence exists for the alternative: that decision makers are swayed by qualitative results (a good story, compelling images, or sharp graphics). In the absence of research about the decision-making process, one must guess about the effectiveness of quantitative versus qualitative data. It is understood that different stakeholders have different views—that there can be different, valid stories about the same place. Values-based preservation theory and the theory of multiple intelligences help explain how the design of historic

6 Randall Mason, ed., *Economics and Heritage Conservation* (Los Angeles: Getty Conservation Institute, 1999); Randall Mason, "Beware and Be Interested: Joining Economic Valuation and Heritage Conservation," *International Journal of Heritage Studies* 14, no. 4 (July 2008): 303–318.

7
Molly Sauter, "Google's Guinea-Pig City," *The Atlantic*, February 13, 2018, https://www.theatlantic.com/technology/archive/2018/02/googles-guinea-pig-city/552932.

8
Tim Adams, "Interview: Jaron Lanier: 'The Solution Is to Double Down on Being Human,'" *Guardian*, November 12, 2017.

places matters to how they are experienced. It has also been demonstrated that there are different, incommensurable valuation techniques that produce different kinds of assessments (qualitative and quantitative)—but how these assessments and data are *received* by decision makers has not been demonstrated.

Behavioral research on what people and institutions (especially decision makers) value about historic places and their functions in society—and how they value it—would shine light on what remains a black box. The epistemological makeup of the kinds of data we seek is a very important matter for those of us most engaged with governance and politics around decisions. To illuminate this subject, a pair of research efforts underway by my research team at the University of Pennsylvania seeks to understand details of historic preservation decision-making by collecting data directly from decision makers. We are researching decision-making using conjoint analysis, contingent valuation, and other stated-preference techniques; at the same time, we are doing qualitative interviews of decision makers about the relative importance of qualitative and quantitative findings in reaching decisions about preservation policies and preservation-development controversies.

● LOOMING ISSUES OF DATA AND POWER

The policy and preservation worlds will surely become more data rich. Governance will remain the primary system for decision-making, and so we must understand the culture and evolution of historic preservation and urban policy more broadly in order to understand how more and better data might help navigate these tricky waters. More data and new data do not erase the need to map and respect the idiosyncratic and political realities of governance.

Burgeoning data availability and new modes of analysis raise practical questions and demand a flexible methodology. How our data-rich future might enable greater integration with other fields should remain a critical focus of research. But conceptual and political contexts cannot be ignored.

New data opportunities also raise issues of power and ownership, comprising yet another front of research, practice, and advocacy. Foregrounding the effects of data on power is an issue of governance that is beyond the scope of this essay, but it looms over preservation just as it does in other sectors. Again, the reporting on Sidewalk Toronto provides a glimpse of how this issue is already unfolding.[7] And there are plenty of skeptics—most floridly, writer and futurist Jaron Lanier, who noted we have the means to "create algorithmic systems that capture knowledge, that exercise wisdom. I thought that was a huge trap—that it would turn into this house of mirrors that could be manipulated by whoever was the biggest asshole."[8] Not a good thing for the commons. For historic preservation, as for other urban, environmental, and design fields, the promises of a data-rich future are likewise shadowed by questions of who will own, control, and use new data and analyses for private and partial ends—rather than for the public good.

 Appendices

As part of the Urban Heritage and Data in the 21st Century symposium, contributors to this volume brainstormed priority actions for reinforcing the data-policy relationship in the field of preservation. The ideas generated do not constitute a consensus in the field, nor do they represent a formal set of recommendations. Rather, these recommendations reflect the creative thinking of those gathered around the table. In this sense, they serve as an impromptu agenda for action and an effort to promote innovation and connections within and beyond the field.

Build Trust Through Data

Data is a tool through which we seek truth. But data can be used in various ways—for one, it can underpin various truths that often change over time as cities and their communities evolve. For the preservation enterprise to capitalize effectively on the new data landscape, it must use data to build trust among those who engage in or are affected by preservation decision-making.

Be Conscious of Power

Everyone learns or understands data differently; everyone has different power to use data. Preservationists need to be conscious of these differences as they move across varying scales of engagement and decision-making, from data collection to outcomes research and from individual citizens to government agencies.

Take Risks

Preservation inherently recognizes the long arc of history, and by protecting existing elements of the built environment, it fundamentally promotes a "look before you leap" approach. However, the new data horizon is evolving rapidly, and the field of preservation must adopt a "take risks" attitude in order to capitalize on opportunities and overcome barriers.

Educate for Data Fluency

The bulk of urban-scale, community data that can be used to better understand and direct preservation policy is not produced or analyzed by preservationists. Building data fluency within the heritage field will enhance our capacities to learn from and to better guide policy decision-making.

Improve Data Standards and Data Sharing

Much can be done to improve data standards for preservation: for example, publishing metadata, clearly identifying data sources and contexts, publishing data with research, and enhancing the visualization of data in research. Fostering a culture of working in the open will help develop a community that shares more.

Build Networks

Data is a new area of practice and research within preservation; it is important to establish connections among those working in this area and to build networks that can support individual and institutional collaboration.

Promote Data Access and Transparency

More and more municipalities are implementing open data laws, but access and usability vary widely. Preservationists should work toward the creation of open data portals or platforms, data dashboards, web interfaces, resource centers, and other resources that enhance access to and transparency of preservation-related data for many types of users—from neighborhood residents to researchers.

Cultivate Allies

Preservationists can forge stronger connections between data creation/collection and research by cultivating "middlemen": tech and heritage practitioner-translators who can help bridge the gaps among communities, government bureaucrats, and scholars. Allies can be cultivated through partnerships beyond the usual built-environment professions (planners, architects, etc.) to leverage agency.

Co-Create Data

Preservationists are witnessing an increase in opportunities to promote citizen-created and/or co-produced data for heritage. Through hackathons, crowdsourcing, gamifying, preservation data camps, and so on, the field can forge a digital toolbox and new avenues of data collection and generation that also raise awareness of preservation.

Think Beyond the Building

A better understanding of the social-spatial relationships that preservation engenders is one of the most exciting prospects of the new data landscape. This understanding compels preservationists to think beyond the building and ask different kinds of questions, from why people decide to preserve or not, to how preservation impacts neighborhood change, to who benefits from preservation.

Assess Outcomes

Data has the potential to support a new era in preservation through the evaluation of what has effectively been a half century of policy implementation. By creating evidence-based feedback loops that show the strengths and weaknesses of preservation policies, the field can establish indicators of success to inform sustainable and community-responsive policy changes.

Be Agents of Change

While evidence-based feedback is a vital tool of learning, it does not, in and of itself, create change. Research must still be translated to guide the evolution of the preservation field effectively. The "last mile" connection to policy can happen only with the support of intermediaries—in the public, private, and not-for-profit sectors, as well as in academia—who are also working toward change.

Data and Evaluative Criteria in Historic Preservation: A Literature Review and Annotated Bibliography

Jenna Dublin
Shreya Ghoshal
Erica Avrami

Historic preservation is an urban practice increasingly engaged with policies for housing, land use, and equitable neighborhood change.[1] As a discipline concerned with historical and social issues embodied in the materiality of cities—from the scale of brownstone stoops to the formal and spatial qualities of older neighborhoods to the physical city as a holistic entity—historic preservation has significant roles to play in contemporary social equity and urban sustainability. Preservationists' tools of surveying, landmarking, historic district zoning, and transfer of development rights, among others, are some of the many forces physically transforming cities. Breaking from the modernist tradition of preservation as a generalized reaction against the destruction of older neighborhoods, at the turn of the twenty-first century preservationists returned to the Progressive Era roots of urban preservation. Since then, preservationists have positioned themselves as change agents in urban policy with an eye toward community building.[2] Today, there are many opportunities to integrate historic preservation into long-range, future-oriented planning and urban policy-making.[3] And with emergent technologies, big data, and powerful statistical analysis tools, the discipline is poised to do so.

There is a rich body of literature that demonstrates the positive impacts of historic designation on urban economic and community development, especially on property value change.[4] Scholars have also challenged the advocacy-oriented approach of this research, arguing that urban historic preservation may have socially detrimental effects. Historic preservationists' tools may contribute to gentrification, inequity in access to the benefits of historic tax credits, and race and class segregation under the "banner of historical authenticity."[5] Contemporary land use and housing scholarship has gone a step further by empirically testing the relationships between historic district designation and a broad variety of social and neighborhood indicators. Through the use of counterfactuals—such as comparisons with nondesignated adjacent neighborhood areas—researchers have been able to approximate the differences between what has occurred in designated neighborhoods over time and what might have happened if the neighborhood were never made a historic district.[6]

Quantifying the economic and neighborhood-level impacts of historic preservation is a relatively new research avenue.[7] Traditionally, historic preservation scholarship has evaluated the aesthetic, spiritual, social, historical, and symbolic values of historic places.[8] Thus, a comprehensive agenda for studying the relationships between historic preservation and community must encompass both quantitative numerical data and qualitative data that examines individuals' experiences to

1
Randall Mason, *The Once and Future New York: Historic Preservation and the Modern City* (Minneapolis: University of Minnesota Press, 2009), 240.

2
Mason, *Once and Future New York*, 246; Stephanie Ryberg-Webster and Kelly L. Kinahan, "Historic Preservation and Urban Revitalization in the Twenty-First Century," *Journal of Planning Literature* 29, no. 2 (May 2014): 122.

3
William Baer, "When Old Buildings Ripen for Historic Preservation: A Predictive Approach to Planning," *Journal of the American Planning Association* 61, no. 1 (Winter 1995).

4
Donovan Rypkema, *The Economics of Rehabilitation* (Washington, DC: National Trust for Historic Preservation, 1991); David Listokin, Barbara Listokin, and Michael Lahr, "The Contributions of Historic Preservation to Housing and Economic Development," *Housing Policy Debate* 9, no. 3 (May 1998): 431–478; Paul K. Asabere, Forrest E. Huffman, and Seyed Mehdian, "The Adverse Impacts of Local Historic District Designation: The Case of Small Apartment Buildings in Philadelphia," *Journal of Real Estate Finance and Economics* 8, no. 3 (May 1994): 225–234; N. Edward Coulson and Robin M. Leichenko, "The Internal and External Impact of Historical Designation on Property Values," *Journal of Real Estate Finance and Economics* 23, no. 1 (July 2001): 113–124; N. Edward Coulson and Michael L. Lahr, "Gracing the Land of Elvis and Beale Street: Historic Designation and Property Values in Memphis," *Real Estate Economics* 33, no. 3 (Fall 2005): 487–507.

5
Neil Smith, "Housing Policy Debate Comment on David Listokin, Barbara Listokin, and Michael Lahr's 'The Contributions of Historic Preservation to Housing and Economic Development': Historic Preservation in a Neoliberal Age," *Housing Policy Debate* 9, no. 3 (1998): 479–485; Robert Weyeneth, "Ancestral Architecture: the Early Preservation Movement in Charleston," in *Giving Preservation a History: Histories of Historic Preservation in the United States*, eds., Max Page and Randall Mason (New York: Routledge, 2004), 257–281.

6
Vicki Been, Ingrid Gould Ellen, Michael Gedal, Edward Glaeser, and Brian J. McCabe, "Preserving History or Restricting Development? The Heterogeneous Effects of Historic Districts on Local Housing Markets in New York City," *Journal of Urban Economics* 92 (March 2016): 16–30; Ingrid Gould Ellen, Brian McCabe, and Eric Stern, *Fifty Years of Historic Preservation in New York City* (New York: New York University Furman Center, 2016); Brian J. McCabe and Ingrid Gould Ellen, "Does Preservation Accelerate Neighborhood Change? Examining the Impact of Historic Preservation in New York City," *Journal of the American Planning Association* 82, no. 2 (Spring 2016): 134–146; Stephanie Ryberg-Webster and Kelly L. Kinahan, "Historic Preservation in Declining City Neighbourhoods: Analysing Rehabilitation Tax Credit Investments in Six US Cities," *Urban Studies* 54, no. 7 (May 2017): 1673–1691.

7
Ryberg-Webster and Kinahan, "Historic Preservation and Urban Revitalization," 123.

answer "why" and "how" questions. Some studies are innovative in their application of social science methodologies to historic preservation.[9] But there are opportunities to develop research approaches that complement the quantitative "by how much" questions with qualitative methods that examine community- and people-oriented interests in historic preservation, civic engagement, and bureaucratic decision-making, among other social processes.

Practitioners and scholars of historic preservation have also identified specific limitations to establishing new, community-oriented evaluation criteria, particularly for city agencies. Urban-oriented research tends to focus on how designation benefits the residents or owners of historically designated properties, leaving out how it can effect a wider public good. Furthermore, commonly available municipal data on the aged built environment, such as property values, tends to support reactionary evaluations of historic preservation's social contributions only after designation decisions have been made. The preservationists' toolbox should have the capacity to analyze potential future effects of present-day decisions. There is also an opportunity to better understand just what the characteristics of older urban neighborhoods contribute to communities. In other words, by applying social science methods to Jane Jacobs's neighborhood dictums, researchers may determine correlative relationships between the physical and social dimensions of older urban neighborhoods.

These limitations also open up a series of questions: If urban policy codifies historic preservation as beneficial to economic growth and social well-being, what are better ways to assess how all residents benefit from the city's historic places? What contributions do aged places make on their own, without historic preservation planning or designation, to our shared social and environmental needs? What data should we be collecting to operationalize, track, and evaluate these contributions? Finally, heritage decision-making isn't solely attributable to historical significance, so how can we identify informal determinants that shape decision-making—such as the social, economic, and spatial factors of places?

The purpose of this review is to examine contemporary scholarship that empirically evaluates historic preservation's contributions to a variety of human and environmental needs. Organized around themes connecting historic preservation to human experiences, the discussion will highlight the data and methodological approaches developed to answer these questions.

The first theme "Sense of Community Purpose and Place Distinctiveness" is concerned with how the features of older neighborhoods contribute to residents' sense of attachment to places and the potential benefits of this attachment, such as increasing residents' levels of engagement in urban politics. The second theme, "Developing Common Agendas," will discuss contemporary research studies that evaluate the social, economic, and environmental impacts of aged places. Particularly, the research demonstrates often unaccounted for relationships between historic places and desirable community outcomes. These types of empirical studies in historic preservation can help us to better understand just what historic preservation policy may be capable of in terms of achieving equity, justice, and sustainability. Finally, the theme of "Patterns in Decision Making"

189

will discuss the literature that uncovers the often-overlooked factors beyond historic criteria that influence historic designation decisions.

● SENSE OF COMMUNITY AND PLACE DISTINCTIVENESS

Certain features of older neighborhoods can contribute to beneficial social processes, such as residents' quality of life and sense of civic responsibility.

Arts and Cultural Experiences

Economic development discourse identifies the arts and cultural venues as assets that contribute to neighborhood uniqueness and, by extension, that influence communities' ability to attract new residents and businesses. [10] Similarly, cultural studies scholars demonstrate the value of local arts and culture as assets by integrating the spatially oriented theories of geographic clustering. There is a long history of US cities growing outward, away from the historic mixed-use downtown areas, which are characterized by the long-term clustering of theaters, arts venues, and main street small businesses. However, these areas accumulate significant social and economic capital. [11] For example, Mark J. Stern and Susan C. Seifert interpret Philadelphia's downtown Old City neighborhood as a case of an unplanned cultural cluster that is now a critical hub of urban activity in the city. [12]

Data-driven arts and culture studies collect survey data and utilize publicly available demographic, occupation, and housing data. Carl Grodach and Anastasia Loukaitou-Sideris take an institutional approach to the significance of arts and culture as local assets and conduct a comprehensive survey of the municipal agencies leading this trend across the United States. The study finds that, first, public agencies prefer cultural development strategies that leverage existing and centrally located arts and culture venues. Second, these urban areas contribute to residents' quality of life by supporting social and economic public goods. [13]

The Stern and Seifert study of Philadelphia utilizes 2001–2006 US Census American Community Survey microdata and the explanatory power of multivariate regression to test for causal relationships between the presence of cultural clusters and neighborhood socioeconomic conditions. The authors find a significant relationship between the presence of clustered cultural assets and positive housing market conditions. Furthermore, neighborhoods of Philadelphia with modest cultural clusters are associated with higher levels of local and regional civic engagement, increases in population, and decreases in poverty with "little evidence of displacement." [14]

Cultural Mapping

Cultural mapping is a method of spatial inquiry that identifies, documents, and analyzes intangible historical resources, thereby complicating historic preservation's bias toward buildings and monuments as arbiters of the past. Community members act as the main informants for cultural mapping studies. Researchers interview community members

8
Erica Avrami, Randall Mason, and Marta de la Torre, *Values and Heritage Conservation: Research Report* (Los Angeles: The Getty Conservation Institute, 2000); Marta de la Torre, ed., *Assessing the Values of Cultural Heritage: Research Report* (Los Angeles: The Getty Conservation Institute, 2002); Randall Mason, *Economics of Historic Preservation: A Guide and Review of the Literature* (Washington, DC: Brookings Institution, Metropolitan Policy Program, 2005); David Throsby, *Economics and Culture* (Cambridge, UK: Cambridge University Press, 2001).

9
Been et al., "Preserving History or Restricting Development?"; Ellen et al., *Fifty Years of Historic Preservation*; McCabe and Ellen, "Does Preservation Accelerate Neighborhood Change?"

10
James Carr and Lisa Servon, "Vernacular Culture and Urban Economic Develop- ment: Thinking Outside the (Big) Box," *Journal of the American Planning Association* 75, no. 1 (January 2009): 28–40.

11
Ryberg-Webster and Kinahan, "Historic Preservation and Urban Revitalization," 128.

12
Mark J. Stern and Susan C. Seifert, "Cultural Clusters: The Implications of Cultural Assets Agglomeration for Neighborhood Revitalization," *Journal of Planning Education and Research* 29, no. 3 (March 2010): 263.

13
Carl Grodach and Anastasia Loukaitou- Sideris, "Cultural Development Strategies and Urban Revitalization: A Survey of US Cities," *International Journal of Cultural Policy* 13, no. 4 (November 2007): 365.

14
Stern and Seifert,
"Cultural Clusters," 262.

15
Raquel Freitas,
"Cultural Mapping as a
Development Tool," City,
Culture, and Society
7, no. 1 (March 2016):
9–16.

16
Nancy Duxbury, W.
F. Garrett-Petts, and
David MacLennan, eds.,
Cultural Mapping as
Cultural Inquiry (New
York: Routledge, 2015).

17
Alys Longsley and
Nancy Duxbury,
"Introduction: Mapping
Cultural Intangibles,"
City, Culture, and
Society 7, no. 1 (March
2016): 1–7.

18
Cited in Duxbury,
Garrett-Petts, and
MacLennan, Cultural
Mapping as Cultural
Inquiry, 7.

19
Guy Debord, ed.,
Internationale
Situationniste 1 (June
1958).

20
Darko Radović,
"Measuring the
Non-Measurable: On
Mapping Subjectivities
in Urban Research,"
City, Culture, and
Society 7, no. 1 (March
2016): 17–24.

21
Kuah Li Feng and
Mahani Musa,
"Initiating An Oral
History Project In A
Multicultural UNESCO
World Heritage Site Of
George Town, Penang,
Malaysia: Challenges
And Outcomes," Kajian
Malaysia 34, no. 2,
(2016): 123–143.

about their everyday practices—religious, adaptive, and communicative, with reference to history and otherwise—that are deeply embedded in place. Although it has been stated that the main objective of cultural mapping is to turn intangible cultural practices into more standardized indicators for preservation planning, the applications of cultural mapping vary. 15 In terms of people-centered interests, the collected information can substantiate the many contributions of a place beyond its economic valuation, such as attachment to places and types of holistic, local knowledge. Cultural mapping is also an approach that intentionally collects the views of marginalized social groups whose histories were never or are no longer represented by the built environment. Perhaps the greatest appeal of cultural mapping for this literature review is twofold: the way it incorporates both quantitative and qualitative data, and its multidisciplinary uses across urban design, art and culture, geography, sociology, architecture, cultural policy, and historic preservation.

The anthology *Cultural Mapping as Cultural Inquiry* identifies five main trajectories, or applications, of cultural mapping data: community empowerment and counter-mapping, cultural policy, municipal governance, mapping as artistic practice, and mapping as academic inquiry. 16 Cultural mapping has also been demonstrated to be an effective tool for supporting resident participation in public planning and decision-making. 17 For example, in a 1997 UNESCO report for international policy, authors Tony Bennett and Colin Mercer identify cultural mapping as a catalyst for more inclusive approaches to cultural heritage planning. 18 In this case, university academics and residents collaborated to bridge the "town and gown" divide of municipal governance. Bennett and Mercer ask informants questions like, "What sites or monuments in the landscape hold the most meaning to the community as a whole? How do people interact with cultural heritage and how does the community create meaning at these places?" Responses to questions such as these became standardized indicators of community values.

Many cultural mapping projects use the *dérive* (literally, "drifting") method of experience mapping to extract memories tied to landscapes. Theorist Guy Debord states that a drifting, unplanned journey can force people to drop their everyday associations with sites and to instead develop deeper, more meaningful attachments in the urban environment. 19 Drawing upon these theories, between 2011 and 2014 an architecture and urban research laboratory at Keio University, Tokyo, and academic partners from Tokyo, Hong Kong, Bangkok, and Singapore designed a series of experiments to gather the feelings, intuitions, and sensualities that participants associated with their home city. By considering the *dérive*, the project asked participants to avoid purposive destinations and instead to arrive at destinations of emotional significance. The result of the study is a series of maps that identify common monuments and landscapes important to all of the participants. 20

"Cherita Lebuh Chulia: Living on Chulia Street" is a municipal government project that took place in Penang, Malaysia, in 2013–2014, to collect, document, and disseminate community values. The project used cultural mapping as a method of identifying the intangible cultural heritage of the city through oral histories, historic photographs, and maps. 21

Important sites were chosen based on how often they were mentioned in the interviews. Selected memories were then paired with historic photographs and maps and were published in order to convey their perceived importance. Other cultural mapping projects exhibit similar methods of community-based participation as a means of identifying heritage. [22]

Place Attachment

Studies demonstrate that the physical age of a neighborhood contributes to place attachment and the sense of community for both local residents and people who frequent these neighborhoods. The majority of data-driven place attachment studies analyze rural environments under threat by development. [23] Elizabeth Lokocz, Robert L. Ryan, and Anna Jarita Sadler undertook a survey of five hundred randomly sampled Massachusetts residents to elicit their attachments to the landscape and their attitudes toward conservation and land use planning. The survey data was interpreted using descriptive statistics and t-tests to examine the demographic differences in responses. The study also expands findings on place attachment by showing that when places disappear, the emotional sense of loss increases place attachment. Lokocz, Ryan, and Sadler replicate the methodology used in a study by Amanda J. Walker and Robert L. Ryan, indicating the significance of this methodology. [24]

Urban studies on these sentiments are far fewer in number and consider historic character to be a contributor to a "sense of community," rather than to "place attachment." Jeremy C. Wells and Elizabeth D. Baldwin conduct a comparative analysis of historic Charleston and a nearby New Urbanist development, I'On, which uses an inductive research design, purposive sampling, interviews, and photo elicitation to analyze the significance of neighborhood age to all who experience historic Charleston, not just residents or property owners. [25] The authors are mainly interested in the "authenticity" of experiences rather than the authenticity of the original historic fabric. The findings indicate that the public perception and value of I'On and Charleston neighborhoods are similar, but it is historic landscape features—such as gates, trees, and gardens—rather than buildings that evoke a strong sense of community attachment. According to Rocco Pendola and Sheldon Gen, "a popular theory in modern day urban planning is that the existence of a neighborhood main street can help bring about a strong sense of community." [26]

Contingent valuation methods (CVM) measure the value of public goods that are not readily captured by market prices, like historic character. [27] But there are few published applications of contingent valuation to the historic environment. [28] CVM studies typically are formulated as surveys that ask participants their willingness to pay for some project or resource and their willingness to accept compensation for the loss of a resource. The responses to these surveys can then be aggregated across larger populations to determine a community's overall sentiments about a proposal. Douglas S. Noonan argues that CVM methods can be critical for preservation studies that analyze residents' sense of responsibility to maintain or restore certain cultural resources, and for estimating how the public would value new projects that may affect or provide cultural resources. [29] Robert W. Kling, Charles F. Revier, and Karin Sable also point

22
L. Hadzic et al., "Participatory Imaging Mapping of Cultural Heritage Across Internal Borders: Stolac, Bosnia and Herzegovina," *International Archives of the Photogrammetry, Remote Sensing, and Spatial Information Sciences* 40, no. 5W7 (2015): 195–200.

23
Gregory Brown and Christopher Raymond, "The Relationship Between Place Attachment and Landscape Values: Toward Mapping Place Attachment," *Applied Geography* 27, no. 2 (April 2007): 89–111; Amanda J. Walker and Robert L. Ryan, "Place Attachment and Landscape Preservation in Rural New England: A Maine Case Study," *Landscape and Urban Planning* 86, no. 2 (May 2008): 141 152; Elizabeth Lokocz, Robert L. Ryan, and Anna Jarita Sadler, "Motivations for Land Protection and Stewardship: Exploring Place Attachment and Rural Landscape Character in Massachusetts," *Landscape and Urban Planning* 99, no. 2 (February 2011): 65–76.

24
Lokocz, Ryan, and Sadler, "Motivations for Land Protection and Stewardship"; Walker and Ryan, "Place Attachment and Landscape Preservation."

25
Jeremy C. Wells and Elizabeth D. Baldwin, "Historic Preservation, Significance, and Age Value: A Comparative Phenomenology of Historic Charleston and the Nearby New-Urbanist Community of I'On," *Journal of Environmental Psychology* 32, no. 4 (December 2012): 384–400.

26
Rocco Pendola and Sheldon Gen, "Does 'Main Street' Promote Sense of Community? A Comparison of San Francisco Neighborhoods," *Environment and Behavior* 40, no. 4 (July 2008): 546.

27
Douglas S. Noonan, "Valuing Arts and Culture: A Research Agenda for Contingent Valuation," *Journal of Arts Management, Law, and Society* 34, no. 3 (Fall 2004): 205–221.

28
Robert W. Kling, Charles F. Revier, and Karin Sable, "Estimating the Public Good Value of Preserving a Local Historic Landmark: The Role of Non-Substitutability and Citizen Information," *Urban Studies* 41, no. 10 (September 2004): 2025–2041.

29
Noonan, "Valuing Arts and Culture."

30
Kling et al., "Estimating the Public Good Value."

31
Daniel J. Levi, "Does History Matter? Perceptions and Attitudes Toward Fake Historic Architecture and Historic Preservation," *Journal of Architectural and Planning Research* 22, no. 2 (Summer 2005): 148–159.

32
Juan J. Rivero, "'Saving' Coney Island: The Construction of Heritage Value," *Environment and Planning A* 49, no. 1 (January 2017): 65–85.

33
Rhonda G. Phillips and Jay M. Stein, "An Indicator Framework for Linking Historic Preservation and Community Economic Development," *Social Indicators Research* 113, no. 1 (August 2012): 1–15.

out the importance of public history education to this methodology. [30] Valuation studies are not necessarily accurate if the sample of respondents has not been exposed to site-specific education. The authors find that when respondents know more about the history of places, then demand for preservation remains consistent even if the cost of maintaining and protecting historic places increases.

Daniel J. Levi's essay "Does History Matter? Perceptions and Attitudes toward Fake Historic Architecture and Historic Preservation" is also representative of urban-based inquiry but demonstrates the challenges of external validity to such studies. [31] The sample of survey participants—166 general studies students at Cal Poly—is most likely not representative of the San Luis Obispo community. Juan J. Rivero examines the historic Coney Island Boardwalk and extends the concept of "sense of community" into a more dynamic social practice. [32] The preservation controversy at Coney Island led New York City residents, who were not necessarily locals, to engage in a process of community formation and a process of constructing new heritage values.

● DEVELOPING COMMON AGENDAS

Expanding the data and methodologies used to analyze aged places, both designated and undesignated, can help contribute to social, economic, and environmental needs. Studies into this possibility are concerned with determining causality between physical qualities of aged places and social and environmental indicators. Furthermore, the literature points to research avenues for standardizing what data on historic places should be collected so that governments, organizations, and residents can make apples-to-apples comparisons when analyzing trends over time. Innovative data-collection methods also demonstrate how citizens and mobile technologies can help city agencies to collect large amounts of historic survey data and to better integrate this information into planning policy.

Data Collection

In order to understand the social and environmental effects of older places, researchers must determine which measurable aspects—called indicators—will tell us more about aspects of people and places that may be only indirectly measurable. For example, it may not be possible to directly measure the sense of well-being among the large numbers of people who experience an older place, but we can use readily collectable data such as neighborhood educational attainment, percent below poverty level, and crime rate as approximate indicators of well-being. Indicators are also useful for standardizing data collection and assessments.

Rhonda G. Phillips and Jay M. Stein address the contributions of historic preservation to community and environmental needs by developing a conceptual "community indicator framework." [33] The authors conduct a literature review to develop four major indicator categories that can be used to assess the built environment and the roles that it plays for people and places, and they emphasize the issue of measurement.

193

The four indicators are gauging (related to type and amount, perceptions and values), protecting (ordinances and regulations), enhancing (partnerships and incentives), and interfacing (uses). There is a need for additional research into indicator frameworks in order to provide clear guidance on how specific indicators are selected, collected, and evaluated. Methodologies to collect and assess proposed indicators are not specified in the article.

According to Ken Bernstein and Janet Hansen, "local governments can find comprehensive, community-wide historical surveys daunting to execute both financially and logistically." [34] The Getty Foundation and the Los Angeles Office of Historic Resources created an innovative public participation and mapping platform named SurveyLA, which enables a range of people across Los Angeles to collect information on places of social, cultural, and historical significance. Initiated in 2005, SurveyLA is an example of innovation with widespread relevance to planners and preservationists. As directors of the initiative, Bernstein and Hansen examine and contextualize the development of SurveyLA. The project included the organization of two hundred volunteers, the launching of a "virtual town hall," and organizing by community members within their own neighborhoods to survey the places that they found significant. The article concludes by examining how urban planners are using SurveyLA data to revise community plans and growth patterns around the region's new transit lines, to assist environmental reviews, and to develop new neighborhood planning tools, such as overlay zones and context-sensitive zoning. These varied uses also underscore the potential of "urban dashboards" as a technology that can simultaneously integrate and display data from multiple city agencies, facilitating holistic decision-making. [35]

Social Effects of Older Neighborhoods

There is limited but influential literature focused on understanding the contributions of older buildings and intermixed old and new buildings to neighborhood vitality. The preservation of older neighborhoods is not necessarily an impediment to growing urban economies. One study by Michael Powe, Jonathan Mabry, Emily Talen, and Dillon Mahmoudi develops a conceptual model that ties neighborhood building characteristics in four US cities to social and economic indicators and tests to see if there are significant relationships between the two. [36] Seattle, San Francisco, Tucson, and Washington, DC, are the case cities of the 2016 study. The authors' methodology builds on literatures of public health, criminology, and environmental psychology that similarly test for significant relationships between attributes of the built environment and social indicators, such as individual health and a sense of well-being. [37] The authors demonstrate that physical and social dimensions are, in fact, interrelated, but they do so through fixed landmarks in the built environment, such as parks and liquor stores.

What is novel about this study is its creation of continuous, city-wide indexes of building morphology, based on age, size, and the mix of old and new buildings. [38] The morphology index is then spatially matched to a variety of demographic and economic datasets. Using regression analysis, the authors find that areas with smaller buildings

34
Ken Bernstein and Janet Hansen, "SurveyLA: Linking Historic Resources Surveys to Local Planning," *Journal of the American Planning Association* 82, no. 2 (Spring 2016): 88–91.

35
Shannon Mattern, "Mission Control: A History of the Urban Dashboard," *Places Journal*, March 2015, 1–20.

36
Michael Powe, Jonathan Mabry, Emily Talen, and Dillon Mahmoudi, "Jane Jacobs and the Value of Older, Smaller Buildings," *Journal of the American Planning Association* 82, no. 2 (Spring 2016): 167–180.

37
R. Araya et al., "Perceptions of Social Capital and the Built Environment and Mental Health," *Social Science and Medicine* 62, no. 12 (June 2006): 3072–3083; Fuzhong Li, K. John Fisher, Ross C. Brownson, and Mark Bosworth, "Multilevel Modelling of Built Environment Characteristics Related to Neighbourhood Walking Activity in Older Adults," *Journal of Epidemiology and Community Health* 59, no. 7 (July 2005): 558–564; Lynne C. Manzo and Douglas D. Perkins, "Finding Common Ground: The Importance of Place Attachment to Community Participation and Planning," *Journal of Planning Literature* 20, no. 4 (May 2006): 335–350; Douglas D. Perkins, Barbara B. Brown, and Ralph B. Taylor, "The Ecology of Empowerment: Predicting Participation in Community Organizations," *Journal of Social Issues* 52, no. 1 (Spring 1996): 85–110; Robert J. Sampson and Stephen W. Raudenbush, "Systematic Social Observation of Public Spaces: A New Look at Disorder in Urban Neighborhoods," *American Journal of Sociology* 105, no. 3 (November 1999): 603–651.

38
Powe et al., "Jane Jacobs and the Value of Older, Smaller Buildings."

39
Erica Avrami, "Making Historic Preservation Sustainable," *Journal of the American Planning Association* 82, no. 2 (Spring 2016): 104–112.

40
Mark Holland, "Conserving the Future: The Need for Sustainability in City Planning and Preservation," *APT Bulletin* 43, no. 1 (2012): 3–6.

41
Avrami, "Making Historic Preservation Sustainable."

42
Kathryn Rogers Merlino, "[Re]Evaluating Significance: The Environmental and Cultural Value in Older and Historic Buildings," *Public Historian* 36, no. 3 (August 2014): 70–85.

43
Merlino, "[Re]Evaluating Significance."

and mixed-vintage blocks support more jobs in new businesses, small businesses, and businesses in creative industries. Areas with older, smaller buildings also have more racial and ethnic diversity. Based on these findings, the authors recommend that planners support the preservation and reuse of older buildings and the integration of old and new buildings. Other recommendations include adaptive reuse ordinances, performance-based energy codes, context-sensitive form-based coding, and the deregulation of parking requirements.

Environmental Effects of Older Neighborhoods

The field of preservation is grappling with the need to more effectively contribute to environmental, economic, and social sustainability. Historic preservation and sustainability literatures indicate that while it was once assumed that preservation is a sustainable practice, the relationship of preservation to sustainability is in fact much more complex. [39] There are significant shortcomings in the data, research methods, and policies necessary to evaluate and demonstrate the sustainability of historic preservation, and these shortcomings hinder preservation practice. The evaluation of sustainability goals today is increasingly left to green rating systems, such as the US Green Building Council's LEED rating program. [40] However, the complexity of historic building systems requires a greater degree of specificity and expanded indicators than what is captured by the current rating system.

Energy consumption data, in terms of embodied and operational energy, also needs to be further contextualized and evaluated in order to determine the true contributions of older buildings. Preservation organizations have undertaken life cycle assessments (LCAs) to evaluate the impacts of embodied energy—the sum of energy consumed to extract and prepare materials for building construction and to develop the labor force. LCAs also evaluate buildings' operational energy, which is the energy consumed by heating, lighting, and other utilities throughout the life cycle of a building. [41] Kathryn Rogers Merlino offers a significant research avenue. [42] LCA is the strongest research avenue for developing the standardized and robust indicators that will credibly measure the environmental and human health impacts of historic buildings.

Reframing the sustainability discussion around the reuse of existing buildings also posits a new definition of sustainable development: reusing existing buildings necessitates fundamental changes in the way we consider buildings' value and significance. Reuse of existing buildings often aligns with political and community values. Evaluating buildings through more inclusive agendas helps to build consensus during complex decision-making processes. [43]

● PATTERNS IN DECISION-MAKING

Social, Economic, and Spatial Designation Criteria

This literature reveals the social determinants of municipal landmark designation beyond the formal criteria of historical significance. This is critical information in metropolitan areas that are undergoing rapid transformation; historic district and landmark designation are highly politicized processes. In a city like New York, not all historic places eligible for landmarking are necessarily designated, so what are the intervening factors that do determine preservation? Although the following is a rural case, the findings are instructive. Vishakha Maskey, Cheryl Brown, and Ge Lin statistically test the relationships between the number of National Register listings in West Virginia and social, economic, geographical, and institutional variables.[44] The authors find that the rural character of the county and the presence of multiple historic preservation organizations and colleges positively influence the rate of houses listed. Results show statistically significant and negative relationships between designation and median age, poverty rate, and the Gini coefficient of income inequality.

Stephanie Ryberg-Webster and Kelly L. Kinahan present a compelling study of the geographic distribution of federal historic tax credit activity between 2000 and 2010 in six legacy cities: Baltimore, Cleveland, Philadelphia, Providence, Richmond, and St. Louis.[45] Through analysis of National Park Service Technical Preservation Services data and a statistical measure of concentration, the authors find that federal historic tax credit investments are, in fact, highly concentrated and are used to build market-rate housing predominantly in very low and low income neighborhoods.

Douglas S. Noonan and Douglas J. Krupka focus specifically on the urban environment of Chicago.[46] By sampling approximately 1,700 historically and/or culturally significant properties in Chicago, the authors find, remarkably, that historical quality appears to be negatively correlated to the likelihood of historic designation. Individually designated properties tend to be older properties in less historic neighborhoods, while designated districts tend to be in poorer neighborhoods with more historical resources. The authors also find that district designation depends on the density of the cultural fabric, among other things. The article argues that the causal interactions between neighborhood demographics and preservation policy may offer a window into the decision-making processes of preservation program administrators and the long-term effects of those decisions on the neighborhoods they regulate.

● DATA-DRIVEN PRESERVATION

As posited by William Baer in "When Old Buildings Ripen for Historic Preservation: A Predictive Approach to Planning," the discipline of historic preservation must develop the data and techniques necessary for addressing problems before they arise and for projecting the social outcomes of preservation decisions. Baer writes, "The techniques [would] assist planners in thinking about preservation in the long term—in thinking about how extensive preservation might become, the cumulative effects of its growth, and the difference it will make in other realms of our urban experience."[47] This is a future-looking project. Equally, historic preservation must be readily present at the bargaining tables and involved in making community policy. The purpose of this literature review was to present one approach to strengthening the contributions of historic preservation: data-driven research methods and techniques.

44
Vishakha Maskey, Cheryl Brown, and Ge Lin, "Assessing Factors Associated with Listing a Historic Resource in the National Register of Historic Places," *Economic Development Quarterly* 23, no. 4 (November 2009): 342–350.

45
Ryberg-Webster and Kinahan, "Historic Preservation in Declining City Neighbourhoods."

46
Douglas S. Noonan and Douglas J. Krupka, "Determinants of Historic and Cultural Landmark Designation: Why We Preserve What We Preserve," *Journal of Cultural Economics* 34, no. 1 (February 2010): 1–26.

47
Baer, "When Old Buildings Ripen."

48
Baer, "When Old
Buildings Ripen"; Smith,
"Housing Policy Debate
Comment"; Mason,
*Once and Future New
York.*
As suggested in the literature, such people-oriented evaluative criteria will allow the discipline to progress from the binary of preservation "successes" or "failures" and "gentrification" or "antigentrification" to better evaluate how historic preservation influences neighborhoods. The impacts of historic designation on property values are well represented, but as scholars such as Baer, Smith, and Mason remind us, municipal historic preservation is a powerful but often overlooked force in urban transformation.[48] These provocations bring the discipline back to the fundamental concern of how, exactly, historic preservation functions as an inclusive public good beyond its financial benefits to property owners and residents within the immediate vicinity of designated places.

The three organizing categories of this review, "Sense of Community and Place Distinctiveness," "Developing Common Agendas," and "Patterns in Decision-Making," present contemporary scholarship that asks the more challenging questions often relegated to the peripheries of historic preservation and urban planning. These are questions about the role of historic preservation in environmental sustainability, inclusive urban development, and socio-spatial justice in increasingly divided cities. The literature demonstrates how the integration of the strong qualitative, perceptive, and experience-based aspects of historic preservation can use data-driven empirical evidence to return the field to its Progressive Era roots as a change agent in urban policy and city development.

● BIBLIOGRAPHY

Araya, Ricardo, Frank Dunstan, Rebecca Playle, Hollie Thomas, Stephen Palmer, and Glyn Lewis. "Perceptions of Social Capital and the Built Environment and Mental Health." *Social Science and Medicine* 62, no. 12 (June 2006): 3072–3083.
The complex ways in which the social and built environment affect mental health is a little explored realm of research. This article investigates how physical contexts affect individual perceptions by conducting a cross-sectional household survey in South Wales, United Kingdom, to measure the relationship between the quality of the built environment and social capital.

Asabere, Paul K., Forrest E. Huffman, and Seyed Mehdian. "The Adverse Impacts of Local Historic District Designation: The Case of Small Apartment Buildings in Philadelphia." *Journal of Real Estate Finance and Economics* 8, no. 3 (May 1994): 225–234.
There is an ongoing debate regarding the economic impact of local historic preservation regulations. The authors conducted a regression study on historically designated apartment buildings in the central business district of Philadelphia to determine if the impact of designation on property values is positive or negative.

Avrami, Erica. "Making Historic Preservation Sustainable." *Journal of the American Planning Association* 82, no. 2 (Spring 2016): 104–112.
The field of preservation is grappling with how preservation policy and practice need to evolve to contribute effectively to environmental,

197

economic, and social sustainability. This article reviews the literature of the "preservation-sustainability nexus" and examines how preservation policy and practice may support or inhibit sustainability goals.

Avrami, Erica, Randall Mason, and Marta de la Torre. *Values and Heritage Conservation: Research Report*. Los Angeles: Getty Conservation Institute, 2000.
This report provides the background behind a Getty Conservation Institute initiative to understand the role that conservation plays in social and cultural development. The report consists of essays regarding the future of conservation in relation to society, as well as potential future research that is necessary to understand the effect of preservation in the long run.

Baer, William. "When Old Buildings Ripen for Historic Preservation: A Predictive Approach to Planning." *Journal of the American Planning Association* 61, no. 1 (Winter 1995): 82–94.
Historic preservation should not be a piecemeal endeavor and should instead work with long-range planning efforts to anticipate and describe future trends influenced by the designation of urban places. This paper illustrates examples of long-range preservation planning throughout the twentieth century and proposes studies of the production and durability of historic structures.

Been, Vicki, Ingrid Gould Ellen, Michael Gedal, Edward Glaeser, and Brian J. McCabe. "Preserving History or Restricting Development? The Heterogeneous Effects of Historic Districts on Local Housing Markets in New York City." *Journal of Urban Economics* 92 (March 2016): 16–30.
This paper develops a theory that landmarking has heterogeneous impacts across neighborhoods. It analyzes historic district designation in New York City to identify the effects of preservation policies on residential property markets. The authors test their hypothesis of varying impacts by using a model that compares data on residential transactions during a fixed period.

Bernstein, Ken, and Janet Hansen. "SurveyLA: Linking Historic Resources Surveys to Local Planning." *Journal of the American Planning Association* 82, no. 2 (Spring 2016): 88–91.
Local governance can find comprehensive, community-wide historical surveys daunting to execute, financially and logistically. The authors sought to develop innovative methods for making surveys feasible and integrating available information on historic resources with planning policy. This resulted in SurveyLA, partially funded by the Getty Foundation, which implemented new methods of collecting, interpreting, and displaying data on mobile devices to engage a diverse public.

Brown, Gregory, and Christopher Raymond. "The Relationship Between Place Attachment and Landscape Values: Toward Mapping Place Attachment." *Applied Geography* 27, no. 2 (April 2007): 89–111.

Place attachment is created through therapeutic experiences in aesthetic and natural landscapes. The authors of this study test whether or not mapped landscapes can be used as proxies for scale-based measures of place attachment to prove that a willingness to associate spiritual value with a landscape is the best predictor of the psychological sense of place attachment.

Coulson, N. Edward, and Robin M. Leichenko. "The Internal and External Impact of Historical Designation on Property Values." *Journal of Real Estate Finance and Economics* 23, no. 1 (July 2001): 113–124.

Despite mixed evidence regarding the direct effects of local designation on property values, preservation is also thought to have positive external effects on homes and neighborhoods in and around designated properties. This article seeks to find positive internal and external benefits of historical designation and to calculate an aggregate impact on property values.

Coulson, N. Edward, and Michael L. Lahr. "Gracing the Land of Elvis and Beale Street: Historic Designation and Property Values in Memphis." *Real Estate Economics* 33, no. 3 (Fall 2005): 487–507.

Designation of historic places can stimulate growth in older neighborhoods, but empirical studies on whether or not this is a net positive or negative effect are complicated. This study develops a series of models to highlight the role of designation in appreciation rates by testing if historic property values appreciate at a significantly different rate from that of undesignated properties.

Duncan, Terry E., Susan C. Duncan, Hayrettin Okut, Lisa Strycker, and Hollie Hix-Small. "A Multilevel Contextual Model of Neighborhood Collective Efficacy." *American Journal of Community Psychology* 32, no. 3/4 (December 2003): 245–252.

This paper extends previous research by examining the hierarchical nature of neighborhood efficacy and the contextual influences of the social hierarchy. Using a multilevel technique allows for the simultaneous analysis of perceptions of collective efficacy at the individual, family, and neighborhood levels.

Ellen, Ingrid Gould, Brian J. McCabe, and Eric Stern. *Fifty Years of Historic Preservation in New York City.* New York: New York University Furman Center, 2016.

This white paper offers a descriptive account of historic preservation in New York City to reveal investment and socioeconomic trends. The authors compare historic districts with similar non-regulated tax lots in order to argue that historic districts tend to have stronger rental markets.

Feng, Kuah Li, and Mahani Musa. "Initiating an Oral History Project in a Multicultural UNESCO World Heritage Site of George Town, Penang, Malaysia: Challenges and Outcomes." *Kajian Malaysia* 34, no. 2 (2016): 123–143.

This article describes the methodologies of an oral history project that identified elements of intangible cultural heritage in George Town. The project integrated oral histories with historic maps and photographs as a means of creating a comprehensive understanding of heritage in Penang.

Freitas, Raquel. "Cultural Mapping as a Development Tool." *City, Culture and Society* 7, no. 1 (March 2016): 9–16.
Cultural mapping is an important tool for the preservation of culture, but it can also be used as a tool for development. This article highlights the different development models, levels of analysis, and visions of culture that make up cultural mapping and interprets how worldviews and intentions affect the structure and types of information collected.

Grodach, Carl, and Anastasia Loukaitou-Sideris. "Cultural Develop-ment Strategies and Urban Revitalization: A Survey of US Cities." *International Journal of Cultural Policy* 13, no. 4 (November 2007): 349–370.
This article is a product of a national survey with cultural agency department heads to understand what cultural development and urban regeneration strategies are being used across US cities. The research addresses the prevalence of the downtown clustering of arts and cultural happenings and investigates what types of cultural activities municipal governments support as mechanisms for economic development.

Hadzic, L., A. Dzino-Suta, R. Eppich, A. Vezic, and J. L. Izkara Martinez. "Participatory Imaging Mapping of Cultural Heritage Across Internal Borders: Stolac, Bosnia and Herzegovina." *International Archives of the Photogrammetry, Remote Sensing, and Spatial Information Sciences* 40, no. 5W7 (2015): 195–200.
Participatory and cultural mapping involves the representation of community landscapes in two or three dimensions from the perspective of locals. This study analyzes a cultural mapping exercise in which participants were asked to photograph tangible heritage in order to create an online, collaborative depiction of the most significant places in their community.

Holland, Mark. "Conserving the Future: The Need for Sustainability in City Planning and Preservation." *APT Bulletin* 43, no. 1 (2012): 3–6.
Green building and sustainable infrastructures have been key points in the discussion of the built environment since the Bruntland Commission in 1987. This article outlines a series of global concerns related to sustainable development, and calls for consideration of the existing built environment as part of conversations about the future.

Kitchin, Rob, Sophia Maalsen, and Gavin McArdle. "The Praxis and Politics of Building Urban Dashboards." *Geoforum* 77 (December 2016): 93–101.
Through a study of the authors' own development of an urban dashboard for the city of Dublin, this article examines the social and political implications of making urban dashboards. The authors critique the assumed realist

epistemology and instrumental rationality of urban dashboards to highlight the emergent politics and praxes of urban data and dashboard design.

> Kling, Robert W., Charles F. Revier, and Karin Sable. "Estimating the Public Good Value of Preserving a Local Historic Landmark: The Role of Non-Substitutability and Citizen Information." *Urban Studies* 41, no. 10 (September 2004): 2025–2041.

This article analyzes the process of designation to examine how public valuation of historic landmarks is influenced by enhanced information on these resources and on the proposed financing tools. Unlike previous preservation studies, this research uses a referendum-style dichotomous-choice approach and helps explain discrepancies in value when measured as willingness to pay and willingness to accept.

> Levi, Daniel J. "Does History Matter? Perceptions and Attitudes Toward Fake Historic Architecture and Historic Preservation." *Journal of Architectural and Planning Research* 22, no. 2 (Summer 2005): 148–159.

Downtown San Luis Obispo, California, is a mixture of historic, contemporary, and "fake historic" buildings. The author argues that architects, historians, and preservationists need to better understand imitation historic architecture, rather than simply dismissing it. The author conducted a study to determine public perception of aesthetics and to determine whether the community distinguished between the historic and non-historic architecture.

> Li, Fuzhong, K. John Fisher, Ross C. Brownson, and Mark Bosworth. "Multilevel Modelling of Build Environment Characteristics Related to Neighbourhood Walking Activity in Older Adults," *Journal of Epidemiology and Community Health* 59, no. 7 (July 2005): 558–564.

Walking is commonly accepted to be a popular activity—whether for leisure or for health. This study uses a cross-sectional, cluster, multi-sampling technique to understand if certain characteristics of the built environment are positively related to the promotion of healthy activity, focusing on the walking habits of older populations.

> Listokin, David, Barbara Listokin, and Michael Lahr. "The Contributions of Historic Preservation to Housing and Economic Development." *Housing Policy Debate* 9, no. 3 (1998): 431–478.

This article studies the contributions of historic preservation to housing, economic development, and revitalization. The authors explore the notion that historic preservation is a key housing and economic development strategy with negative externalities that often are not considered but should be.

> Lokocz, Elizabeth, Robert L. Ryan, and Anna Jarita Sadler. "Motivations for Land Protection and Stewardship: Exploring Place Attachment and Rural Landscape Character in Massachusetts." *Landscape and Urban Planning* 99, no. 2 (February 2011): 65–76.

Rural landscapes are facing significant economic, social, and demographic changes. Rural planners need to understand what residents value in different landscapes, but definitions of "rural character" are often hard to articulate. The authors study residents' attachment to rural landscapes in Massachusetts through a photo-questionnaire survey with representative images to be rated by the residents.

Longsley, Alys, and Nancy Duxbury. "Introduction: Mapping Cultural Intangibles." *City, Culture, and Society* 7, no. 1 (March 2016): 1–7.

This article reviews a selection of papers that explore conventional and alternative methods to mapping cultures and communities. The authors emphasize cultural mapping as an interdisciplinary and participatory tool that can be used identify intangible cultural assets.

Manzo, Lynne C., and Douglas D. Perkins. "Finding Common Ground: The Importance of Place Attachment to Community Participation and Planning." *Journal of Planning Literature* 20, no. 4 (May 2006): 335–350.

This paper connects literature on place attachment with literature on community participation and planning, examining participation in community events in order to understand the impact of collective emotions and behaviors. The authors emphasize the importance of grassroots-driven community development that engages sociocultural, economic, and political contexts in ways that can inform the planning process.

Markusen, Ann, and Anne Gadwa. "Arts and Culture in Urban or Regional Planning: A Review and Research Agenda." *Journal of Planning Education and Research* 29, no. 3 (March 2010): 379–391.

The purpose of this article is to review current research on arts and cultural projects as an urban or regional development tool. The authors address the lack of studies that demonstrate the impacts, risks, and opportunity costs of the ways these projects are financed.

Maskey, Vishakha, Cheryl Brown, and Ge Lin. "Assessing Factors Associated with Listing a Historic Resource in the National Register of Historic Places." *Economic Development Quarterly* 23, no. 4 (November 2009): 342–350.

The underlying reasons that some communities pursue historic place designation and others do not are still not well understood. This article compares the relationship between the number of national register listings and demographic and spatial variables, analyzing socioeconomic and spatial factors that may influence designation beyond historical significance.

Mason, Randall. *Economics of Historic Preservation: A Guide and Review of the Literature.* Washington, DC: Brookings Institution, Metropolitan Policy Program, 2005.

This article reviews literature on the economics of historic preservation, outlining three dominant strands of research: evaluations of individual projects, property value effects, and local and/or regional economic impact studies. The author identifies the typical methods used, including basic cost studies, economic impact studies, regression analyses, stated-preference studies, choice modeling, and case studies.

> Mattern, Shannon. "Mission Control: A History of the Urban Dashboard." *Places Journal*, March 2015, 1–20.

The urban dashboard embodies the many ways of representing and contextualizing data to make it intelligible to an audience that likely has only a limited understanding of how the data are derived. This article addresses the relatively understudied transformation of urban dashboard information from knowledge to action and asks how urban dashboards have increased in complexity since the Bloomberg Terminals of 1982.

> McCabe, Brian J., and Ingrid Gould Ellen. "Does Preservation Accelerate Neighborhood Change? Examining the Impact of Historic Preservation in New York City." *Journal of the American Planning Association* 82, no. 2 (Spring 2016): 134–146.

This investigation of how historic districts change after designation was conducted in order to gain a better understanding of the impact of designation on neighborhoods. The study focused on bringing together socioeconomic metrics at census tract level with historic district data to track whether or not designation influenced socioeconomic status.

> Merlino, Kathryn Rogers. "[Re]Evaluating Significance: The Environmental and Cultural Value in Older and Historic Buildings." *Public Historian* 36, no. 3 (August 2014): 70–85.

Reusing existing buildings is a critical component of sustainable development that changes the ways we consider buildings' value and significance. Through observation and quantitative discourse analysis, the author finds that the inclusion of environmental significance with historical significance and the use of real-time data collection on building performance warrants new criteria for preservation significance.

> Noonan, Douglas S. "Contingent Valuation and Cultural Resources: A Meta-Analytic Review of the Literature." *Journal of Cultural Economics* 27, no. 3–4 (2003): 159–176.

Although popular in other socioeconomic fields, the use of contingent valuation methodology in the cultural arena is recent and underdeveloped. This article reviews the practice, explaining the concepts of contingent valuation and cultural clustering, and sets out a research agenda.

> Noonan, Douglas S. "Valuing Arts and Culture: A Research Agenda for Contingent Valuation." *Journal of Arts Management, Law, and Society* 34, no. 3 (Fall 2004): 205–221.

The author introduces contingent valuation of arts and culture—measuring economic value that is not captured readily by market prices—and frames the existing literature into categories: admissions fee studies undertaken at cultural institutions or heritage sites; preservation studies that look at willingness to pay to maintain or restore certain cultural icons; alternate funding studies that estimate willingness to pay in lieu of the status quo funding; and studies that estimate values for new projects that affect or provide cultural resources.

Noonan, Douglas S., and Douglas J. Krupka. "Determinants of Historic and Cultural Landmark Designation: Why We Preserve What We Preserve." *Journal of Cultural Economics* 34, no. 1 (February 2010): 1–26.
While academics seem to have a limited interest in modeling the historic designation process itself, research seems to overemphasize the price effects of preservation. This article argues that the causal interactions between neighborhood demographics and preservation policy may offer a window into the decision-making processes of preservation program administrators and the effects of those decisions on the neighborhoods they regulate.

Pendola, Rocco, and Sheldon Gen. "Does 'Main Street' Promote Sense of Community? A Comparison of San Francisco Neighborhoods." *Environment and Behavior* 40, no. 4 (July 2008): 545–574.
Through a comparative study of four San Francisco neighborhoods, this article examines the associations between "main street" and "sense of community." Researchers found and surveyed neighborhood residents, developed a place attachment scale, and conducted two regression models—one with additional dummy variables, in order to determine whether the existence of a main street does, in fact, correspond to a stronger sense of community.

Perkins, Douglas D., Barbara B. Brown, and Ralph B. Taylor. "The Ecology of Empowerment: Predicting Participation in Community Organizations." *Journal of Social Issues* 52, no. 1 (Spring 1996): 85–110.
This paper examines predictors of individual participation in grassroots organizations, focusing on the physical, economic, and social environment, through a comparative analysis. The authors compare resident survey data and independent observational ratings of the physical environment to predict residents' voluntary association in grassroots community organizations engaged in block and neighborhood improvement activities.

Phillips, Rhonda G., and Jay M. Stein. "An Indicator Framework for Linking Historic Preservation and Community Economic Development." *Social Indicators Research* 113, no. 1 (August 2012): 1–15.
The authors ask how a conceptual model of a community indicator framework can bridge the aims of community revitalization and historic preservation. The article reviews relevant literature with four major framework categories that emphasize the issue of measurement, including gauging, protecting, enhancing, and interfacing.

Powe, Michael, Jonathan Mabry, Emily Talen, and Dillon Mahmoudi. "Jane Jacobs and the Value of Older, Smaller Buildings." *Journal of the American Planning Association* 82, no. 2 (Spring 2016): 167–180.

Economists and urban developers have argued that preservation is an impediment to growing, diverse, urban economies. Scholars rarely study the role of older buildings and the importance of a mix of old and new buildings in supporting neighborhood vitality. The authors develop a conceptual model tying building characteristics to social and economic diversity and density. The concept is operationalized for quantitative study by a lattice grid sized to one or two square city blocks in four major US cities.

> Radović, Darko. "Measuring the Non-Measurable: On Mapping Subjectivities in Urban Research." *City, Culture, and Society* 7, no. 1 (March 2016): 17–24.

Many approaches to urban studies and analyses of the built environment rely on reductive descriptions of neighborhood characteristics. The author outlines an alternative method of subjective mapping, using a study conducted in Tokyo as an example of how subjective mapping practices should be used to understand and describe the urban fabric.

> Rivero, Juan J. "'Saving' Coney Island: The Construction of Heritage Value." *Environment and Planning A* 49, no. 1 (January 2017): 65–85.

This paper examines how the heritage field catalyzes processes of community formation and concomitant community-based heritage values through the case of the Coney Island Thunderbolt amusement park ride demolition. The author makes a case for the importance of qualitative, in-depth interviews for understanding the formation of heritage values by publics that are not necessarily community-based.

> Ryberg-Webster, Stephanie, and Kelly L. Kinahan. "Historic Preservation and Urban Revitalization in the Twenty-First Century." *Journal of Planning Literature* 29, no. 2 (May 2014): 119–139.

A major problem for preservation advocacy is the lack of empirical research demonstrating that preservation is a key driver in urban revitalization. The authors review the literature on the intersection of historic preservation and urban development, as well as recent research on urban preservation. The authors then develop a research agenda focused on historic preservation and find four leading discourses within the literature: The New American City; Place Matters; Anchor Institutions; and Legacy Cities.

> Ryberg-Webster, Stephanie, and Kelly L. Kinahan. "Historic Preservation in Declining City Neighbourhoods: Analysing Rehabilitation Tax Credit Investments in Six US Cities." *Urban Studies* 54, no. 7 (May 2017): 1673–1691.

This article addresses the lack of empirical studies of the federal historic rehabilitation tax credit. The authors argue that no existing studies examine disaggregated activity at the neighborhood level. The article examines rehabilitation tax credit activity from 2000 to 2010 in six legacy cities—Baltimore, Cleveland, Philadelphia, Providence, Richmond, and St. Louis—in order to understand the role of tax credits in rehabilitation across tracts of various incomes.

Smith, Neil. "Housing Policy Debate Comment on David Listokin, Barbara Listokin, and Michael Lahr's 'The Contributions of Historic Preservation to Housing and Economic Development': Historic Preservation in a Neoliberal Age." *Housing Policy Debate* 9, no. 3 (1998): 479–485.
The author critiques the article by Listokin, Listokin, and Lahr for inflating the achievements of historic preservation in community development. The underlying argument is that the institutionalization of historic preservation rewards investment cycles that are not natural but rather are induced by developers.

Stern, Mark J., and Susan C. Seifert. "Cultural Clusters: The Implications of Cultural Assets Agglomeration for Neighborhood Revitalization." *Journal of Planning Education and Research* 29, no. 3 (March 2010): 262–279.
This paper argues for alternative uses of the arts for community development: cultivating neighborhood clusters with modest concentrations of cultural providers can use arts to engage residents. The authors develop a cultural asset index that determines census block groups with the highest density of cultural assets. The method concentrates on the behavior of individuals and of informal and commercial cultural groups.

Throsby, David. *Economics and Culture*. New York: Cambridge University Press. 2001.
This book begins with an etymological analysis of neoclassical economics and the cultural context of economics. The author explains the notion of cultural capital as a means of understanding particular problems in cultural heritage.

Walker, Amanda J., and Robert L. Ryan. "Place Attachment and Landscape Preservation in Rural New England: A Maine Case Study." *Landscape and Urban Planning* 86, no. 2 (May 2008): 141–152.
Little research has been done on the psychological impacts of sprawl. Data gathered from photo interpretation and mail-out surveys indicates that higher levels of place attachment predicted increased support for protecting highly valued landscapes. The study expands findings on place attachment by determining that an emotional sense of loss when places change or disappear increases place attachment.

Wells, Jeremy C., and Elizabeth D. Baldwin. "Historic Preservation, Significance, and Age Value: A Comparative Phenomenology of Historic Charleston and the Nearby New-Urbanist Community of I'On." *Journal of Environmental Psychology* 32, no. 4 (December 2012): 384–400.
Through a comparative analysis of historic Charleston and the I'On New Urbanist development, this study mainly uses photo elicitation and interviews with informants, selected from a sampling of people already present in public space, to analyze the significance that neighborhood age holds for residents. The authors are mainly interested in the authenticity of landscape experiences rather than the authenticity of original historic fabric.

Weyeneth, Robert. "Ancestral Architecture: The Early Preservation Movement in Charleston." In *Giving Preservation a History: Histories of Historic Preservation in the United States* eds., Max Page and Randall Mason (New York: Routledge, 2004), 257–281.
This article offers a comprehensive examination of the historic preservation movement in Charleston, South Carolina in order to understand the context in which the Historic Charleston Foundation was established. The author then discusses why Charleston became such a beacon for early preservation efforts in the United States.

● THURSDAY, FEBRUARY 8

Opening Remarks and Introductions

— Erica Avrami, Graduate School of Architecture, Planning, and Preservation
— Jacqueline Klopp, Center for Sustainable Urban Development – Earth Institute
— Nicholas Hamilton, The American Assembly
— Lisa Ackerman, World Monuments Fund

SESSION 1
Data for Managing the Historic Built Environment
Moderator: Erica Avrami

— Meenakshi Srinivasan, Lisa Kersavage, Daniel Watts – *NYC Landmarks Preservation Commission's Historic Building Data Project*
— Lisa Ackerman – *Documentation: The Most Essential Preservation Tool*
— Janet Hansen – *SurveyLA and HistoricPlaceLA: Contemporary Strategies for Historic Resource Data Collection and Management for Urban Planning*
— Matthew Hampel – *Historic Complexity: Data in the Service of Preservation*

SESSION 2
Measuring and Communicating the Qualitative
Moderator: Nicholas Hamilton

— Alicia Rouault – *Civic Technology and Community Partnership Models for Qualitative Data Collection*
— Jeremy C. Wells – *Big and Deep Heritage Data: The Social HEritage Machine (SHEM)*
— Marco Castro Cosio – *Mapping Experiences in the Digital and Physical Landscape*

SESSION 3
Crossing Divides in Data Access, Accuracy, and Expertise
Moderator: Jacqueline Klopp

— Andrew S. Dolkart – *The Pitfalls of Big Data*
— Jennifer L. Most – *The Case for Data Analytics in Preservation Education*
— Chris Whong – *Open(ish) Data: Perspectives on the Civic Data Landscape*
— Vicki Weiner – *Democratizing Data: Pratt Center's Neighborhood Data Portal*

PUBLIC SESSION
Evidence-Building for Preservation: How can historic preservation, in an era of urban data, address the challenges of twenty-first century cities?
Moderator: Erica Avrami

A panel discussion exploring how institutional actors and new avenues of research inform public and private investment in preservation.

— Meenakshi Srinivasan, New York City Landmarks Preservation Commission
— Eduardo Rojas, Inter-American Development Bank
— Randy Mason, University of Pennsylvania School of Design
— Michael Powe, National Trust for Historic Preservation's Preservation Green Lab

● FRIDAY, FEBRUARY 9

SESSION 4
Understanding the Social, Economic, and Environmental Role of Heritage
Moderator: Erica Avrami

— Stephanie Ryberg-Webster – *The Possibilities and Perils of Data-Driven Preservation Research: Lessons from a Multiyear Study of Federal Historic Tax Credits*
— Amanda L. Webb – *Examining the Use of Municipal Energy Benchmarking Data in Historic Preservation Planning and Policy*
— Michael Powe – *Using Public Data to Demonstrate the Contributions of Older Buildings*
— Emily Talen – *Historic Buildings and Mom-and-Pop Retail: Quantifying the Link*

SESSION 5
Informing Policy Research and Decision-Making
Moderator: Jacqueline Klopp

— Douglas S. Noonan – *Perspectives on Data in Urban Historic Preservation Policy*
— Randall Mason – *Positioning Preservation in Urban Policy Research*
— Eduardo Rojas – *Involving All Social Actors in the Conservation of the Urban Heritage, a Condition for Sustainability*

Breakout discussions

Concluding discussion and recommendations

LISA ACKERMAN is the executive vice president and chief administrative officer of World Monuments Fund, an international preservation organization that raises funds and provides expertise for heritage conservation projects throughout the world. Ackerman is a visiting assistant professor at Pratt Institute and previously served as executive vice president of the Samuel H. Kress Foundation, which funds projects related to European art and architecture. Ackerman holds an MS in historic preservation from Pratt Institute, an MBA from New York University, and a BA from Middlebury College. She currently serves on the boards of Historic House Trust of New York City and the New York Preservation Archive Project; she previously served on the boards of the St. Ann Center for Restoration and the Arts, Partners for Sacred Places, US/ICOMOS, and the Neighborhood Preservation Center. In 2007 she received the Historic District Council's Landmarks Lion award. In 2008 Ackerman was named the first recipient of US/ICOMOS's Ann Webster Smith Award for International Heritage Achievement. She lectures frequently on cultural heritage, conservation, and philanthropy.

ALLISON ARLOTTA is a recent graduate of Columbia University's MS in Historic Preservation Program. As a data fellow for the Landmarks Preservation Commission, she contributed to the addition of robust designation report information to the agency's Discover New York City Landmarks interactive online map of the city's thirty-six thousand buildings with historic designation. Arlotta wrote her award-winning thesis on the reciprocal relationship and areas of potential collaboration between historic preservation and waste management. In her research, she is interested in how heritage can contribute to larger social aims of sustainability, resilience, and equity.

ERICA AVRAMI is the James Marston Fitch Assistant Professor of Historic Preservation at Columbia University's Graduate School of Architecture, Planning, and Preservation. She was formerly the director of research and education for World Monuments Fund and a project specialist at the Getty Conservation Institute. Avrami earned both a BA in architecture and an MS in historic preservation at Columbia and a PhD in planning and public policy at Rutgers University. She was a trustee and secretary of US/ICOMOS from 2003 to 2010 and currently serves on the editorial advisory board of the journals *Change Over Time* and *Future Anterior.*

VANILSON BURÉGIO is adjunct professor of systems and software engineering in the Department of Statistics and Informatics at Federal Rural University of Pernambuco in

211

Brazil. He has a PhD and an MSc in computer science from Informatics Center of Federal University of Pernambuco (CIn-UFPE). As a researcher, he focuses on social machines, enterprise 2.0, software engineering, software architecture, and software reuse. Burégio has more than fifteen years of experience in the development of several large-scale web-based information systems. He performed roles such as P&D researcher, software architect, engineer, system analyst, and team leader for private companies and government agencies such as the Recife Center for Advanced Studies and Systems, the Information Technology Agency of Pernambuco, and the Federal Data Processing Service.

MARCO CASTRO COSIO graduated from the Interactive Telecommunications Program at the Tisch School of the Arts at New York University and has worked as a curator of exhibitions and art festivals in New York and Mexico. He was MediaLab director at the Metropolitan Museum of Art, where he helped the museum to imagine art and its audiences from innovative perspectives. Prior to that, he worked as the first visitor experience manager at the Queens Museum, where he also conducted workshops on developing interactive experiences for diverse communities. As an artist, his work—such as his project Bus Roots, which seeks to furnish the roofs of urban buses with lush gardens— nourishes urban communities in practical and playful ways.

Castro Cosio contributed to the Rio+20 series proposed by the UN, spoke at the TEDx conference in Cape May, New Jersey, and is a member of the Climate and Urban Systems Association. He was a TED speaker in residence. He is currently a research fellow at the Brown Institute for Media Innovation, based at the Columbia University School of Journalism, and an artist in residence at NYU-POLY incubator.

SARA DELGADILLO CRUZ has a master's degree in heritage conservation from the University of Southern California. She is the data coordinator for Los Angeles's historic resource inventory system, HistoricPlacesLA. In her role with the City of Los Angeles, Delgadillo Cruz works in partnership with the Getty Conservation Institute's Arches project team on planned improvements to HistoricPlacesLA and the Arches heritage inventory platform. She also has experience conducting research on sites associated with underrepresented communities in the National Park Service's Pacific West Region, and she serves on the executive committee of Latinos in Heritage Conservation, the leading organization for the preservation of Latino places, stories, and cultural heritage in the United States.

ANDREW S. DOLKART is a professor of historic preservation at the Columbia University Graduate School of Architecture, Planning, and Preservation. He is a preservationist and historian specializing in the architecture and development of New York City, with particular interest in the common yet overlooked building types that line the city's streets. Dolkart is the author of several award-winning books, including *Morningside Heights: A History of Its Architecture and Development*, which received the Association of American Publishers' award for best scholarly book in architecture and urban design; *Biography of a Tenement House in New York City: An Architectural History of 97 Orchard Street;* and *The Row House Reborn: Architecture and Neighborhoods in New York City, 1908–1929*, which won the Society of Architectural Historians' prestigious Antoinette Forrester Downing Award in 2012.

JENNA DUBLIN is a PhD student in urban planning at Columbia University. Her research examines how and why community-based groups utilize historic district designation as a means to affect neighborhood trends of socioeconomic change and gentrification. Currently she is a research manager at the National Trust for Historic Preservation Research and Policy Lab, and for the past two years, she has been a Columbia University teaching fellow in urban economics. In 2016 Dublin participated in the US/ICOMOS International Exchange Program; she lived in Delhi, India, and contributed to the heritage-based infrastructure upgrading plan for the city of Amritsar, located in northwestern Punjab. Dublin graduated with dual master's degrees in urban planning and historic preservation from the University of Maryland, and she has a BFA from the Cooper Union School of Art.

SHREYA GHOSHAL is a current dual master's candidate in historic preservation and urban planning at Columbia University. She is interested in the intersection of preservation and planning policies, especially in the integration of preservation efforts with new development in cities. She has published original research on the ways architecture affected student protests on university campuses during the Vietnam War era, and she has facilitated other research topics related to architectural history, preservation, and land use issues. Ghoshal is currently an intern with the San Francisco City Planning Department, where she is conducting a citywide survey of historic resources using Arches.

NICHOLAS HAMILTON serves as director of urban policy at the American Assembly, Columbia University's bipartisan policy institute. There, he works closely with city leaders, researchers, and civil society groups around the country to develop more equitable, sustainable, and economically vibrant communities. His work has focused on legacy cities, neighborhood revitalization, and historic preservation. Recent writing includes coauthoring a chapter in *On the Edge: America's Middle Neighborhoods* that discusses the role of historic preservation as a tool for the revitalization of legacy city neighborhoods. Hamilton previously served as an architectural and urban designer for Davis Brody Bond, advancing the firm's work on university laboratory buildings and US embassies.

MATTHEW HAMPEL is a senior software architect with Loveland Technologies. He works with governments, non-profits, newspapers, universities, and other organizations to build tools for the public good. A native of Ann Arbor, Michigan, he is now based in Brooklyn. Hampel works with Loveland clients on projects ranging from citywide surveys and historic inventories to voter engagement. He supports projects, builds web and mobile apps, and works with the parcel team to improve Loveland's nationwide dataset. Before joining Loveland, Hampel cofounded the startup LocalData, was a Code for America fellow in Detroit, and worked as a technology project manager at the University of Michigan.

JANET HANSEN holds an MA in historic resources management from the University of California, Riverside, and has over twenty-five years of experience working in the field in both the public and the private sector. She is the deputy manager of the City of Los Angeles Office of Historic Resources and the project manager for SurveyLA, the citywide historic resources survey. In that capacity, Hansen developed and implemented survey methods and tools and collaborated with the Getty Conservation Institute to develop HistoricPlacesLA, the city's historic resources inventory and management system. She has coauthored several articles on the citywide survey project and has lectured at conferences and other venues nationally. She is also a governor-appointed commissioner on the California State Historical Resources Commission.

LISA KERSAVAGE is the director of special projects and strategic planning at the New York City Landmarks Preservation Commission, where she supervises the work of the Research, Archaeology, and Environmental Review Departments, manages special research projects, and executes planning exercises related to high-level agency and interagency projects. Before joining the commission, she was the project manager of Changing Course, an ambitious global design competition to reimagine a more sustainable Lower Mississippi River Delta, which was sponsored by the Environmental Defense Fund and the Van Alen Institute. Prior to that, Kersavage was the senior director of preservation and sustainability at the Municipal Art Society, where she also served as the director of advocacy and policy and the Kress/RFR fellow. She has also held positions as a public policy consultant to the William Penn Foundation in Philadelphia and as executive director of both the Fitch Foundation and Friends of the Upper East Side Historic Districts. Kersavage received an MS in historic preservation from Columbia University and a BA in art history from Pennsylvania State University.

KELLY L. KINAHAN, AICP, is an assistant professor in the Department of Urban and Public Affairs at the University of Louisville. Her research and teaching focus on the intersection of historic preservation with neighborhood change, urban revitalization, and housing policy. Kinahan holds a PhD from Cleveland State University's Levin College of Urban Affairs.

JACQUELINE KLOPP is currently an associate research scholar at the Center for Sustainable Urban Development at Columbia University, a Volvo Research and Education Foundation Center of Excellence in Future Urban Transport. She taught for many years at the School of International and Public Affairs and now teaches in the Sustainable Development Program at Columbia University. Her research focuses on the intersection of sustainable transport, land use, accountability, data, and technology. Klopp is the author of numerous academic and popular articles on land and the politics of infrastructure, with a focus on Africa, and she is increasingly exploring the potential of new technologies to impact transportation for the twenty-first century. She is also a founder of Digital Matatus, a consortium that mapped and created open data for bus routes in Nairobi, Kenya, part of a global movement to create open data for improved planning.

RINALDO LIMA is adjunct professor in the Department of Statistics and Informatics at the Federal Rural University of Pernambuco in Brazil. He received a PhD in computer science from the Federal University of Pernambuco (UFPE) in 2014. He received an MS in artificial intelligence from the same university in 2010. From 2005 to 2010, Lima worked as a business intelligence consultant for telecommunication companies, engaged in several projects on data mining and data warehousing. He participated as a P&D researcher in several projects on automatic text summarization at the Informatics Center/UFPE. He has published several papers in international journals and conferences on topics including information extraction, automatic text summarization, machine learning, ontology population, and the semantic web. His more recent research interests are in natural language processing and sentient analysis.

RANDALL MASON plays several roles at the University of Pennsylvania School of Design: senior fellow at PennPraxis; associate professor of city and regional planning; and, until recently (2009–2017), chair of the Graduate Program in Historic Preservation. Mason was educated in geography, history, and urban planning (PhD, Columbia University); his published work includes *The Once and Future New York*. His professional practice includes projects at many scales, addressing planning, preservation, and public space issues, commissioned by organizations including the Getty Conservation Institute, William Penn Foundation, Brookings Institution, the City of Philadelphia, and the National

Park Service. Mason lives in Philadelphia and was a Rome Prize Fellow in 2012–2013.

KERRY MCCARTHY is the program director of Thriving Communities/Arts and Historic Preservation for the New York Community Trust. Before joining the trust in 2009, McCarthy ran a consulting company serving city nonprofit arts organizations. She has more than twenty years of experience in museum and performing arts administration with organizations as varied as the Queens Museum of Art and Jim Henson Productions. She has curated exhibitions for the New York Public Library for the Performing Arts at Lincoln Center and Atlanta's Center for Puppetry Arts. McCarthy holds an MA in folk art studies from New York University and a BA from Sewanee: The University of the South. She is a graduate of Coro's Leadership New York Program and former cochair of the city's Dance Funders Group and of New York Grantmakers in the Arts. Currently she is vice-chair of Grantmakers in the Arts; board member of Women's Studio Workshop; and member of the New York City Department of Education's arts education committee.

JENNIFER L. MOST has worked since 2014 as a city planner for the New York City Department of Transportation, where she presently serves as design manager for the agency's WalkNYC Wayfinding Program. From 2011 to 2017, she developed and taught the course GIS for Preservation at Columbia University's Graduate School of Architecture, Planning, and Preservation. Previously, Most worked for the New York City Landmarks Preservation Commission, where she held the positions of data and mapping administrator and architectural historian. She has also worked for the New York City Department of Housing Preservation and Development as a GIS mapper and program analyst. Most holds a degree in architecture from MIT and a master's in historic preservation and urban planning from Columbia University.

DOUGLAS S. NOONAN is professor of public and environmental affairs at Indiana University's School of Public and Environmental Affairs (SPEA). His research focuses on a variety of policy and economics issues related to the urban environment, neighborhood dynamics, and quality of life. He has published on the economics of historic preservation, studying both the determinants of landmark designation and the impacts of such designations. His current research centers on arts and cultural districts and the intersection of arts, entrepreneurship, and innovation. He is the coeditor of the *Journal of Cultural Economics* and serves on the board of directors of the Association of Cultural Economics International. Noonan joined SPEA after spending over a decade on the faculty at the School of Public Policy at Georgia Institute of Technology. He earned a PhD in public policy at the University of Chicago.

TETSUHARU OBA received his PhD degree in 2006 from Kyoto University, Japan. His research interests include urban policy and planning, transportation and land use, urban and environmental economics, and policy analysis. He is currently an associate professor in the department of Urban Management at Kyoto University and a part-time instructor in the graduate school of Urban Management at Osaka City University. He was a visiting scholar at the School of Public Policy at Georgia Institute of Technology from 2012 to 2013.

MICHAEL POWE is the director of research for the National Trust for Historic Preservation's Research and Policy Lab. Powe conducts research empirically assessing the contributions that existing buildings and blocks offer communities. In 2014 he led work on the lab's Older, Smaller, Better project, which used maps and statistics to demonstrate the critical role that older, smaller buildings play in supporting the social, cultural, and economic vitality of urban neighborhoods, and in 2016 he led efforts to expand this work to include a total of fifty US cities in the *Atlas of ReUrbanism*. Powe also played a significant role in the National Trust's Partnership for Building Reuse with the Urban Land Institute, steering policy conversations focused on strengthening building reuse opportunities in Baltimore, Philadelphia, Chicago, Detroit, and Louisville. He holds master's and doctoral degrees in urban and regional planning and planning, policy, and design from the University of California, Irvine.

EDUARDO ROJAS is an independent consultant on urban development and a lecturer on historic preservation at the School of Design of the University of Pennsylvania. He was the principal specialist in urban development at the Inter-American Development Bank, and prior to that, he worked at the Regional Development Department of the Organization of American States and the Urban Development Corporation of the government of Chile. Rojas was the deputy director of the Institute of Urban Studies of the Catholic University of Chile and lectured at the institute's master's program in urban studies. He holds a degree in architecture from the Catholic University of Chile; an MPhil in urban and regional planning from the University of Edinburgh; an MBA from Johns Hopkins University; and a doctor of urbanism degree from the Universidade Lusófona in Portugal.

ALICIA ROUAULT is a technology professional working at the intersection of urban planning, data, and interactive design. She currently works at 18F, a digital services agency within the US government. Formerly, Rouault led the Digital Services Group in Boston's Metropolitan Area Planning Council. In the recent past, she worked in San Francisco as senior advisor to the executive director at Code for America, a national leader in municipal innovation and technology. Rouault was CEO and cofounder of LocalData, a technology company that works with municipalities and universities to collect and understand urban data. She has worked as a researcher with MIT's Civic Data Design Lab and at the MIT Media Lab. Her academic background is in political science at the University of Toronto and in city and regional planning and urban information systems at the Massachusetts Institute of Technology. Rouault is a winner of the 2012 Knight News Challenge for Data Innovation.

STEPHANIE RYBERG-WEBSTER is an associate professor in the Department of Urban Studies at Cleveland State University's Levin College of Urban Affairs, where she also directs the Master of Urban Planning and Development Program. Her work addresses the intersections of historic preservation and urban development. Ryberg-Webster's current work explores the 1970s-era history of historic preservation within the context of Cleveland's escalating urban decline. She has also published research on preservation and community development, African American heritage, historic rehabilitation tax credits, and preservation amid urban decline. She holds a PhD in city and regional planning from the University of Pennsylvania, a master's degree in historic preservation from the University of Maryland, and a bachelor's degree in urban planning from the University of Cincinnati.

MEENAKSHI SRINIVASAN served as both chair and commissioner of the New York City Landmarks Preservation Commission until June 2018. She was appointed by Mayor Bill de Blasio in 2014 and managed a staff of approximately seventy-five architects, archaeologists, preservationists, historians, attorneys, and administrators. Srinivasan is a planner and urban designer with a longstanding commitment to public service. She has more than two decades of experience working in various aspects of New York City's land use process. Prior to her Landmarks Preservation Commission appointment, Srinivasan served for ten years as the chair and commissioner of the Board of Standards and Appeals and worked for the Manhattan office of the Department of City Planning in various capacities, including as deputy director. An architect by training, Srinivasan holds a BArch from the School of Planning and Architecture in New Delhi, India, and earned an MArch and a master of city planning from the University of Pennsylvania.

EMILY TALEN is professor of urbanism at the University of Chicago. She holds a PhD in urban geography from the University of California, Santa Barbara, and a master's in city planning from Ohio State University. She is a fellow of the American Institute of Certified Planners and the recipient of a Guggenheim Fellowship. Talen has written extensively on the topics of urban design, New Urbanism, and social equity. She has published over seventy peer-reviewed articles and four books (*New Urbanism and American Planning, Design for Diversity, Urban Design Reclaimed*, and *City*

218

Rules). Her most recent book is titled *Neighborhood* (Oxford University Press, 2018).

DANIEL WATTS is a GIS administrator and planning analyst for the New York City Landmarks Preservation Commission. He coordinates GIS and geospatial data analysis projects for the commission. During his three years with the commission, much of his work has focused on the creation and use of data to grow the role of analytics in the preservation process. Watts holds an MUEP from the University of Virginia and an MS in historic preservation from Clemson University.

AMANDA L. WEBB is an assistant professor in the Department of Civil and Architectural Engineering and Construction Management at the University of Cincinnati, where her research focuses on the energy performance of historic buildings. She is a committee member of ASHRAE's Guideline 34, *Energy Efficiency Guideline for Historic Buildings*, and a US task expert for the International Energy Agency's Task 59, Renovating Historic Buildings Towards Zero Energy. Webb holds a PhD in architectural engineering from Pennsylvania State University and a master's degree from MIT's Building Technology Program.

VICKI WEINER is currently deputy director of Pratt Center for Community Development, where she develops and oversees initiatives that meet the center's mission to create a more just, equitable, and sustainable New York City. She came to the center in 2004 to lead projects that explore connections between preserving culturally important places and creating more equitable communities, and she has conducted studies in Fulton Street Mall in downtown Brooklyn, Manhattan's East Village, and Cypress Hills/East New York in Brooklyn. Prior to her tenure at Pratt Center, Weiner served as director of two historic preservation organizations and as a consultant to community organizations and government agencies. She received a James Marston Fitch Mid-Career Grant to study the community development and historic preservation movements. An adjunct associate professor at Pratt since 2001, Weiner teaches graduate courses in historic preservation research methods, policy analysis, and community planning. She has a BA from Drew University and an MS in historic preservation from Columbia University.

JEREMY C. WELLS is an assistant professor in the Historic Preservation Program at the University of Maryland, College Park, and a Fulbright Scholar. His research explores ways to make built heritage conservation practice more responsive to people through the use of applied social science research methods from environmental psychology, humanistic geography, anthropology, and community development/public health. Wells is currently the chair of the Environmental Design Research Association (EDRA), where he is leading efforts to integrate evidence into heritage conservation practice. At EDRA, he created the Historic Environment

Knowledge Network to engage academics and practitioners in addressing the person/place and environment/behavior aspects of heritage conservation. Wells runs the heritagestudies.org website, which explores how to evolve heritage conservation practice using critical heritage studies theory to better balance meanings and power between experts and most stakeholders.

CHRIS WHONG is an urbanist, mapmaker, data junkie, and full-stack web developer. As founder and director of the progressive technology team NYC Planning Labs, he is promoting open technology, open-source software, and open data at the New York City Department of City Planning. Whong is a leader in the city's civic technology community and a former Code for America brigade leader. He holds a master's degree in urban planning from NYU Wagner and a BS in geography from the University of Maryland.

Acknowledgments

This book emerged from the work of Urban Heritage, Sustainability, and Social Inclusion, a research initiative co-sponsored by the Columbia Graduate School of Architecture, Planning, and Preservation; Center for Sustainable Urban Development – Earth Institute; and The American Assembly. The initiative is generously funded by the New York Community Trust. This collaborative research examines historic preservation as a form of public policy. The decisions we make about what to preserve or protect within the built environment have profound implications in terms of who participates in the process and how the outcomes of that process affect communities and the environment. Through a series of symposia and related publications, this research works to imagine more socially inclusive processes that can inform the next generation of preservation policy.

A two-day symposium in February 2018 convened twenty-six scholars and practitioners in New York City to explore how the preservation enterprise is engaging, shaping, learning from, and capitalizing on the new landscape of urban data. This dialogue served as a platform for the exchange of ideas and the development of lines of inquiry. Over the spring and summer, these conversations further developed through interviews and participant-authored texts.

Jacqueline Klopp of the Center for Sustainable Urban Development – Earth Institute and Nicholas Hamilton of The American Assembly were key collaborators in the development of the symposium and this volume. Jesse Connuck, from Columbia Books on Architecture and the City, was our amazingly skilled managing editor. Jenna Dublin, Allison Arlotta, and Shreya Ghoshal served as our indispensable graduate research assistants.

We are especially grateful for the support and vision of the Graduate School of Architecture, Planning, and Preservation and Dean Amale Andraos. Special thanks go to the New York Community Trust, in particular Kerry McCarthy, for investing in preservation's future and for funding the collaborative processes needed for policy thinking. World Monuments Fund generously provided the venue for the symposium, and we thank Lisa Ackerman for her programmatic commitment to this effort, as well as all the World Monuments Fund staff who provided logistical support over the two-day event. Finally, we are indebted to all of the authors who contributed to this volume and to the symposium participants for lending their time and insight to this endeavor.

Columbia Books on
Architecture and the City

Columbia University
1172 Amsterdam Ave
407 Avery Hall
New York, NY 10027
arch.columbia.edu/books

Distributed by Columbia
University Press
cup.columbia.edu

*Preservation and
the New Data Landscape*
Edited by Erica Avrami

Graphic Designer
Common Name

Copyeditor
Erica Olsen

978-1-941332-48-1

This book has been produced
through the Office of the Dean,
Amale Andraos, and the Office
of Publications at Columbia
University GSAPP.

Director of Publications
James Graham

Assistant Director
Isabelle Kirkham-Lewitt

Managing Editor
Jesse Connuck

Library of Congress
Cataloging-in-Publication Data

Names: Avrami, Erica C., editor.
Title: *Preservation and the new data
landscape*/edited by Erica Avrami.
Description: New York: Columbia Books
on Architecture and the City, 2019.
Series: Issues in preservation policy |
Includes bibliographical references.
Identifiers: LCCN 2018050849 |
ISBN 9781941332481 (pbk.: alk. paper).
Subjects: LCSH: Architecture—
Conservation and restoration. |
Historic preservation—Social
aspects. | Historic preservation—
Economic aspects.
Classification: LCC NA105 .P75 2019 |
DDC 720.28/8—dc23.
LC record available at
https://lccn.loc.gov/2018050849